Principle B, VP Ellipsis, and
Interpretation in Child
Grammar

Principle B, VP Ellipsis, and Interpretation in Child Grammar

Rosalind Thornton and Kenneth Wexler

The MIT Press
Cambridge, Massachusetts
London, England

This book was set in Times New Roman by Asco Typesetters, Hong Kong and was printed and bound in the United States of America.

Library of Congress Cataloging-in-Publication Data

Thornton, Rosalind.
  Principle B, VP ellipsis, and interpretation in child grammar / Rosalind
  Thornton and Kenneth Wexler.
      p.   cm. — (Current studies in linguistics ; 31)
  Includes bibliographical references and index.
  ISBN 0-262-20119-4 (hc. : alk. paper). — ISBN 0-262-70069-7
  (pbk. : alk. paper)
    1. Language acquisition. 2. Grammar, Comparative and general—
  Pronoun. 3. Grammar, Comparative and general—Syntax.
  4. Government-binding theory (Linguistics) I. Wexler, Kenneth.
  II. Title. III. Series: Current studies in linguistics series ; 31.
  P118.T49   1999   98-51296
  401'.93—dc21   CIP

Contents

Acknowledgments

Thanks are due to many people, but most of all to Stephen Crain for extensive input throughout all phases of this project, from help with the initial design and piloting of the experiments to editing the final manuscript. This book would never have reached completion without his continuing help and support.

We would also like to thank Yu-Chin Chien for her collaboration over a number of years with Ken Wexler on experiments investigating the binding theory, which underlie our work on the topic of this book.

To the following individuals, we extend special thanks: to Yoichi Miyamoto and especially Carole Boster, for help and discussion at the pilot stage of the experiment; to Sergey Avrutin, Irene Heim, Howard Lasnik, and Juan Uriagereka, for helpful discussion on theoretical issues; to Danny Fox, for reading the manuscript closely for us, and for his expert advice; to Meghan Durham, Carrie O'Leary, Maia Singer, and Julie Solomon, for many hours of help in carrying out the experiment; to Laurel Laporte-Grimes and Carole Boster, for videotaping a sample of the stimuli; to the director, teachers, and children of Another Place to Grow (Arlington, MA), Lesley Ellis School for Children (Arlington, MA), and The University of Connecticut Child Development Laboratories (Storrs, CT), for their cooperation and welcome; and to two anonymous reviewers, for helpful comments.

This research was supported by NSF grant DBS 9121291 to Ken Wexler and by postdoctoral support to Rosalind Thornton. Ken Wexler would like to thank the Bellagio Rockefeller Study Center for a delightful month's stay, which allowed him to concentrate on writing much theoretical analysis. Oh, to return!

Ken Wexler would like to thank Sherry Wexler for her love, support, and help over many years of work; she provided the kind of emotional support that makes life worth a great deal. It was always important to Ken that after long work hours there was a great person to share relaxing moments with. Likewise, Paul Wexler, Stephanie Wexler Coutu, and Chris Coutu were indispensable for the love and happiness they provided.

Rozz Thornton thanks Stephen Crain and daughter Aurora Luisa Thornton Crain, for spending many Sundays without her, while this book was being completed.

Finally, we would like to thank Anne Mark, whose expert hand vastly improved the readability of this work.

Chapter 1

Introduction

1.1 The Framework

This book examines children's interpretation of pronouns. The investigation is carried out within the theory of Universal Grammar in the generative framework (Chomsky 1981, 1986, 1995). A basic tenet of this theory is that much linguistic knowledge is part of the child's genetic makeup, leading to the expectation that this knowledge will be manifested in all the world's languages—that is, that it will be "universal." This knowledge is encoded in the form of universal principles. These principles help to explain the fact that any normally developing child can learn any natural language. Moreover, they help to explain other aspects of language development—for example, the fact that language acquisition proceeds at a characteristic pace, outdistancing other complex cognitive abilities, and the fact that children make few errors in the course of language development, considering the vast number of logically possible errors that could occur.

In the principles-and-parameters model of Universal Grammar, it is also maintained that certain aspects of language variation are encoded in the biological endowment of the species. More specifically, Universal Grammar endows each child with a number of parameters that account for language variation. These parameters can take different values within children's grammars depending on the language to which they are exposed.

Among the innate linguistic principles assumed by the theory of Universal Grammar are a set of properties known as the binding theory. These properties will be the focus of this book. Since Aristotle, language has been viewed as a mapping between sound and meaning. Within sentence grammar, the relevant mapping is between sentences and their associated meanings. The principles of the binding theory constrain this mapping in two ways. First, they establish well-formedness conditions on sentences that contain noun phrases. Second, they place limitations on the range of interpretations that sentences with different kinds of noun phrases can and cannot have. In some instances, the binding principles exclude interpretations that might otherwise be expected to be assigned to sentences, given the range of meanings that can be assigned to related sentences. Our concern in this book is children's knowledge of the range of interpretations for three kinds of sentences that fall under the auspices of the binding theory: sentences with ordinary pronouns, ones with referring expressions, and ones in which a verb phrase has been elided.

An important assumption of this research is that the architecture of the language faculty is modular; in other words, the language module is "sealed off" from other cognitive systems (see Fodor 1983; Crain and Steedman 1985). On this view, the grammar cannot be influenced by performance factors, in most circumstances. Of course, even adults can be exposed to circumstances that cause them to fail a particular task. However, performance factors mask children's (and adults') grammatical knowledge for the most part only when they are tested in infelicitous circumstances. Thus, we reject a view in which the child's response in an experimental situation is taken to reflect a composite of competing factors of which the grammar is only one factor among many (for a critique of this view, see Crain and Thornton 1998; Crain and Wexler 1999). Our assumptions about modular architecture also put our approach at odds with psycholinguistic approaches such as that of Fodor, Bever, and Garrett (1974), which view children's linguistic behavior as the by-product of "strategies," for example.

On a modular view of the language faculty, the architecture of the grammatical system is invariant; information from the incoming speech stream is fed to the syntactic component. The output of the syntax is in turn fed to the semantics. The principles and parameters of Universal Grammar are housed within this architecture. Extending the view that linguistic knowledge is innately given, we also assume that children have access to a sentence-processing mechanism, a parser, that is uniform across the species. The parser transfers information from one component to the other and resolves ambiguities that arise within the syntactic and semantic components. So, we make the twofold assumption that the properties of Universal Grammar and the properties of the parser do not differ for children and adults. That children and adults have a common set of parsing principles is another assumption that is not shared by all language acquisition researchers who work within the generative tradition. We take this to be the null hypothesis, however, in light of the learnability problems that would otherwise ensue. If children and adults have different parsing systems, for example, then we would have to ask how the child system changes so as to converge on the adult system.

Another difference between our approach and that of others in the field is methodological. We seek to investigate children's grammatical knowledge through experimental means, rather than relying on transcripts of their spontaneous speech, for example. Experimental techniques are now refined enough to be able to separate children's linguistic competence from the vagaries of performance, revealing their grammatical knowledge in many domains, including both syntax and semantics. One method that has been particularly successful at testing children's grammatical knowledge is the truth value judgment task (see Crain and McKee 1985 for the earliest use of the task, and Crain and Thornton 1998 for extended discussion of its design features).

The truth value judgment task is ideally suited to testing constraints such as the principles of the binding theory. In this task, events are acted out for children with toys and props in real time. Provided that rigorous attention is paid to methodology, nonadult behavior, should it be uncovered, cannot be ascribed to experimental artifacts; some other account for the behavior must be sought. A version of the truth value judgment task is used in this book to evaluate the interpretations children allow pronouns to have in a range of matrix and VP ellipsis sentences. In several instances, children's linguistic behavior is found to differ from that of adults. Therefore, much of the resulting discussion concerns the differences between children's and adults' linguistic knowledge.

According to the model of the language faculty we have outlined, children's nonadult responses in an experimental task should not be relegated to failure of the language-processing system, whenever possible. That is, every attempt is made to avoid exonerating the grammar of responsibility for children's nonadult behavior by laying the blame within their performance system. This is motivated by our supposition that children and adults share the same (universal) parser. In the absence of an articulated theory of the parser, blaming the parser for children's nonadult responses is a "nonexplanation." Worse still, learnability of properties of the parser becomes an issue: How does the child make the transition from a nonadult parsing system to an adult one?

This is not to say that the processing system has no place in explaining behavior uncovered in linguistic experiments. Where it is relevant, however, it will be a source of explanation for the performance of both children and adults. In this book, we will appeal to the processing system to explain both children's and adults' responses to experimental items governed by one of the binding principles, Principle C. Given that failure of the language processor cannot be used to explain *differences* between children and adults, however, our approach is to seek an account of children's nonadult behavior elsewhere.

One avenue for explaining young children's nonadult linguistic behavior is to invoke the grammar itself. Given the assumption that children are equipped with the principles of Universal Grammar, however, the kinds of grammatical mechanisms to which the variation between children and adults can be attributed is severely limited. These limits are dictated by the Strong Continuity Hypothesis (see Hyams 1986; Pinker 1984; Poeppel and Wexler 1993; Wexler and Culicover 1980), according to which children's grammars can differ from their target grammar only in those ways in which the grammars of different languages differ from each other. For example, an English-speaking child's grammar may reflect a parameter setting that is appropriate for some language other than English. In this case, the child's task is to identify the triggers, the data that express the "cues" for correct setting of the target language parameters (see Gibson and Wexler 1994; Lightfoot 1998).

Another possible source of differences between child and adult language is compatible with a slightly weakened version of the Strong Continuity Hypothesis: namely, that the principles of Universal Grammar remain intact, but specific grammatical operations undergo maturational change, becoming operational only at some later age (e.g., Borer and Wexler 1987, 1992; Radford 1990; Rizzi 1993; Wexler 1999). Still another possible source of difference is consistent with the architecture we are assuming: namely, that although the principles of Universal Grammar remain intact and operational, children differ from adults in pragmatic, or real-world, knowledge. This is the approach to children's nonadult behavior developed in some earlier research on the binding theory (e.g., Chien and Wexler 1990; Wexler and Chien 1985), and it is the approach we extend in this book.

1.2 Constraints and Negative Evidence

The technical implementation of the binding theory has changed as the theory of generative grammar has evolved, and it is still in flux as the

Minimalist Program is being developed (Chomsky 1995; Hornstein 1995; Uriagereka 1998). The exact implementation of the binding principles is not crucial to us, however. What is crucial is that the binding theory, however formulated, is part of the language apparatus and, presumably, part of children's innate knowledge. For our purposes, the following definitions of the binding principles will suffice to illustrate how they prohibit certain interpretations of sentences (see Chomsky 1981). The three principles deal separately with (1) reflexive and reciprocal phrases (e.g., *himself, herself, each other*), (2) pronouns (e.g., *him, her, they*), and (3) names or referring expressions (R-expressions) (e.g., *John, the table*).

(1) *The binding theory*
 a. *Principle A*
    A reflexive must be bound in its clause.
 b. *Principle B*
    A pronoun must be locally free (not bound).
 c. *Principle C*
    An R-expression must be free.

According to Principle A, a reflexive must have an antecedent in the same clause that both c-commands it and is coindexed with it. Consider the examples in (2).

(2) a.   John$_i$ laughed at himself$_i$.
    b. *John$_i$ said that Mary$_j$ laughed at himself$_i$.

Sentence (2a) manifests the requirements of Principle A: the antecedent is in the same clause and c-commands the reflexive. In (2b), the reflexive has a c-commanding antecedent that is coindexed with it, but the antecedent is not local enough; it is not in the same clause as the reflexive. Therefore, (2b) violates Principle A and is deviant on the indicated interpretation; in other words, Principle A prevents (2b) from meaning that John said that Mary laughed at John. In this particular case, not only does Principle A rule out an illicit interpretation of the sentence; the sentence form itself is ungrammatical.

The examples in (3) illustrate facts relevant to Principle B.

(3) a. *John$_i$ laughed at him$_i$.
    b.   John$_i$ laughed at him$_j$.
    c.   John$_i$ laughed at his$_i$ joke.
    d.   John$_i$ said that Mary$_j$ laughed at him$_{i/k}$.
    e.   John$_i$ said that he$_{i/k}$ laughed at Mary$_j$.

In (3a), the pronoun is coindexed with a local c-commanding antecedent, where *local* means 'in the same clause'. The example is ruled out by Principle B because a pronoun may not have a local antecedent. Instead, the pronoun must refer to some other individual, as shown by the indexing in (3b). The differing indices on the pronoun and the name are usually interpreted as meaning that the two noun phrases (NPs) do not have the same reference; they are disjoint in reference. Thus, *John laughed at him* is a grammatical sentence form, but it cannot have the meaning in which John laughs at himself (cf. (3a)). In (3c), however, the pronoun may have an antecedent in the same clause. In this sentence, it is the larger NP *his joke* that counts as the local domain for Principle B. Since the pronoun is free within this NP, it can be coreferential with a higher c-commanding coindexed NP in the same clause, such as *John*. The pronoun is also free in (3d) and (3e), where its antecedent is in a higher clause. In structures of this sort, the pronoun may refer to an antecedent in the higher clause or to some individual not mentioned in the sentence, as shown by the indices.

In contrast to reflexives and pronouns, names (and other R-expressions) cannot have a coindexed, c-commanding antecedent at all. This observation is captured by Principle C, as illustrated in (4).

(4) a. *He_i laughed at $John_i$.
    b. *He_i said that $Mary_j$ laughed at $John_i$.
    c. He_k laughed at $John_i$.
    d. He_k said that $Mary_j$ laughed at $John_i$.

Examples (4a) and (4b) show that the locality of the antecedent is not a factor. Whether the antecedent is in the same clause or a higher clause makes no difference; coreference between the name and the c-commanding pronoun is ruled out. Principle C rules out an interpretation of (4a) in which John laughs at himself, and an interpretation of (4b) in which John said that Mary laughed at John. In both examples, the pronoun must refer to an individual not mentioned in the sentence, as shown by the indices in (4c) and (4d).

The principles of the binding theory are often called *constraints* because they impose limits on the sentence forms and meanings that can be generated by the grammar. Constraints have assumed a central position in theories, such as Chomsky's theory of Universal Grammar, that endow the child with innate knowledge of syntactic properties. This is because the information conveyed by constraints is unlikely to be learned. Notice that constraints, by their nature, are negative statements, in the sense that they

in line with the predictions of Universal Grammar; that is, for the most part, children have been found to adhere to Principles A and C. Principle B, however, stands out as an empirical problem area. Specifically, some children have been found to allow a nonadult interpretation of sentences like (6). Although ruled out by Principle B, an illicit reading of (6), according to which Mama Bear washes herself, is often accepted by children.

(6) Mama Bear is washing her.

If children have innate knowledge of Principle B, then the fact that some children accept an interpretation that adults do not assign raises a language learnability puzzle (see, e.g., Wexler and Chien 1985; Manzini and Wexler 1987; Montalbetti and Wexler 1985; Wexler and Manzini 1987). How do children abandon this illicit interpretation, so as to converge on the adult grammar, in the absence of negative evidence?

There were hints about the relevant empirical phenomenon in earlier studies, but the first systematic reports of children's nonadult interpretation of sentences governed by Principle B are due to Jakubowicz (1984) and Wexler and Chien (1985). Jakubowicz (1984) suggested that the error in interpretation arises because children miscategorize pronouns as reflexives. As part of their study on the learning of binding parameters, Wexler and Manzini (1987) showed that Jakubowicz's hypothesis did not handle certain facts: for example, the same children who permitted a nonadult interpretation of sentences like (6) also permitted an interpretation according to which the pronoun referred to an individual not mentioned in the sentence. This deictic interpretation is not possible for reflexive pronouns (but see McKee, Nicol, and McDaniel 1993, which reports findings showing a small number of children did allow deictic interpretations of reflexives).

Studies by Wexler and Chien (1985) compared children's acquisition of Principles A and B. These studies showed that by no later than age 4, children responded correctly to sentences governed by Principle A. Since Principle A seems as abstract and difficult to learn as Principle B, the recalcitrant data on Principle B were a real puzzle. Moreover, Wexler and Chien's study showed that children's correct responses to Principle A sentences increased in the way one would expect if young children (at age 2;6, for example) had difficulty with the experiment but knew the principle. By contrast, behavior on Principle B constructions remained remarkably flat over a period of 4 years. There were divergent curves in the distributions of responses by children to sentences governed by Principles A and B. This suggested that lack of mastery of the principle may have been responsible for children's responses, not difficulty with the task. However, even in this very first presentation of the data, Wexler and Chien argued on learnability grounds that children probably knew Principle B. They also offered an alternative account of the errors and proposed tests to examine the question experimentally.

Over a number of years, a scientific drama played out. For language learnability reasons, most researchers have continued to assume that children have knowledge of the binding principles, including Principle B, and have sought alternative explanations for the way in which children interpret pronouns in syntactic configurations governed by Principle B. Wexler and Chien focused on the pragmatic conditions associated with the interpretation of pronouns. This led to a series of empirical investigations, the results of which consistently showed that children apparently lack knowledge of Principle B but do have knowledge of Principles A and C. These studies looked closely at the pragmatic conditions that accompany pronominal use and considered other formulations of the binding theory, beyond that given above. In chapter 2, we examine some of these investigations.

1.4   Further Interpretations of Pronouns

Partly as a result of the findings from these experimental investigations of child language, linguists and psycholinguists realized that more distinctions were needed concerning the possible interpretations for sentences like (6), repeated here, and sentences like (7). Consider the possible interpretations of (7).

(6) Mama Bear is washing her.

(7) Mama Bear is washing her face.

As with (5a), two interpretations of (7) immediately come to mind: one in which Mama Bear is washing someone else's face, and one in which she is washing her own face. It turns out that in order to make headway on the puzzle of why children allow (6) to have an illicit meaning, three interpretations that can be associated with (7) need to be distinguished. The three interpretations are given in (8). In an attempt to make the intuitions clearer about how these interpretations come about, we use arrows and initials as an informal way of indicating the real-world referents of the NPs.

(8) Mama Bear is washing her face.

a. Mama Bear is washing her face   (deictic)

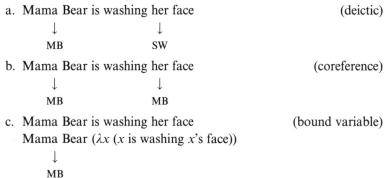

    ↓   ↓

    MB   SW

b. Mama Bear is washing her face   (coreference)

    ↓   ↓

    MB   MB

c. Mama Bear is washing her face   (bound variable)

   Mama Bear (λx (x is washing x's face))

    ↓

    MB

The interpretation on which the pronoun refers to an individual not mentioned in the sentence is called the *deictic* interpretation. In (8a), this is the interpretation on which Mama Bear washes, say, Snow White's (SW) face. The interpretations given in (8b) and (8c) are difficult to tell apart, because these interpretations yield the same truth conditions. Both interpretations express the proposition that Mama Bear is washing Mama Bear's face. The syntax gives rise to these truth conditions in different ways, however. On the *coreference* reading in (8b), the pronoun picks out Mama Bear (MB) as its referent. By contrast, in (8c) the pronoun is interpreted as a *bound variable*; that is, it is bound by a lambda operator. The lambda expression is a function that takes individuals as its argument. Its denotation is a set, namely, the set of individuals who wash their own faces. When this function is applied to an argument, in this case the NP *Mama Bear*, the result is a proposition that is true if Mama Bear is in that set of individuals, and false otherwise. The bound variable reading is only possible if the pronoun is c-commanded by its antecedent, as it is in (8).

Let us return now to example (6), where Principle B is operative. So far, we have suggested that these sentences have only one possible interpretation, on which the pronoun is used deictically. This will change shortly. For now, we will assume that the coreference reading is excluded by pragmatic rules. (We will expand on this in chapter 2.) The bound variable interpretation is excluded by Principle B. The potential range of interpretations for (6) is illustrated in (9).

(9) Mama Bear is washing her.

a. Mama Bear is washing her   (deictic)

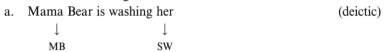

    ↓   ↓

    MB   SW

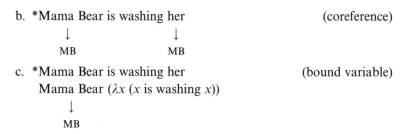

b. *Mama Bear is washing her   (coreference)

  ↓   ↓

  MB   MB

c. *Mama Bear is washing her   (bound variable)

  Mama Bear (λx (x is washing x))

  ↓

  MB

At this point, it becomes relevant to consider the antecedent of the pronoun. The antecedent can be a name (i.e., a referential NP), as in (9). It can also be a quantificational expression, as in (10) below. This distinction is important because when quantificational NPs are the antecedents of pronouns, one reading—the coreference interpretation of the pronoun—is eliminated. We explain why in the next section.

1.5 The Antecedents of Pronouns

We have described three interpretations of pronouns. First, a pronoun may be used deictically to refer directly to an individual or set of individuals. Second, a pronoun may be interpreted as referring to an individual (or set) that has been introduced by a preceding NP. In both of these cases, the pronoun comes to pick out an individual (or individuals) as its referent. Third, a pronoun may be interpreted as a bound variable. In this case, despite being anaphorically linked to an antecedent, a c-commanding quantificational NP, a bound pronoun does not inherit any individual as its reference: because quantificational NPs do not have inherent reference, they are incapable of transmitting a referent to the variables (bound pronouns) that they bind.

The lack of inherent reference of quantificational NPs is perhaps best illustrated by those with the determiner *no,* such as *no bear.* In a sentence like *No bear is washing his face,* the NP *no bear* is clearly not referential. Therefore, the pronoun it binds cannot pick up a referent. The same holds for universally quantified NPs (e.g., *every bear*), as the logical form of sentences containing such NPs indicates. Consider the example *Every bear is washing her* in (10). The deictic interpretation is illustrated in (10a). Here, the pronoun refers to an individual, Snow White (SW). The pronoun cannot make reference to an individual or set of individuals in (10b), however. It cannot corefer with the NP, because there is no set picked out by the NP *every bear.*[2] The same is true of the bound variable interpretation in (10c). The NP *every bear* is the antecedent of a conditional statement to the effect that if anything is a bear, then it is washing itself.

(10) Every bear is washing her.

    a.   Every bear is washing her   (deictic)

$$\downarrow$$

SW

    b. *Every bear is washing her   (coreference)

    c. *Every bear is washing her   (bound variable)

       $\forall x$ (bear $(x) \rightarrow x$ is washing x)

The distinction between referential NPs and quantificational NPs turns out to be important for the study of child language because it allows us to probe the source of children's misinterpretations of sentences like *Mama Bear is washing her*. Wexler and Chien observed in their 1985 paper that when children allowed this sentence to have the interpretation in which Mama Bear washes herself, the source of the error was unclear. One possible source of the error is the absence of Principle B. If this is the source of children's nonadult behavior, then they should also accept an illicit interpretation of sentences with quantificational antecedents, such as *Every bear is washing her*.

Another possible source of children's nonadult responses to sentences like *Mama Bear is washing her* is that they could be permitting a coreference interpretation of the pronoun. As noted earlier, we are assuming that in ordinary circumstances, some principle of pragmatics excludes this interpretation, although we will also discuss certain pragmatic contexts in which it is available. The second source of children's nonadult behavior, therefore, could reside at the level of pragmatics, outside the computational system. Wexler and Chien argued that if pragmatics were the source of children's nonadult linguistic behavior, then they should respond in an adultlike manner to sentences such as *Every bear is washing her* with quantificational NPs as the linguistic antecedent for the pronoun. If children did not allow the illicit reading for such sentences, then we could conclude that they were not violating Principle B in response to sentences with referential NPs. Having exonerated the syntax, we would have to look elsewhere, presumably to pragmatics, in seeking an account of children's nonadult behavior.

Chien and Wexler 1990 was the first study to investigate this issue. Other findings are reported by Avrutin and Wexler (1992), Avrutin and Thornton (1994), McDaniel, Cairns, and Hsu (1990), McDaniel and

Maxfield (1992), and Thornton (1990), among others. The experimental finding was that those children who allow illicit readings of sentences like *Mama Bear is washing her* do not allow illicit readings of ones like *Every bear is washing her.*

1.6 Overview of the Book: Binding, Coreference, and VP Ellipsis

In the remainder of this chapter, we introduce the ideas on which the rest of the book is based.

1.6.1 Chapter 2: Overview of Previous Research

Children's knowledge of Principle B has engendered a great deal of research. The scientific events that have unfolded are noteworthy in several respects. The experimental investigation of children's nonadult responses to sentences governed by Principle B shows that linguistic theory and language acquisition, taken as two parts of the same field (the study of the human language capacity), benefit from the mutually informative interaction between theory and experiment. In chapter 2, we introduce the results of earlier investigations of Principle B, beginning with the study by Chien and Wexler (1990). Then we discuss various interpretations of these results and others represented in the research of Grodzinsky and Reinhart (1993), Grimshaw and Rosen (1990), McDaniel and Maxfield (1992), Avrutin (1994), and Cardinaletti and Starke (1995).

1.6.2 Chapter 3: A New Account

In chapter 3, we present our own updated account of children's behavior on sentences governed by Principle B. In brief, we maintain the conclusion originally reached by Chien and Wexler (1990), that children's misinterpretations of pronouns in sentences like *Mama Bear is washing her* are not violations of Principle B but result because children's knowledge of pragmatics is incomplete. As a consequence, children accept coreference between a pronoun and a name, what we will be terming a *local coreference interpretation*, in circumstances in which an adult would not.

What pragmatic knowledge do children lack? Broadly speaking, children appear to have difficulty evaluating other speakers' intentions. This has consequences in both production and comprehension of language. As speakers, children fail to distinguish between their knowledge and that of listeners. They seem to assume that listeners have the same mental model as they do. Children's failure to take the hearer's knowledge (or lack of it) into account explains their inappropriate use of pronouns, for example.

More specifically, children use pronouns without first ensuring that a referent has been introduced into the conversational context (by an indefinite NP or a name). This leads to violations of the pragmatic principle known as the *familiarity condition* (Heim 1982). In short, children typically make the error of assuming that new information is old information. This explains the observation that children may announce "He hit me" instead of "A boy hit me" or "John hit me."

Children's failure to take into account the knowledge of other participants in a conversation has consequences in comprehension too. As listeners, children appear to assign interpretations to other speakers' utterances that require special contextual support to be felicitous for adults; that is, children assign these interpretations in the absence of the relevant contextual support. This too, can be chalked up to children's failure to distinguish between their own mental model of the conversational context and that of other participants. We believe this is why they allow local coreference interpretations for sentences like *Mama Bear is washing her*. Even when speakers have not established the special context that licenses a coreference interpretation, children are nonetheless able to assign it. What children lack, then, is real-world knowledge about which special situations initiate local coreference. They must also learn how speakers inform hearers about the intended interpretation of their utterances. In the cases of sentences like *Mama Bear is washing her*, speakers indicate that local coreference is intended by stressing the pronoun, in addition to providing special pragmatic context. Which structures are associated with focus, and the language-specific mechanisms for bringing linguistic material into focus (e.g., movement, contrastive stress), must also be acquired on the basis of positive input.

In chapter 3, we discuss several special pragmatic contexts that make a local coreference interpretation available for adults. These special situations override the usual pragmatic rules that disallow coreference in sentences governed by Principle B. Work by Heim (1998) figures prominently in that discussion. Adopting Heim's approach, we maintain that adults allow a local coreference interpretation of sentences governed by Principle B when the same individual is presented in two different *"guises."* The prototypical case is called an *identity debate*, where the question is whether someone being referred to under one guise (e.g., someone delivering a speech, or wearing certain dress-up clothes, or holding a martini) is a particular person known to the conversational participants.

There are other cases in which an individual can take on different guises. In certain contexts, for example, the fact that an individual is exhibiting uncharacteristic behavior can give rise to a local coreference interpretation of a pronoun. Essentially, the idea is that it is possible to assign a coreference interpretation even for sentences like *Mama Bear is washing HER* (where uppercase letters indicate that the pronoun bears stress), in a context in which Mama Bear is washing herself, if this event is understood to be uncharacteristic of Mama Bear or of bears generally.

The upshot of these observations is that a fourth interpretation—coreference under different guises, shown here in (11d)—needs to be added to the inventory of possible interpretations for sentences like *Mama Bear is washing her*. Interpretation (11d) represents those special pragmatic situations in which the name, *Mama Bear*, and the pronoun, *her*, pick out the same individual, Mama Bear, in the conversational context under two different guises.

(11) Mama Bear is washing her.

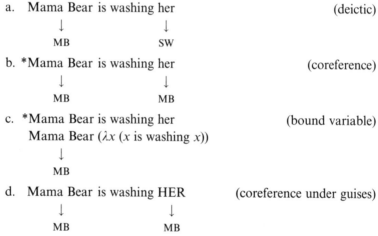

a. Mama Bear is washing her   (deictic)
       ↓   ↓
      MB   SW

b. *Mama Bear is washing her   (coreference)
       ↓   ↓
      MB   MB

c. *Mama Bear is washing her   (bound variable)
    Mama Bear (λx (x is washing x))
       ↓
      MB

d. Mama Bear is washing HER   (coreference under guises)
       ↓   ↓
      MB   MB

With (11d) added to the inventory of interpretive options for sentences with pronouns, two licit interpretations of (11) are now possible: one in which the pronoun is interpreted deictically, and one involving knowledge of the special pragmatic conditions (e.g., guises and typicality) under which a pronoun can directly refer to the same individual mentioned earlier in a sentence.

Children are not skilled at interpreting when speakers intend local coreference under guises, that is, when interpretations as in (11d) are intended. We term children's overacceptance of coreference under guises *extended guise creation.* In order to converge on the adult grammar children have to acquire more knowledge about what speakers and hearers, as participants in conversations, can assume about each other's knowledge states. They have to sharpen their real-world knowledge of the situations in which a local coreference interpretation is permitted—for example, situations in which the same individual appears in different guises or is performing an action that is not typical for the individual or for individuals of that type. This pragmatic/real-world knowledge takes time to acquire.

Where children are most vulnerable, in our view, is in identifying what constitutes characteristic and uncharacteristic behavior for particular individuals or types of individuals. Without a complete dossier on conventional knowledge, children may infer that the speaker had in mind two guises of an individual when, in fact, a local coreference interpretation of a sentence was not intended. The difficulty children experience in identifying a speaker's intended interpretation is compounded by the fact that many children have trouble interpreting contrastive stress and understanding how it is linked to particular sentence interpretations. This also takes time to learn. Children's full understanding of pronominal use is not in place until these aspects have been mastered. Fundamentally, it is pragmatic knowledge that is at issue.

1.6.3   Chapter 4: The Experiment

In chapter 4, we present our investigation of children's knowledge of the binding theory. This investigation tests the same children in a wide variety of experimental conditions, allowing within-subject comparison of different properties of the binding theory. The experiment begins with a replication of Chien and Wexler's (1990) original test of children's interpretation of pronouns with referential and quantificational NP antecedents in matrix sentences. This replication uses a different version of the truth value judgment task. Instead of looking at a picture and saying whether a statement describes it truthfully or not, children judge a puppet's statement following a scenario acted out with toys.

The results obtained from replicating Chien and Wexler's test are used as a yardstick for comparing children's responses when the inquiry is extended to Principle C sentences and VP ellipsis structures. We compare children's interpretation of pronouns in matrix sentences like (12a), governed by Principle B, with their responses to sentences like (12b), governed by Principle C.

(12) a. Mama Bear is washing her.
      b. She is washing Mama Bear.

As in earlier studies, the finding is that some children, unlike adults, allow the pronoun and the name in (12a) to corefer. This nonadult pattern of behavior does not extend to sentences like (12b), however. This difference in behavior is unexpected on some accounts (see chapter 2).

We also compare children's interpretation of pronouns in matrix sentences like (12a) with their interpretation of pronouns in VP ellipsis sentences. VP ellipsis sentences are coordinate structures in which the VP of the second conjunct is replaced by an auxiliary verb such as *did*, as in (13a). Because our immediate concern is the interpretation of pronouns, children (and adults) were tested using sentences in which the elided VP contains a pronoun, as shown in (13b).

(13) Papa Bear ate pizza and Brother Bear did too.

    a. Papa Bear ate pizza and Brother Bear ~~ate pizza~~ too

                                   did

    b. Papa Bear wiped his face and Brother Bear ~~wiped his face~~ too

                                   did

Like the pronoun in matrix sentences, the pronoun in VP ellipsis structures like (13b) is multiply ambiguous. At least three interpretations can be distinguished: a deictic interpretation, a coreference interpretation, and a bound variable interpretation. In matrix sentences, it is not easy to separate the coreference reading from the bound variable reading because the two interpretations are true in the same circumstances (cf. (8b) and (8c)). Sentences with VP ellipsis circumvent this problem, making it easier to see the difference between coreference and bound variable interpretations (see Reinhart 1983, 1986). In VP ellipsis structures, the truth conditions corresponding to the coreference interpretation and the bound variable interpretation are different; the sentence may be true on one interpretation and false on the other. Consider (14).

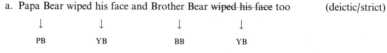

(14) Papa Bear wiped his face and Brother Bear did too.

    a. Papa Bear wiped his face and Brother Bear ~~wiped his face~~ too   (deictic/strict)

       ↓   ↓   ↓   ↓

      PB   YB   BB   YB

    b. Papa Bear wiped his face and Brother Bear ~~wiped his face~~ too   (coreference/strict)

       ↓   ↓   ↓   ↓

      PB   PB   BB   PB

c. Papa Bear wiped his face and Brother Bear ~~wiped his face~~ too   (bound

Papa Bear (λx (x wiped x's face)) and Brother Bear ~~(λx (x wiped x's face))~~ variable/

↓   ↓   sloppy)

PB   BB

Both (14a) and (14b) illustrate what are known as *strict* interpretations. In (14a), the pronoun in each conjunct refers deictically to some particular individual not mentioned in the sentence—say, Yogi Bear (YB). Example (14b) shows the coreference interpretation of the pronoun, where the overt pronoun picks out Papa Bear and the pronoun in the elided clause is anaphorically linked to the overt pronoun. On the bound variable interpretation, (14c), known as the *sloppy* interpretation, the pronoun is bound in both conjuncts (but by different operators), so it picks out a different individual in each conjunct. Roughly, this interpretation can be paraphrased as follows: Papa Bear is a member of the set of self-face-wipers, and Brother Bear is too. Thus, it can be seen that in VP ellipsis structures, unlike in matrix sentences such as (8), the coreference and bound variable interpretations give rise to different truth conditions. On the strict coreference interpretation, the sentence expresses the proposition that both Papa Bear and Brother Bear wiped Papa Bear's face. By contrast, the bound variable interpretation expresses that Papa Bear and Brother Bear wiped their own faces.

The VP ellipsis structures that will be the focus of our investigation are ones in which the pronoun in the elided VP is subject to Principle B or C of the binding theory. This is illustrated in (15), where Principles B and C are relevant in the elided VPs of (15a) and (15b), respectively.

(15) a. Papa Bear licked him and Brother Bear ~~licked him~~ too

↓

did

b. Papa Bear licked Brother Bear and he ~~licked Brother Bear~~ too

↓

did

What is striking about VP ellipsis structures is that the binding principles are applying to linguistic structure that is not phonologically realized. Therefore, showing that children know the range of interpretations that can and cannot be assigned to elided VPs would constitute evidence bearing on the innate specification of the binding principles. Such results could not be explained by learning, since ellipsis does not provide the positive input necessary for acquiring the relevant facts from experience.

In VP ellipsis structures like (15), our concern once more is the range of interpretations possible for adults, and whether it matches the range of interpretations that children assign. If children treat pronouns in VP ellipsis structures on a par with pronouns in matrix sentences, they might be expected to allow nonadult interpretations in cases like (15). As in our exploration of the properties of pronouns in simple matrix sentences, in order to understand how children interpret pronouns in VP ellipsis structures, it is crucial to distinguish the contributions of the syntax and the pragmatics.

In structures governed by Principle B, such as (15a), the alternation between referential NP antecedents and quantificational NP antecedents again proves to be instrumental in separating syntactic knowledge from pragmatic knowledge. Consider the VP ellipsis examples in (16). In (16a), the antecedent of the pronoun in the elided clause is a quantificational NP, and in (16b), the antecedent of the pronoun is a referential NP.

(16) a. Papa Bear licked him and every dog licked him too

                                                    ↓

                                                   did

    b. Papa Bear licked him and Brother Bear licked him too

                                                    ↓

                                                   did

Given the findings from matrix sentences, we expect children to prohibit the interpretation of (16a) according to which Papa Bear licked himself and every dog licked himself. That is, the results of the study of children's understanding of sentences like (16a) should establish the extent to which they interpret the pronoun in the elided conjunct as a bound variable. This finding thus demonstrates the extent of children's adherence to Principle B; moreover, sentences of this type serve as a yardstick for comparing children's responses to sentences like (16b). In sentences like (16b), the pronoun cannot be interpreted as a bound variable; only the deictic interpretation is possible. Therefore, if children permit illicit interpretations for some other reason, they can be seen as lacking pragmatic or real-world knowledge, and not knowledge of Principle B.

VP ellipsis sentences containing pronouns offer several potential interpretations; the array of possibilities for one type of sentence is reviewed in (17). Determining which of these interpretations children entertain is a major goal of our VP ellipsis experiments. Of special interest is whether children allow a local coreference interpretation of pronouns and their antecedents inside VP ellipsis structures.

(17) Papa Bear licked him and Brother Bear did too.

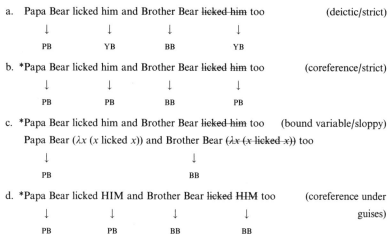

a.   Papa Bear licked him and Brother Bear ~~licked him~~ too   (deictic/strict)

PB   YB   BB   YB

b. *Papa Bear licked him and Brother Bear ~~licked him~~ too   (coreference/strict)

PB   PB   BB   PB

c. *Papa Bear licked him and Brother Bear ~~licked him~~ too   (bound variable/sloppy)

Papa Bear (λx (x licked x)) and Brother Bear (λx (x licked x)) too

PB   BB

d. *Papa Bear licked HIM and Brother Bear ~~licked HIM~~ too   (coreference under

PB   PB   BB   BB   guises)

For adults, the only possible interpretation is (17a). That is, this sentence can only mean that Papa Bear and Brother Bear licked someone else—say, Yogi Bear (YB). Adults reject the interpretations indicated in (17b), (17c), and (17d). The strict coreference interpretation illustrated in (17b), on which Papa Bear and Brother Bear both lick Papa Bear, is excluded by pragmatic rules, just as in matrix sentences (see (11b)). For familiar reasons, the bound variable interpretation illustrated in (17c), in which Papa Bear licks himself and Brother Bear licks himself, is disallowed by Principle B.

This brings us to the fourth interpretation, (17d). Here, one individual, under two guises, is named in the first conjunct, and another individual, under two guises, is named in the second conjunct. In other words, the pronoun is given a local coreference interpretation in each conjunct of the VP ellipsis structure. As mentioned earlier, one advantage of looking at the interpretations children assign to VP ellipsis structures is that the truth conditions for the coreference interpretation and the bound variable interpretation can be teased apart. Unfortunately, the two-guises interpretation threatens to take away this advantage. If this interpretation were possible, the result would be an interpretation with the same truth conditions as (17c), the bound variable interpretation; once more, these two interpretations would be difficult to distinguish.

It turns out, however, that the two- guises interpretation in (17d) is ruled out in the adult grammar, for two reasons. First, for adults, local coreference interpretations are usually possible only with heavy stress on the pronoun. In a VP ellipsis structure like (17), however, only the first pronoun can bear stress; the second is phonologically silent (by definition). Second, the interpretation in (17d) is excluded by a constraint that is independent of the binding theory, known as the parallelism constraint (e.g., Chomsky and Lasnik 1993; Chomsky 1995; Fox 1998; Lasnik 1972). The parallelism constraint applies to VP ellipsis structures, and also to coordinate structures with a "downstressed" second conjunct (i.e., a second clause that has flat intonation, with no stressed elements). It does *not* apply to coordinate structures that contain stressed pronouns. The effect of the parallelism constraint on VP ellipsis structures like (17) is to force referential pronouns (i.e., pronouns that are not bound variables) to pick out the same referent in each clause. For this reason, it is not possible in (17d) for *HIM* to pick out Papa Bear in the first clause and Brother Bear in the second clause. Thus, the two-guises interpretation, in which the pronoun finds its referent within the clause, should be prohibited for VP ellipsis sentences like (17), even though it is possible for pronouns in matrix sentences like *Mama Bear is washing her*.

It is one thing to expect adults to have knowledge of all the conditions relevant to parallelism. It is quite another thing to expect this of children. Because children have to learn the pragmatic conditions associated with the parallelism constraint, some children, at least, may allow interpretations like (17d) to be assigned to sentences with VP ellipsis. The findings of a study of both children's and adults' behavior on this construction are reported in chapter 4. The results will support the hypothesis that syntactic aspects of parallelism are known to children but that pragmatic aspects take longer to develop. In turn, the results from language acquisition may lead to a finer-grained theory of parallelism in the adult grammar. Thus we argue for another instance of experimental results from language acquisition studies having the capacity to influence the theory of Universal Grammar (Wexler 1998).

Chapter 2

The Acquisition of
Principle B

2.1 Introduction

In this chapter, we review previous research on the acquisition of Principle B. There is a substantial literature on children's knowledge of this principle (see, e.g., Avrutin 1994; Avrutin and Thornton 1994; Avrutin and Wexler 1992; Chien and Wexler 1990; Chien, Wexler, and Chang 1993; Deutsch, Koster, and Koster 1986; Grimshaw and Rosen 1990; Grodzinsky and Reinhart 1993; Hamann, Kowalski, and Philip 1997; Hirsh-Pasek et al. 1994; Jakubowicz 1984, 1991; Jakubowicz et al. 1996; Kaufman 1988, 1994; Koster 1993, 1994; Lee and Wexler 1987; Matsuoka 1997; McDaniel, Cairns, and Hsu 1990; McDaniel and Maxfield 1992; McKee 1988, 1992; Philip and Coopmans 1996; Rosen and Rosen 1994; Sigurjónsdóttir and Coopmans 1996; Sigurjónsdóttir and Hyams 1992; Thornton 1990; Varela 1989; Wexler and Chien 1985). We cannot do justice to all of the literature here. Instead, we review a handful of accounts of children's acquisition of Principle B that represent the range of proposals that have been made.

The basic findings on which we focus here come from a study by Chien and Wexler (1990). Specifically, Chien and Wexler found that some children allow (1) to have an interpretation in which Mama Bear is washing herself, in apparent violation of Principle B. When a quantificational NP like *every bear* is in subject position as in (2), however, children do not allow the interpretation that every bear is washing herself. In many of the early studies, these interpretations were inferred from children's responses to the yes/no question versions of (1) and (2).

(1) Mama Bear is washing her./Is Mama Bear washing her?

(2) Every bear is washing her./Is every bear washing her?

Chien and Wexler's interpretation of the experimental findings was that children lack certain pragmatic knowledge. After we introduce their account, we consider five alternatives. (a) Grodzinsky and Reinhart (1993) agree with Chien and Wexler that children's failure to reject the illicit reading of (1) has its source in pragmatic knowledge. Ultimately, however, Grodzinsky and Reinhart's account rests on processing: they claim that children have the appropriate pragmatic knowledge but fail to implement it because of a broad-based processing deficiency. (b) Grimshaw and Rosen (1990) are unsympathetic to the claim that children's nonadult behavior stems from lack of pragmatic competence. In their view, children's syntactic and pragmatic knowledge are both intact. Among other suggestions, they propose that the contrast between children's responses to (1) and their responses to (2) may be an artifact of experimental design. (c) McDaniel and Maxfield (1992) suggest that children's nonadult interpretations have a perceptual basis: on their view, the children who produce nonadult responses are insensitive to stress. (d) Avrutin (1994) proposes that children respond incorrectly to (1) because they have difficulty interpreting the intentions of other speakers. Like Grodzinsky and Reinhart, Avrutin claims that the root of the problem children experience is a processing overload. (e) Cardinaletti and Starke (1995) propose a syntactic account. They appeal to crosslinguistic differences in the typology of pronouns, claiming that nonadult responses by children to sentences like (1) appear only in languages in which strong pronominal forms are homophonous with weak forms.

2.2   Chien and Wexler 1990

2.2.1   The Principle P Account

We begin with the work of Chien and Wexler (1990), whose experimental investigations with children were designed to evaluate the distinction between binding and coreference. This distinction has been discussed by a number of syntacticians (see, e.g., Evans 1980; Fiengo and May 1994; Higginbotham 1980; Montalbetti and Wexler 1985; Reinhart 1983, 1986). As noted in chapter 1, coreference .pertains to pronouns with referential NPs as antecedents. Because quantificational NPs lack inherent reference, the anaphoric relation between pronouns and quantificational NP antecedents cannot be one of coreference; instead, it must be one of pronominal binding, where the pronoun is interpreted as a bound variable.

Recall that a sentence like (1) has three potential interpretations: deictic, coreference, and bound variable, as shown in (3). In fact, in the adult grammar only the deictic interpretation is available for this particular syntactic configuration of a pronoun and a name. Some as yet unspecified principle of pragmatics is assumed to rule out the coreference reading, and Principle B of the binding theory rules out the bound variable reading. Because coreference is not even at issue for sentences like *Every bear is washing her*, only two interpretations—deictic and bound variable—need be considered. As illustrated in (4), the bound variable interpretation is again ruled out by Principle B.

(3) Mama Bear is washing her./Is Mama Bear washing her?

   a. Mama Bear is washing her   (deictic)

       ↓   ↓

      MB   SW

   b. *Mama Bear is washing her   (coreference)

       ↓   ↓

      MB   MB

   c. *Mama Bear is washing her   (bound variable)

      Mama Bear (λx (x is washing x))

      ↓

     MB

(4) Every bear is washing her./Is every bear washing her?

   a. Every bear is washing her   (deictic)

                ↓

              SW

   c. *Every bear is washing her   (bound variable)

      $\forall x$ (bear $(x) \rightarrow x$ is washing x)

In an earlier experiment Wexler and Chien (1985) had observed that some children allowed nonadult interpretations of (3), and proposed that the error was pragmatic in nature. They predicted that children would not make errors on pronouns with quantificational antecedents. Chien and Wexler (1990) included quantificational NPs, thus enabling them to probe the source of children's misinterpretations.

Recall that children's nonadult interpretation of (3), in which Mama Bear washes herself, was difficult to evaluate, because the source of the nonadult behavior was unclear: either these children were allowing the coreference interpretation of the pronoun, in violation of some pragmatic rule, or they were violating a syntactic principle, Principle B. Sentences like (4) eliminated this ambiguity. Acceptance of the nonadult interpretation of (4) in which every bear washes herself amount to a violation of Principle B. Therefore, children's rejection of this interpretation for sentences like (4) attests to their adherence to Principle B. Children's acceptance of sentences like (3) could then be attributed to difficulty with pragmatics. The comparison between sentences like (3) and ones like (4) was the backbone of experiment 4 in Chien and Wexler's (1990) study.

The methodology used in the experiment was a picture version of the truth value judgment task.[1] The experimenter showed the child a picture, made a statement introducing the relevant characters, and asked a question about the picture; the child's task was simply to say "Yes" or "No." For example, showing the child the picture, the experimenter said, "Look at this picture. This is Mama Bear; this is Goldilocks. Is Mama Bear washing her?" The sentence preceding the target question provided the potential linguistic antecedents (here, *Mama Bear, Goldilocks*) for the pronoun (here, *her*). The experimenters were instructed not to stress the pronoun but to lightly stress the verb.

The target questions (e.g., (1) *Is Mama Bear washing her?* and (2) *Is every bear washing her?*) were each tested twice, in "match" and "mismatch" conditions. For example, the target question *Is Mama Bear washing her?* was posed once paired with a picture in which Mama Bear was washing herself, but not Goldilocks, and it was posed a second time when paired with a picture in which Mama Bear was washing Goldilocks. (In reality, children did not see two pictures with identical characters; instead, they saw two similar pictures, one with, say, Papa Smurf and Gargamel and one with Mama Bear and Goldilocks.)

Interspersed among the target questions were a number of control sentences, such as (5)–(7).

(5) Is Mama Bear/every bear washing Goldilocks?

(6) Is Mama Bear/Are all the bears washing Goldilocks?

(7) Is Mama Bear/every bear washing herself?

The control sentences were also tested in match and mismatch conditions. Examples like (5) were included to ensure that children responded accurately to sentences containing names instead of pronouns in object position. The mismatch picture for (5) with the quantificational NP depicted only two of three bears washing Goldilocks; this was used to assess whether or not children understood the universal quantifier *every*. Examples like (6) tested a different quantifier, *all*, and examples like (7) ensured that children could accept a bound variable (i.e., *herself*) in the same position as the pronoun in *Is every bear is washing her?* In the mismatch condition for sentences like (7), containing a referential antecedent, Mama Bear was not washing herself, but was washing Goldilocks.

A large number of children participated in the experiment: 177 altogether, ranging in age from 2;6 to 7;0. In addition, a control group of 20 adults was tested on the same experimental materials. The adults performed perfectly, or near perfectly, on all conditions.

The results from the control questions containing *every* and *all* were as follows. Only the children who were 5 years old or older correctly responded "No" to questions like (5) in the mismatch condition with about 90% accuracy. In responding to sentences with reflexive pronouns, such as (7), children younger than 5 proved to be overaccepting, permitting an illicit (deictic) interpretation of the pronoun in the mismatch condition; this pattern of responses was more robust for the questions with quantificational NP antecedents than for ones with referential NP antecedents. This response pattern suggests that children younger than 5 had some difficulty with the task. As figure 2.1 indicates, by 5 years of age, children were correctly giving negative answers over 80% of the time in the mismatch condition to both *Mama Bear is washing herself* and *Every*

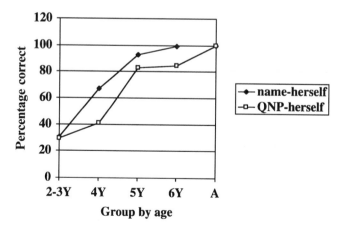

Figure 2.1
Percentage of correct "No" responses by group ($N = 177$) on reflexive condition; Y = years of age; A = adult; QNP = quantified noun phrase (adapted from Chien and Wexler 1990)

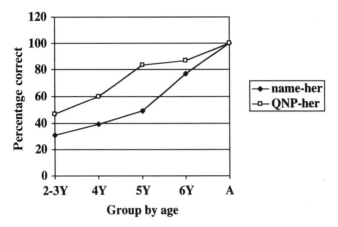

Figure 2.2
Percentage of correct "No" responses by group ($N = 177$) on pronoun condition
(adapted from Chien and Wexler 1990)

bear is washing herself (92.8% for the name and 83.0% for the quantificational NP). Overall, the results from the control conditions suggested that
knowledge of the universal operators *all* and *every* does not become fully
operative until age 5 and that 5 is the critical age at which children's
knowledge of Principle B can be assessed accurately.

The level of correct negative answers for the test questions (1) and (2) is
presented in figure 2.2. It can be seen that at 5 years of age, children avoid
the illicit meaning of *Every bear is washing her* in which every bear washes
herself about 85% of the time, whereas they avoid the illicit meaning of
(1) only 50% of the time.[2] This is in contrast to the reflexive condition,
where children responded "No" to both the questions with a name and
the ones with a quantificational NP at rates above 80%. The difference
between the two conditions (i.e., between (1) and (2)) was less marked at 6
years, presumably because at this age, some children were converging on
the adult grammar and were therefore correctly rejecting the questions with
a referential NP. As figure 2.2 indicates, Chien and Wexler's hypothesis
that children would respond differently to questions like (1) and (2) was
confirmed; the 5-year-olds, who were the critical group, appeared to
accept (1) frequently, while rejecting the ungrammatical reading of (2).

We turn now to Chien and Wexler's interpretation of the findings,
which were evaluated within Chomsky's version of the binding theory
(1981, 1986). In this theory, Principle B applies to both referential pronouns and pronouns that are bound variables.[3] Thus, the indicated inter-

pretations of the pronouns in both (8) and (9) violate Principle B because in each case, the pronoun is coindexed with, and c-commanded by, its antecedent. (This is now marked by indices on the relevant NPs. Previously, the bound variable interpretations were represented using the lambda operator.)

(8) *Mama Bear$_i$ is washing her$_i$.

(9) *Every bear$_i$ is washing her$_i$.

On the basis of the experimental results with quantificational NPs, Chien and Wexler assumed that children were correctly rejecting the bound variable interpretation of the pronouns in (8) and (9) that violates Principle B. Since the 5-year-old children did not often accept this interpretation of sentences like (9), it follows, other things being equal, that children were not allowing this interpretation of sentences like (8), either. Instead, Chien and Wexler reasoned, they must be permitting the coreference interpretation of sentences with a referential NP antecedent like (8). If so, the source of the problem lies in the pragmatic system, and Principle B is exonerated.[4]

So far, we have represented the coreference interpretation as in (10). Chien and Wexler represent this coreference interpretation as in (11), assigning different indices to *Mama Bear* and the pronoun. Usually NPs with different indices are taken to be disjoint in reference. For Chien and Wexler, the idea is that even though the two NPs are "contraindexed," children take the pronoun to be coreferential with the referential NP, *Mama Bear*.

(10) Mama Bear is washing her

(11) Mama Bear$_i$ is washing her$_j$.

Chien and Wexler point out that the adult grammar sometimes allows coreference between two NPs in the structural configuration in (11), though only in special contexts. They illustrate this with (12a), an identity debate adapted from Higginbotham's (1980) Principle C examples. A sentence like (12a) is appropriate when the speaker is unsure whether the person who looks like John is in fact John.

(12) a. That$_i$ must be John$_j$. At least he$_i$ looks like him$_j$.
       b. ?That must be every senator coming out of the building. At least they look like them.

Notice that such an example is odd if the name *John* is replaced by a quantificational NP such as *every senator* as in (12b). This confirms that it is coreference that is at issue in (12a).

Adults call on a principle of pragmatics, which Chien and Wexler call *Principle P*, to rule out coreference for sentences like *Mama Bear is washing her* in ordinary circumstances.

(13) *Principle P*
      Contraindexed NPs are noncoreferential unless the context explicitly forces coreference.

Adults apply this principle to referential pronouns in representations like (11), thereby excluding the coreference interpretation on which *Mama Bear* and the pronoun pick out the same individual. Thus, for adults, the default interpretation of *Mama Bear is washing her* is one in which *her* refers to someone other than *Mama Bear*. Chien and Wexler contend that children who accept the illicit, coreference interpretation of *Mama Bear is washing her* have not yet learned Principle P and therefore allow coreference between *her* and *Mama Bear* when the NPs are contraindexed.

Heim (1998) interprets cases of apparent Principle B violations in adults in terms of a theory of "guises." Essentially, Principle B only rules out a pronoun when it is locally c-commanded by a coreferential NP *in the same guise* as the pronoun. That is, Heim distinguishes between (14a) and (14b). We will elaborate on this theory in section 2.3.2 and incorporate a guise version of Chien and Wexler's pragmatic idea in the account we present in chapter 3. Avrutin (1994) also refers to Heim's theory of guises, although in a somewhat different way.

(14) Mama Bear is washing her.

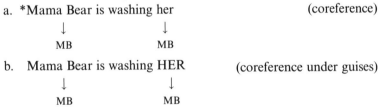

Returning to Chien and Wexler's experimental findings, we are led to ask why children accepted the illicit interpretation of *Mama Bear is washing her* around 50% of the time. Why wouldn't a child who lacked Principle P accept coreference on every occasion? According to Chien and Wexler, the answer lies in the experimental contexts presented to children.

The referent of the pronoun in the test sentences (such as (1)) was not uniquely determined in the pictures children were shown. Instead, the pictures showed two potential referents for the pronoun: Mama Bear and Goldilocks. Children therefore found the test sentences ambiguous, and they selected the two possible referents equally often. This is not to say that children mentally toss a coin to choose the referent of the pronoun. Children will only allow interpretations that are supported by the context. The preference for a particular interpretation will differ across contexts, however. (For details on the factors that conspire to determine the rate of acceptance and rejection of ambiguous sentences, see Crain and Wexler 1999; Crain and Thornton 1998.)[6]

As it is stated, Principle P applies to sentences governed by Principle C, as well as to ones governed by Principle B. If children do not have mastery of Principle P, they should allow coreference between the name and the pronoun in sentences like *She is washing Mama Bear* as well. None of Chien and Wexler's experimental stimuli were designed to test Principle C, and they do not discuss Principle C effects in their paper. In the experiment we present here, we extend the data set to cover Principle C cases. The results of the experiments we report in chapter 4 show that children do not treat the Principle B and Principle C sentences alike: they make errors on *Mama Bear is washing her*, but not on *She is washing Mama Bear*. This asymmetry will be an important factor in our discussion of children's misinterpretation of pronouns. In chapter 3, we develop an account of the differences in interpreting pronouns in subject and object position that complements Chien and Wexler's Principle P.

2.2.2 Replications and Explorations

A number of experimenters, working with English-speaking children and children speaking other languages, have replicated Chien and Wexler's finding that children treat pronouns with a referential NP antecedent differently from pronouns with the quantificational NP antecedent *every* (see, e.g., Chien and Wexler 1991; McDaniel, Cairns, and Hsu 1990 and McDaniel and Maxfield 1992 for English; Avrutin and Wexler 1992 for Russian; Philip and Coopmans 1996 for Dutch).[7] We restrict our attention here to the results of experiments with English-speaking children.

The experiment reported by McDaniel and Maxfield (1992) illustrates the same contrast reported by Chien and Wexler (1990). Variants of sentences (1) and (2) were tested (e.g., *Bert is washing him* and *Every camel is washing him*). Thirty-five children between the ages of 3;1 and 6;10

participated in the study. The experiment consisted of a grammaticality judgment task, with contextual support. That is, children were asked whether the experimenter's utterance matched a situation acted out with props. For example, for the sentence *Every camel is washing him*, children watched the experimenter act out the situation of two toy camels washing themselves, and the experimenter said, "If the two camels are doing this, and Grover is watching, can you say 'Every camel is washing him'?"[8] These sentences were compared with sentences containing referential NPs, such as *Bert is washing him*.

McDaniel and Maxfield do not report results across age groups, so their findings cannot be compared directly with Chien and Wexler's, but it is clear that the two experiments found a similar contrast between sentences with referential NPs and ones with quantificational NPs, at least for some of the subjects tested. Of the 35 children in McDaniel and Maxfield's study, 17 demonstrated adult knowledge of Principle B, correctly rejecting both sentence types. However, 11 children accepted sentences with a referential NP antecedent. Of these children, 2 did not appear to understand the meaning of *every* (as determined by a control item) and were eliminated from the study. Of the 9 remaining children in this group, 8 rejected at least one of the two sentences with a quantificational NP antecedent. Finally, another 6 children showed mixed behavior on both types.

In another experiment, using the operator *who*, Thornton (1990) pursued the prediction that children should reject sentences in which a pronoun is bound by a quantificational NP antecedent (see also Crain 1991). This experiment used a dynamic version of the truth value judgment task, in which children accepted or rejected a puppet's description of a short story acted out with toys. Children were tested on discourse sequences like the one in (15a), and their responses were compared with their acceptance of sentences like (15b), in which the antecedent is a referential NP.

(15) a. *I know who$_i$ scratched them$_i$. Bert and Ernie.
     b. Bert and Ernie scratched them.

In the story preceding the test sentences in (15a) and (15b), Bert and Ernie refuse to help scratch two other characters who have mosquito bites and scratch their own bites instead.

Participants in the study were 12 children between the ages of 3;7 and 4;8. A rejection rate of 96% was found for sentences like (15a),[9] as compared with 51% for referential controls like (15b). This is the distinction predicted by Chien and Wexler. The finding with the operator *who* has been replicated for English by Boster (1994) and for Russian by Avrutin and Wexler (1992).

The hypothesis that children will not allow apparent Principle B violations when the pronoun has a quantificational NP antecedent was further tested in an experiment by Avrutin and Thornton (1994) that investigated children's interpretation of pronouns with plural NP antecedents. The 33 child subjects, aged between 3;10 and 4;10, were tested using a dynamic version of the truth value judgment task. In this experiment, children were presented with sentences like (16) in two different contexts.

(16) The Smurf and the Troll dried them.

Notice that in (16), the antecedent of the pronoun is a plural NP that can be given either a collective or a distributive interpretation. That is, *the Smurf and the Troll* can be treated as a group, or they can be treated as separate individuals who acted on their own. Following Heim, Lasnik, and May (1991), Avrutin and Thornton postulated that in contexts in which the plural NP is collective, children would respond to it as they respond to referential NPs (see the representation in (17)).

(17) [The Smurf and the Troll]$_i$ dried them$_j$.   (collective)

In contexts in which the plural NP is given a distributive interpretation, by contrast, they expected children to treat it as a quantificational NP. This is because in this case the plural NP is hypothesized to have a silent distributive operator (semantically interpreted as *each*) attached to it (as illustrated in (18)).

(18) *[[The Smurf and the Troll]$_i$] D$_j$ dried them$_j$.   (distributive)

The distributive operator (*D*) is coindexed with the pronoun. Therefore, an interpretation of the sentence in which the Smurf and the Troll dry themselves amounts to a Principle B violation.

This means that the same sentence (e.g., (16)), can be used to assess children's coreference and bound variable interpretations of the pronoun, by presenting it in contexts that match either the collective or the distributive interpretation. On some trials in Avrutin and Thornton's study, the characters making up the plural NP were treated as a group ("the collective context"); on other trials, they acted individually ("the distributive context"). For example, the story leading up to the test sentence in (16) features twin clowns who ask to be dried. In the collective context, the

Smurf and the Troll say they can't dry them (i.e., the twin clowns) because they only have one towel. They proceed to wrap the large towel around themselves (i.e., around the two of them) and get dry together. In the distributive context, the Smurf enters the scene alone. When the twins ask the Smurf to dry them, he refuses, saying his towel is too small. He dries only himself and leaves the scene. Next, the Troll enters. He also finds a reason not to dry the twins and dries only himself.

In addition to test sentences like (16), the experiment included controls to check for children's knowledge of distributivity. In these control cases, the contexts were ambiguous between the collective and distributive interpretations. The toy props were simply set out in the workspace, and the experiment tested whether children could accept a collective or distributive answer to questions about them. That is, a puppet made a statement like (19a) or (19b), and the child told the puppet whether he was right or wrong.[10]

(19) Situation: Four bugs are lined up in front of two turtles.
    a. I know how many bugs they have.   Two.   (distributive answer)
    b. I know how many bugs they have.   Four.   (collective answer)

Of the 33 child subjects, 16 accepted the collective interpretation of (16) in the collective context. These 16 children were tested further to explore the hypothesis that a distributive context would trigger the distributive interpretation of Principle B sentences, as represented by (18). That is, the prediction was that these children would accept the collective interpretation of *The Smurf and the Troll dried them* in the context that supported the collective reading of the plural NP, *the Smurf and the Troll*, but reject the distributive interpretation of the same sentence, as a Principle B violation, in contexts that supported the distributive interpretation.

For the most part, the findings were as predicted. Of the 16 children who accepted the collective interpretation of (16), 12 demonstrated knowledge of distributivity in the control situations (i.e., (19)). These children accepted the collective interpretation of (16) 93% of the time, but accepted the distributive interpretation only 27% of the time, supporting the earlier finding by Chien and Wexler (1990).[11]

Further confirmation for the finding that children misinterpret pronouns with referential NP antecedents, but not with quantificational ones, comes from a recent study by Savarese (1999). Savarese investigated children's interpretation of sentences with negative quantificational antecedents like *no bear* and *none of the bears*. Unlike a quantifier phrase such as *no bear*, a partitive quantifier phrase such as *none of the bears* presupposes that there exists a set of bears. The question posed by Savarese was whether the presuppositional nature of the partitive quantifier phrase might make children more likely to accept a nonadult reading of the test sentences. The test sentences were matrix sentences like (20a) and (20b), and children's interpretation of these sentences was compared with control sentences like (20c), containing referential NP antecedents.

(20) a. No bear washed her.
     b. None of the bears washed them.
     c. Mama Bear washed her.

Twenty-four children between the ages of 3;5 and 5;11 participated in the study. Children's interpretation of the pronoun in these sentences was tested using the dynamic truth value judgment task. To begin with the results from the control sentences: The group of children permitted the illicit reading of (20c) (in which Mama Bear washed herself) 28% of the time. However, 15 of the 24 children responded as adults to the control items; the nonadult responses came from just 9 of the children, who accepted coreference in sentences like *Mama Bear washed her* 69% of the time. All children, including the 9 who permitted coreference in (20c), rejected test sentences with quantificational NPs like *no bear* (e.g., (20a)) on every one of the four trials—a 100% rejection rate. The presuppositional nature of partitive quantifier phrases like *none of the bears* had no effect on children's responses. Children treated negative phrases of this kind as quantificational NPs. Fifteen of the 24 children—among them the 9 children who accepted nonadult readings of sentences like (20c)—were tested on sentences like (20b). Once again, the results speak for themselves. The 15 children rejected a reading of (20b) in which none of the bears washed themselves 100% of the time.

Less clear-cut are results from studies investigating how children interpret the pronoun *it*. This pronoun is of interest for investigations of the binding theory because it has some properties that distinguish it from pronouns like *him* and *her*. It cannot function as a deictic pronoun, for example. One cannot point to an object and say *I want IT*, placing emphasis on the pronoun. Because it cannot function deictically, it is often referred to as a weak pronoun. This has led some researchers to predict that children will not allow the pronoun *it* to refer to a referential NP antecedent in the same sentence. A number of independent pilot studies, by Thornton (1991) and by Michal Starke and Anna Cardinaletti (personal communication, 1994), and a larger study by Savarese (1999) have attempted to test this prediction. In his study, Savarese found that children who allowed coreference in sentences like *Mama Bear washed her* sometimes allowed coreference between *it* and *the fire engine* in sentences like *The fire engine sprayed it.* At face value, the results did not support the theoretical predictions. There are a number of methodological problems inherent in testing sentences containing the pronoun *it*, however, which may have confounded the results.[12] Until these problems can be solved, we must reserve judgment on this prediction.

The hypothesis that children know and correctly apply Principle B, but sometimes misapply Principle P, was also advanced by Avrutin (1994) and Avrutin and Wexler (1999) in a study of the disjoint reference effect for pronominal subjects of embedded subjunctive clauses in Russian. Following a binding theory (Principle B) account of the disjoint reference effect (Avrutin and Babyonyshev 1997), Avrutin and Wexler predicted that the disjoint reference effect should hold for adults, whether the pronominal subject is a bound variable or a referential pronoun. On the other hand, for children who misinterpret pronouns and allow local coreference, the effect should hold only for bound variable pronouns. They confirmed this prediction experimentally, further supporting the theory outlined here.

2.3   Grodzinsky and Reinhart 1993

2.3.1   Grodzinsky and Reinhart's Account

In the rest of this chapter, we consider alternative accounts of Chien and Wexler's findings, beginning with Grodzinsky and Reinhart's (1993) account. This analysis is similar in many respects to that advanced by Chien and Wexler (1990). Grodzinsky and Reinhart agree with Chien and Wexler's basic interpretation of the data. For example, they agree with the claim that children have innate knowledge of Principle B; they link children's acceptance of an illicit interpretation for sentences like *Mama Bear is washing her* to a separate principle; and they agree that as a result of applying Principle B, children should not give nonadult judgments on sentences when the antecedent of the pronoun is a quantificational NP like *every bear.* The disagreement concerns the role of the pragmatic principle in children's misinterpretation of pronouns.

For Grodzinsky and Reinhart, the fact that children respond differently to sentences like *Mama Bear is washing her* and *Every bear is washing her* follows naturally from Reinhart's particular version of the binding theory

(Reinhart 1983, 1986). To show why, we will briefly review Reinhart's proposal.

In Reinhart's system, Principle B applies only to bound pronouns (i.e., pronouns that are interpreted as bound variables). Formally, the bound variable status of a pronoun with respect to its antecedent is indicated by indices on the relevant NPs in the syntactic representation of the sentence. In order to qualify as a bound variable, a pronoun must be c-commanded by its antecedent. The c-commanding antecedent NP may be referential, like *Mama Bear*, or quantificational, like *who* or *every bear*.[13] However, Principle B rules out the representations in (21d)–(21f), so the pronouns in such constructions must be referential.

(21) a. Mama Bear$_i$ is washing her$_i$ face.
    b. Who$_i$ is washing her$_i$ face?
    c. Every bear$_i$ is washing her$_i$ face.
    d. *Mama Bear$_i$ is washing her$_i$.
    e. *Who$_i$ is washing her$_i$?
    f. *Every bear$_i$ is washing her$_i$.

Reflexives are always bound variables, whereas ordinary pronouns need not be; the latter can be interpreted either as bound variables or referentially. Referential pronouns are not constrained by the syntax (e.g., Principle B) in Reinhart's system. Their reference is chosen from the domain of discourse, subject to certain pragmatic constraints. The referent may be mentioned either in the sentence containing the pronoun or in some previous sentence in the discourse. *or non-linguistic*

The distinction between coreference and variable binding is crucial to Reinhart's theory, which makes the following distinction between them: bound pronouns bear indices, referential pronouns do not. Thus, the pronouns in (22)–(24) are all referential pronouns. They can clearly refer to individuals not mentioned in the sentence, but available in the context (although no context is given here). Whether or not coreference is permitted between a pronoun and another NP in each sentence is a separate issue, to be determined by a pragmatic rule, Rule I.

(22) a. Mama Bear is washing her face.
    b. Mama Bear thinks she is a great cook.

(23) a. Most of her friends adore Mama Bear.
    b. A party without Mama Bear would upset her.

(24) a. Mama Bear is washing her.
    b. She is washing Mama Bear.

According to Reinhart, the pragmatic rule, Rule I, is innately specified, presumably because it is a constraint—a sanction against one way of interpreting certain sentences. In the absence of negative evidence, it seems unlikely that Rule I could be learned.

Intuitively, Rule I enforces the pragmatic dictum for speakers to select a construction that unambiguously indicates their intended meaning, if possible (Grice 1975). If the intended meaning of a sentence can be expressed by using a bound variable, such as a reflexive pronoun, then that form of expression is preferred, all other things being equal, because a reflexive pronoun expresses its meaning without ambiguity. Therefore, when a speaker selects an ordinary pronoun (which may be either bound or referential), in a construction in which a reflexive pronoun is also licensed, the inference to be drawn by the hearer is that the speaker purposefully avoided a reflexive pronoun. Therefore, the speaker intended the hearer to interpret the pronoun as referential, but lacked an unambiguous way of transmitting the intended meaning. It follows that the intended interpretation of a sentence like *Mama Bear is washing her* is one of non-coreference between the pronoun and the referential NP. If the speaker had intended coreference he or she would have used a reflexive pronoun in place of the ordinary pronoun. This is just the intuition behind Rule I, however.

Technically, Rule I applies at LF, where Quantifier Raising (QR) occurs. At LF, linguistic expressions that have undergone QR are interpreted (see Heim 1998 for the details of QR and the translation of syntactic representations into semantic representations). Rule I is stated in (25).

(25) *Rule I: Intrasentential Coreference*
     NP A cannot corefer with NP B if replacing A with C, C a variable A-bound by B, yields an indistinguishable interpretation.

In the final part of our introduction to Reinhart's system, we show how Rule I applies to the example sentences in (22)–(24). We give an informal rather than technical statement of the process.

Rule I is designed to determine whether coreference is possible in a particular structure. It may be helpful to think of Rule I as consisting of three steps. Step 1 is to check whether c-command holds between the two NPs. Step 2 verifies whether binding is possible or not. Finally, step 3 compares the binding and coreference representations to see if they are distinguishable. In some cases, the procedure for applying Rule I returns an answer regarding the intended interpretation even before all three steps have been executed. This is true for examples like (22a–b) and (23a–b) but not for (24a–b).

In sentences like (22a–b), Rule I dictates the intended interpretation before all three steps have been completed. To see why, recall the intuition behind Rule I: to opt for variable binding over coreference whenever possible. If a bound variable interpretation of a pronoun is possible, coreference need not be considered. The first two steps of the Rule I procedure indicate that the pronoun in (22a–b) is c-commanded by the antecedent and that the pronoun can be treated as a bound variable. Therefore, the procedure stops at step 2. Coreference is not considered.[14] The procedure for Rule I can be aborted after step 2 for (23a–b) also. Here, the pronoun is not c-commanded by the antecedent. This means that binding is not logically possible; therefore, the pronoun can only be interpreted referentially. There is no point in proceeding to step 3.

The crucial examples, for our purposes, are (24a–b). Here, all of the steps associated with Rule I must be carried out. After steps 1 and 2 are taken, the pronoun is found to be c-commanded by its antecedent. This means that the structural configuration is appropriate for variable binding. However, variable binding is ruled out by a syntactic condition, Principle B. It is therefore necessary to proceed to step 3 to determine whether the bound variable and coreference interpretations can be distinguished. If so, then coreference is permitted. If not, then Rule I dictates that the hearer cannot give a coreferential interpretation to the sentence. The only choice is to interpret the pronoun deictically.

Notice that Rule I compares the logical forms of the bound variable representation with the representation on which the pronoun and its antecedent corefer (although the representation for the bound variable reading is excluded by Principle B). The two LF representations are given in (26) and (27). Arrows indicate the semantic values of both names and pronouns. As in chapter 1, uppercase initials stand for real-world referents.

(26) Mama Bear is washing her   (coreference)

    ↓   ↓

   MB   MB

(27) Mama Bear (λx (x is washing x))   (bound variable)

    ↓

   MB

A comparison of these two LF representations shows that they are indistinguishable. Both have the same truth value—roughly, that Mama Bear washed Mama Bear. Therefore, Rule I applies. Consequently, the coreference interpretation is excluded, at least for adults.

This ends our introduction of the relevant aspects of Reinhart's theory of binding and coreference. We turn now to Grodzinsky and Reinhart's account of the data presented in Chien and Wexler's (1990) experiment.

Let us begin by considering sentences with quantificational NP antecedents, such as *Every bear is washing her*. Recall that in Chien and Wexler's experiment, children responded with considerable success to this sentence type, rejecting the meaning in which every bear washes herself about 85% of the time. Crucially, for Grodzinsky and Reinhart, such sentences are necessarily regulated by the binding theory and not by Rule I. Like Chien and Wexler, Grodzinsky and Reinhart view children as adhering to Principle B; this is attested by the high level at which they correctly reject sentences in which the pronoun is a bound variable. Also like Chien and Wexler, Grodzinsky and Reinhart conclude that children's knowledge of the syntactic principles of the binding theory is intact.

The difference between Chien and Wexler's and Grodzinsky and Reinhart's accounts can now be stated clearly. Grodzinsky and Reinhart interpret children's relatively poor performance in response to sentences like *Mama Bear is washing her* as evidence of a difficulty in applying Rule I.[15] Completion of all three of the steps associated with the application of Rule I entails comparing two alternative syntactic representations simultaneously, to decide whether they yield indistinguishable interpretations. The alternative representations must be maintained in memory long enough for the necessary calculation to take place. According to Grodzinsky and Reinhart, young children sometimes succumb to processing overload in executing the computation needed to apply Rule I, owing to an immature processing system. They state, "[C]hildren know exactly what they are required to do by Rule I, but getting stuck in the execution process, they give up and guess" (1993, 88). This quotation explains why children accept (roughly) 50% of sentences in which the pronoun has a referential antecedent.[16] When children's processing capacity increases, according to Grodzinsky and Reinhart, they are able to make the requisite calculations for Rule I, and they respond more accurately in experimental tasks.

What about other sentences to which Rule I applies? Grodzinsky and Reinhart essentially claim that there is a gradient of processing difficulty for the sentence types shown in (22)–(24). The least taxing structures are ones like (22a–b), in which binding is possible; in this case, the coreference interpretation does not need to be considered. More of a processing burden is imposed by cases like (23a–b), but such sentences are still not beyond the child's resources. Finally, cases like (24a–b) are the most difficult. For such sentences, children must execute all three steps of the Rule I procedure. The idea is that the third step of the calculation exceeds the threshold of children's working memory resources, causing them to guess the intended interpretation.

In Reinhart's theory, Principle C is eliminated, and Principle C effects are handled solely by pragmatics, that is, by Rule I. (For purposes of exposition, however, we will continue to talk of Principle C.) Thus, Rule I is also relevant for examples like (24b), a sentence that would be governed by Principle C in Chomsky's theory (Chomsky 1981, 1986).

Sentences like *She is washing Mama Bear* require all three steps of the Rule I procedure to be calculated. Step 1 determines the c-command relation between the two NPs. Step 2 verifies whether or not variable binding is possible between the pronoun and the name. This point is not discussed in Grodzinsky and Reinhart 1993, but it is taken up in Reinhart 1997, where the suggestion is made that binding does not obtain in the LF representation, because an NP like *Mama Bear* is not a free variable and therefore not the right kind of object to be bound by an operator. Technicalities aside, the assumption is that such sentences require step 3 of Rule I to be computed. For the purposes of this comparison, the free NP *Mama Bear* can be replaced by a variable, and this bound variable representation (shown in (29)) is compared with the coreference representation (shown in (28)).

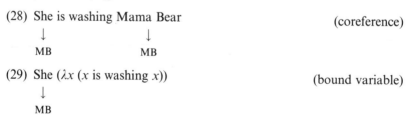

(28) She is washing Mama Bear   (coreference)
      ↓   ↓
      MB   MB

(29) She (λx (x is washing x))   (bound variable)
      ↓
      MB

A comparison of the propositions expressed by the two representations at LF shows that the two cannot be distinguished. Therefore, coreference is ruled out for such sentences. Because this conclusion is based on comparison of the two LF representations, the prediction is that children should experience difficulty executing all three steps of Rule I and therefore should find sentences like *She is washing Mama Bear* as difficult to interpret as *Mama Bear is washing her*.

In short, Grodzinsky and Reinhart propose that children have innate knowledge of both Principle B and Rule I, but their implementation of Rule I is hampered by an immature processing system.

At this point, we take a brief detour to discuss Heim's (1998) analysis of Rule I. Her conclusions prove to be useful in our own account of children's misinterpretation of sentences like *Mama Bear is washing her*, presented in chapter 3.

2.3.2   Heim's (1998) Clarification of Rule I

Heim (1998) points out a number of technical problems with Grodzinsky and Reinhart's account, which lead her to revise Principle B. Since the technical innovations of this revision are not important for our purposes, we do not discuss them here (see Reinhart's (1997) response to Heim). Instead, we concentrate on Heim's discussion of Rule I, in particular the section that clarifies what it means for two interpretations to be "indistinguishable."

Recall Grodzinsky and Reinhart's (1993) statement of Rule I:

(30) *Rule I: Intrasentential Coreference*
      NP A cannot corefer with NP B if replacing A with C, C a variable
      A-bound by B, yields an indistinguishable interpretation.

Heim points out that strictly speaking, not all of the examples considered by Grodzinsky and Reinhart fall under the auspices of Rule I. The ones that do so, in Heim's view, are reviewed below. (Some examples are adapted by Heim so they can be covered by Principle B rather than Principle C.)[17] These examples lead Heim to offer a more detailed account of what it means for two interpretations to be "indistinguishable."

Heim considers three contexts to which Rule I should apply.

(31) *Run-of-the-mill contexts*
      Mama Bear is washing her.

(32) *Identity debate contexts*
      Speaker A   Is this speaker Zelda?
      Speaker B   How can you doubt it? She praises her to the sky. No
      competing candidate would do that.

(33) *Structured-meaning contexts*
      You know what Mary, Sue, and John have in common? Mary
      admires John, Sue admires him, and John admires him too.

As Heim notes, in run-of-the-mill contexts, Rule I seems to function as intended. When the propositions expressed by the LF structures for the bound variable interpretation and the coreference interpretation are compared, the two are found to be indistinguishable. Thus, the coreference interpretation is not permitted, and disjoint reference is the only possibility.

The identity debate examples are problematic, however. Intuition tells us that coreference is legitimate, but a comparison of the LF propositions turns up no difference in interpretation, predicting coreference to be impossible. This is illustrated in (34a) and (34b).[18] In each case, the NP in the LF structure is connected by an arrow to a letter that stands for the referent it picks out in the real world. Both LF structures express the proposition that Z (which picks out *Zelda*) praises Z to the sky.

(34) a. She praises her to the sky   (coreference)
      ↓   ↓
      Z   Z

    b. She (λx (x praises x to the sky))   (bound variable)
      ↓
      Z

Heim suggests that researchers need to consider the context of utterance more closely. She proposes the need to distinguish between the *cognitive value* of a sentence and the *proposition* it expresses. The cognitive value of a sentence provides an account of how the referents are presented in the world. The dialogue in (32) suggests that there are really two presentations of person Z (i.e., *Zelda*) at issue: the particular impression of person Z that the speakers have in their memories from previous events, and the here-and-now visual impression of person Z (who is currently on stage giving a speech). These two presentations of the person are said to be the person in two different "guises." In a sentence like *She praises her to the sky*, Heim proposes, each of the two pronouns (*she* and *her* in (34a)) connects to its referent Z via one of these two presentations. "Therefore, the cognitive value of the sentence *She praises her to the sky* for the hearer in this context is the proposition that whoever causes the visual impression in question praises whomever the pertinent memory entry represents" (Heim 1998, 214). For this reason, the representation of the coreference interpretation should be adapted to include information about each unique presentation of the individual Z, as in (35).

(35) She praises her to the sky   (coreference)

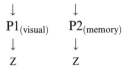

The coreference representation in (35) and the bound variable representation in (34b) now express two different propositions. Rule I gives the right result. The coreference interpretation is not preempted by the bound variable interpretation—coreference is deemed legitimate. (In chapter 1, we represented this more simply and did not take the extra step of illustrating whether each presentation or guise of the individual is visual, memory-based, and so on.)

It can be assumed that run-of-the-mill type examples are not usually uttered in a context rich enough to give rise to two different presentations, or guises, of a person. Therefore, the coreference interpretation will still be overshadowed by the bound variable interpretation, the two being indistinguishable. However, if the sentence (e.g., *Mama Bear is washing her*) is presented in a suitably complex context, with the pronoun bearing heavy stress, it could end up that the two NPs (here, *Mama Bear* and *her*) present different guises of the same individual in the world, that is, the individual indicated by *MB* in (36).[19] This is the interpretation we introduced for such sentences in (11d) in chapter 1.

(36) Mama Bear is washing her   (coreference)

Heim's third context, the structured-meaning context (see (37)), presents a further complication. The adult judgment is that coreference is permissible, yet in Heim's view the sentence type doesn't seem to involve two presentations of the individual (here, John). There must be some way in which the propositions are distinguishable. Heim suggests that although the propositions expressed by the LF representations are the same, the *structured* propositions are different. The interpretation shown in (37) makes it clear that the same property is predicated of each of the three people: in each case, the subject has the property of admiring J. The bound variable interpretation in (38), on the other hand, breaks that pattern. The property attributed to J (i.e., self-admiration) is now different from the property attributed to M and S. According to Heim, this difference in structured propositions is enough to preempt the bound variable interpretation and allow coreference.

(37) Mary admires John, Sue admires him, and John admires him too
$$\downarrow \qquad\qquad \downarrow \quad \downarrow \qquad\quad \downarrow \qquad\quad \downarrow \qquad\qquad\quad \downarrow$$
$$\text{M} \qquad\qquad \text{J} \quad \text{S} \qquad\quad \text{J} \qquad\quad \text{J} \qquad\qquad\quad \text{J}$$

(38) Mary admires John, Sue admires him, and John (λx (x admires x)) too
$$\downarrow \qquad\qquad \downarrow \quad \downarrow \qquad\quad \downarrow \qquad\quad \downarrow$$
$$\text{M} \qquad\qquad \text{J} \quad \text{S} \qquad\quad \text{J} \qquad\quad \text{J}$$

This ends our review of the main cases that Heim considers to allow local coreference interpretations.[20] The idea that in certain circumstances a referent can have two presentations, or guises, will be important in our account of children's misinterpretation of pronouns in chapter 3.

2.3.3 Issues for Grodzinsky and Reinhart's Account

2.3.3.1 The Execution of Rule I and Processing Let us return to the crux of Grodzinsky and Reinhart's proposal concerning children's acceptance of the illicit interpretation of sentences like *Mama Bear is washing her*. In trying to apply Rule I, children are claimed to have difficulty holding two representations in memory long enough to compare them. The "evidential basis" for their claim is a lexical access experiment carried out by Swinney (1979) with nonaphasic adults, by Swinney and Prather (1989) with children, and by Swinney, Nicol, and Zurif (1989) with aphasic adults. In a nutshell, whereas nonaphasic adults are found to access both meanings of an ambiguous lexical item, even in a context that supports only one reading, children and aphasic adults appear to access only one meaning, the one with the higher frequency of occurrence.

We wish to raise several concerns about Grodzinsky and Reinhart's proposal. The first is whether one can compare results from experiments involving ambiguous lexical entries and ones involving competing syntactic representations. As Stephen Crain (personal communication) has pointed out to us, there is an inherent difference between the two phenomena, if we accept Fodor's (1983) account of the priming effects for lexical entries related to either meaning of an ambiguous lexical item. Fodor argues that priming effects are the result of intralexical connections among entries in the mental lexicon, not a comparison of meanings: "The present suggestion is that no such intelligent evaluation of options takes place; there is merely a brute facilitation" of one lexical item by another (Fodor 1983, 81). On the account advanced by Fodor, the fact that children and adult aphasics fail to demonstrate priming effects character-istic of nonaphasic adults would not be viewed as the product of greater processing limitations; rather, it would be interpreted as evidence that the mental lexicons of children and aphasic adults lack certain intralexical connections among entries in their mental lexicons. The differences be-tween children and aphasic adults, on the one hand, and nonaphasic adults, on the other, would be architectural and not due to processing resources.

Another concern is the predictive power of Grodzinsky and Reinhart's proposal. In the absence of an explicit metric of processing complexity, the precise conditions under which children are expected to experience difficulty are unclear. As outlined above, Grodzinsky and Reinhart assume that children are able to compute the referent of pronouns in structures like *Mama Bear is washing her face* and *Most of her friends adore Mama Bear*, but not in structures like *Mama Bear is washing her*. Without a metric of computational complexity, the claim that children have difficulty in determining the referent for the pronoun in one kind of sentence but not another has little force.

Indeed, there are several empirical findings in the literature showing that for many complex structures, children can hold two representations in memory and compare them for the purposes of computing the referent of a pronoun. One example is provided by short discourse sequences testing Principle B in which the pronoun has the operator *who* as its antecedent (Crain 1991; Thornton 1990). Children were presented with an indirect question and answer such as "I know who scratched him. Bert." In order to judge the truth value of the discourse, children not only had to apply Principle B to the first sentence and hold it in memory, but also had to fill in the VP missing in the second sentence and enter this into the computation, again comparing representations. Despite the seeming diffi-culty of this task, children performed at near adult levels.

Further evidence of children's processing capacity comes from a study of discourse binding by Crain and Conway (Conway and Crain 1995a,b; Conway 1997). Children were asked to judge the grammaticality of cross-sentential anaphora in sequences like those in (39a) and (39b).[21]

(39) a. No mouse/Every mouse came to Simba's party. He wore a hat.
     b. A mouse came to Simba's party. He wore a hat.

Such discourse sequences are subject to the closure constraint (Chierchia 1995), which restricts the antecedents that singular pronouns may have in a discourse. According to this constraint, the singular pronoun *he* in the second sentence of the discourses cannot take the quantificational NP *no mouse* or *every mouse* as its antecedent (39a), but it may take the indefinite NP *a mouse* (39b). Children did well at this task, accepting the illicit interpretation of (39a), in which the pronoun was treated as a bound variable, only 19% of the time, and responding correctly to (39b) 93% of the time. Clearly, children must be able to hold both sentences in memory in order to apply the relevant constraint.

We have also found that in experiments testing interpretation of pronouns, children sometimes ask for clarification of the referent. This suggests that they see that the pronoun has more than one potential referent; and clearly, if they see that the pronoun has two possible referents, they must be weighing the two possible representations that enter into the computation of Rule I. A child who is guessing because of processing overload would not be able to ask for clarification of the referent.

As a final example of children's processing capabilities, we would note that children often volunteer an explanation about "what really happened" in the truth value judgment task. For example, in a study by Chierchia et al. (1998), children were asked to judge sentences containing disjunctions, such as *The elephant jumped over the barrel or the fence*, in a situation where the elephant jumped over both the barrel and the fence. Not only were the majority of children able to repeat what the puppet had said; they also went on to tell the puppet what he should have said: "The elephant jumped over the barrel *and* the fence." Clearly, such a response calls upon the child to maintain two representations in mind at the same time.

On Grodzinsky and Reinhart's account, the processing bottleneck that children encounter is "of the sort known to diminish with age" (1993, 91). Thus, they do not share the assumption that children have access to a universal parser (see Crain and Wexler 1999; Crain and Thornton 1998). Rather, the child's processing system has different properties from the adult's, and Rule I remains problematic until this system matures. The prediction, then, is that all children will accept nonadult interpretations of sentences like *Mama Bear is washing her* until maturation occurs. In many experiments, including the one presented in chapter 4, this is not the case.

To verify whether or not all children fall prey to processing difficulty requires examining individual subject data, which are not reported for all experiments. At least in some of the published experiments, however, not all children misinterpreted pronouns. For example, McDaniel and Maxfield (1992) note that 17 out of 35 children (aged between 3;1 and 6;10) did not violate Principle B. The figure was similar in Avrutin and Thornton's (1994) experiment. There, 17 out of 33 children (aged between 3;10 and 4;10) behaved as adults do, rejecting local coreference interpretations. In our view, the number of children who respond like adults depends on the properties of the experimental context, and this is why the number fluctuates from experiment to experiment. In short, it seems that children vary in their performance, which is unexpected if the computational system rather than context is crucial.

As pointed out by Avrutin and Wexler (1992), an important prediction made by Grodzinsky and Reinhart's account is that children will have difficulty with cases in which Rule I returns the answer that coreference is acceptable for adults—for example, the identity debate examples and the structured-meaning examples explored by Heim. Recall the examples that require computation of all the steps of Rule I.

(40) a. Mama Bear is washing her.
      b. [Context] She praises her to the sky.

In (40a), both binding and coreference are excluded. Without specific supporting context, only one guise of Mama Bear is presented, and the coreference and bound variable LF representations cannot be distinguished. The pronoun has to be taken to refer to someone not mentioned in the sentence. Example (40b) is different. Coreference is allowed because the sentence is uttered in a context in which the two instances of the pronoun represent different guises of the referent. In this case, the coreference and bound variable interpretations can be distinguished at LF. Regardless of the final outcome, though, Rule I requires that two representations be compared for both examples (40a) and (40b).

How does the child fare in computing Rule I for examples like (40a) and (40b)? According to Grodzinsky and Reinharts's account, since both examples require comparing two representations, both should cause difficulty for the child. Although no formal studies have been done on identity debate and structured-meaning examples, and there is no empirical evidence either way at the moment, our own account, presented in chapter 3, predicts that children will have no difficulty with such examples.

2.3.3.2 Principle C Effects   Grodzinsky and Reinhart do not present a convincing case that application of Rule I causes children difficulty with both Principle B and Principle C structures. First, let's review the empirical evidence they discuss. They note that in reported experiments, children have not always treated Principles B and C on a par. But they point out that directionality has often been cited as a factor. Compare (41a) and (41b).

(41) a. *He said that Bert touched the box.
     b. Because he heard a lion, Tommy ran fast.

In those studies in which children have been claimed to rule out interpretations governed by Principle C (e.g., sentences like (41a)), Grodzinsky and Reinhart point out that they also reject legitimate cases of backward anaphora like (41b) (Tavakolian 1977; Solan 1978; Lust, Loveland, and Kornet 1980; Lust and Clifford 1982). So, the claim goes, if children don't allow backward anaphora in cases like (41b), the fact that they don't allow it in (41a) does not show that they have knowledge of Principle C.

In our view, there is a clear reason for the directionality effect: it is a product of the experimental methodology. All of the studies that show the directionality effect used either act-out tasks or elicited imitation tasks. Take the act-out task first. If, in acting out a sentence with toy props, children take the pronoun to refer to an individual not referred to in the sentence, this does not imply that the backward anaphora interpretation is missing from their grammars. It merely shows a preference for the alternative, more accessible interpretation. In elicited-imitation studies, children have sometimes been found to avoid repeating (41b) verbatim, instead reversing the order of the pronoun and the name, as in (42).

(42) Because Tommy heard a lion, he ran fast.

Such reversals have been taken to show that children do not allow backward anaphora. As pointed out by Lasnik and Crain (1985), however, children would not be able to rearrange such sentences in this way if they did not have a firm grasp of the coreference relations. Moreover, in Crain and McKee's (1985) study, in which directionality was not a factor, children had no difficulty in accepting a backward anaphora reading.

Further defending the prediction that children should treat cases subject to Principles B and C in the same way, Grodzinsky and Reinhart discuss sentences like (43a–b), which involve reconstruction. The term *reconstruction* describes the fact that in examples like (43a–b), the pronoun or name in the topicalized prepositional phrase is interpreted as if it is in its base position.

(43) a. *Near Ann$_i$, she$_i$ saw a lion.
     b. *Near him$_i$, every hunter$_i$ saw a lion.

When tested on this sentence type, children have been shown to perform poorly (Ingram and Shaw 1981; Taylor-Browne 1983; Lust, Loveland, and Kornet 1980). Grodzinsky and Reinhart attribute this poor performance to difficulty with Rule I.

A closer look at Taylor-Browne's (1983) study reveals that it is premature to blame children's difficulty with sentences like (43) on Rule I; other possibilities must be considered. The methodology of this particular pilot study was that used by Chomsky (1969). Children were shown dolls that corresponded to the NPs in a test sentence and then were questioned about their interpretation of the sentence. However, even the adult controls in this study experienced significant difficulty in ruling out coreference in sentences like (43a), blocking it only 84% of the time. On sentences like those in (44), adults' performance dropped even lower, to 60%.

(44) a. *Across Vicky$_i$'s bed, she$_i$ laid the dress.
     b. *In front of Ken$_i$, on the bus which takes the children home from school, he$_i$ saw a friend.

Clearly, whatever factor is responsible for adults' difficulty with the task is likely to be responsible for children's difficulty with it. In these circumstances, Rule I may be tangential to the difficulties experienced by both groups.

In sum, Grodzinsky and Reinhart's proposal is not able to account for any asymmetry in the findings for Principles B and C. This is important, given that other experimental results (including our own) show that children treat matrix Principle B and C sentences very differently.

We should mention briefly a few studies in which children have demonstrated knowledge of Principle C. Using a truth value judgment task, Crain and McKee (1985) showed that children ruled out backward anaphora (i.e., coreference) when it violated Principle C, but allowed it when it did not.[22] Their subjects were 62 children between 3 and 6 years of age. When the results from three experiments were pooled, the children were found to accept backward anaphora 73% of the time for sentences like (45) and to reject it 88% of the time when it violated Principle C, as in sentences like (46a) and (46b).

(45) When she was outside playing, Strawberry Shortcake ate an ice-cream cone.

(46) a. He washed Luke Skywalker.
    b. He ate the hamburger when the Smurf was in the fence.

A recent study by Guasti and Chierchia (in press) tested Italian-speaking children's knowledge of Principle C in structures subject to reconstruction. They conducted a series of experiments using the truth value judgment task. Eighteen children between the ages of 3;10 and 5;7 were tested on sentences like (47a–b) and (48). In (47a–b), the null pronoun can be interpreted either anaphorically or deictically. In (47a), the direct object follows the verb; in (47b), it precedes it, and a clitic pronoun is used. These examples were the controls. Examples like (48) tested children's knowledge of Principle C, using a structure that required reconstruction (Chierchia 1995).

(47) a. Le scimmie hanno nascosto il   tesoro   di ciascun
       the monkeys have   hidden   the treasure of each/every
       bambino, mentre dormiva.
       child   while   (he) was sleeping
       'The monkeys hid the treasure of every child while he was
       sleeping.'
    b. Il tesoro   di ciascun   bambino, le scimmie lo hanno
       the treasure of each/every child   the monkeys it have
       nascosto, mentre dormiva.
       hidden   while   (he) was sleeping
       'The treasure of every child, the monkeys hid it, while he was
       sleeping.'

(48) Nel   barile di ciascun   pirata con cura ha   messo una
     in-the barrel of each/every pirate with care (he) has put   a
     pistola.
     gun
     'In the barrel of every pirate, he carefully put a gun.'

Children accepted both the anaphoric (i.e., bound variable) and deictic interpretations of examples like (47a–b); the forward anaphoric reading was accepted 86% of the time and the deictic reading 89% of the time. Children demonstrated their knowledge of Principle C by rejecting target sentences like (48) 90% of the time.

Positive knowledge of Principle C is also shown in an experiment testing the constraint on strong crossover (Thornton 1990; Crain and Thornton 1998).[23] Twelve children between the ages of 3;7 and 4;8 were tested using one-clause and two-clause crossover structures like (49a) and (49b).[24]

(49) a. I know who he scratched. Bert.
     b. I know who he said has the best food. Bert and Grover.

The constraint was tested by investigating whether children could treat the pronoun in these structures as a bound variable, instead of as a singular, deictic pronoun. This entailed testing whether children allowed (49a) to mean something like *I know who scratched himself* and whether they allowed (49b) to mean something like *I know who said he has the best food*, where the pronoun *he* picks out multiple individuals from a set of people. In both cases, children rejected the bound variable interpretation: 97% of the time for one-clause structures, and 92% of the time for two-clause structures.

In summary, there are two main problems with Grodzinsky and Reinhart's account of children's interpretation of sentences governed by Principle B. First, there is little or no evidence to support the proposal that some sentences containing pronouns (e.g., *Mama Bear is washing her*) cause a processing overload whereas others (e.g., *Mama Bear is washing her face* and *Most of her friends adore Mama Bear*) do not. Second, there are reliable experimental findings showing that whereas children misinterpret pronouns in Principle B structures, they do not have difficulty with parallel Principle C structures (i.e., *Mama Bear is washing her* vs. *She is washing Mama Bear*). On the Rule I account, both should be equally difficult to process.

2.4 Grimshaw and Rosen 1990

2.4.1 Grimshaw and Rosen's Account
Grimshaw and Rosen (1990) take as the starting point for their account the uncontroversial assumption that Principle B is responsible for excluding illicit interpretations of sentences in which a pronoun is bound by its antecedent inside the sentence. They share this assumption with Chien and Wexler (1990) and Grodzinsky and Reinhart (1993). They differ from these authors, however, in trying to avoid attributing children's nonadult interpretations to lack of pragmatic knowledge (or difficulty with applying a pragmatic rule). Instead, they attribute them to artifactual experimental conditions.

To summarize Grimshaw and Rosen's account: Even though children's performance is poor on sentences like *Mama Bear is washing her*, Grimshaw and Rosen take the experimental results to indicate children's positive knowledge of Principle B. As a result, they must explain why children give a higher level of correct responses to sentences in which the antecedent of the pronoun is a quantificational NP, like *Every bear is washing her*. They claim that children's good performance on such sentences is only superficial: in fact, children have difficulty interpreting bound variables, and it is this difficulty that leads them to reject the sentence. So what looks like good performance on sentences with a quantificational NP antecedent actually reflects a lack of linguistic abilities.

Now let us look at this account in more detail. Recall that both Chien and Wexler (1990) and Grodzinsky and Reinhart (1993) attribute children's high rate of success on sentences containing quantificational NPs to their knowledge of Principle B. On their accounts, what must be explained is children's lower proportion of correct responses to sentences with referential NP antecedents. Grimshaw and Rosen turn the matter around. Although children make roughly 50% errors in responding to sentences with referential NP antecedents, Grimshaw and Rosen contend that children's performance on these sentences does reflect complete adult knowledge. They argue as follows. If children did not have adult knowledge, they would accept coreference between a referential NP and a pronoun under coindexation just as often as they accept disjoint reference. There would be no reason to expect different results for the two interpretations. However, children do accept *Mama Bear is washing her* as a description of a picture in which Mama Bear is washing Goldilocks *more often* than they accept it as a description of a picture in which Mama Bear is washing herself—90% of the time versus 49% of the time, for the 5-year-old group in Chien and Wexler's experiment, as shown in (50). Grimshaw and Rosen conclude that the difference (41%) in the rate of acceptance reflects the contribution of Principle B to children's linguistic performance.

(50) a. Mama Bear is washing her. (her = Mama Bear)
        49% "Yes" responses
     b. Mama Bear is washing her. (her = Goldilocks)
        90% "Yes" responses

Unlike the previous authors, Grimshaw and Rosen contend that children's high rejection rate for sentences with quantificational NP antecedents is not a manifestation of their knowledge of Principle B. In their view, children frequently give the right answer for the wrong reason. They suggest that children often have difficulty accessing bound variable interpretations. The result is that children don't even consider that there could be an anaphoric bound variable relationship between the pronoun and the quantificational NP antecedent. In their words, "Suppose that children find the distributed reading associated with the quantifier–bound variable pair difficult, and construct this interpretation for pronouns less often than the alternative interpretations" (1990, 214). In the face of difficulties in accessing the bound variable reading of the pronoun, children are left with only the deictic interpretation. The picture corresponding to *Every bear is washing her* shows three girl bears washing themselves; Goldilocks is also present, watching them. Children who experience difficulty accessing the bound variable interpretation of the test sentence cannot relate the pronoun *her* to *every bear*; they can only take it to refer to Goldilocks. Since the picture does not depict the bears washing *her* (i.e., Goldilocks), children respond by saying "No." That is, children reject sentences with the universal quantifier because the sentence is false on the only interpretation they can consider. On this view, it only appears that children are obeying Principle B. In reality, their "successful" performance rests on their inability to generate the bound variable representation of the test sentences to which Principle B applies.

As a consequence of children's difficulty in accessing the bound variable interpretation, Grimshaw and Rosen suppose that children should also find it hard to process certain unambiguous sentences—for example, sentences with quantificational NPs that bind reflexive pronouns. To correctly interpret sentences like (51a), for example, the child must understand the reflexive as a bound variable. This "distributed" reading is not required for interpreting (51b), so Grimshaw and Rosen predict better performance on (51b) than on (51a).

(51) a. Every bear is washing herself.
     b. Mama Bear is washing herself.

In Chien and Wexler's experiment, sentences with reflexives like (51a) and (51b) were used as control sentences to ensure that children can accept bound variables in the syntactic position where Principle B excludes bound pronouns. These sentences were tested using the same picture stimuli as for *Mama Bear is washing her* and *Every bear is washing her*. The difference between the test of the pronoun and the test of the reflexive was that the correct interpretation of (51a–b) corresponded to a "Yes" response (because in the picture, every girl bear was in fact washing herself). According to Grimshaw and Rosen, the inaccessibility of the bound variable reading should cause children to reject (51a) some of the time. They should not reject (51b) since it does not require a distributed reading. Grimshaw and Rosen suggest that Chien and Wexler's results show "a small but consistent difference in the predicted direction" (p. 216). We return to this point in the next section.

2.4.2   Issues for Grimshaw and Rosen's Account

Like the other researchers, Grimshaw and Rosen argue that Principle B is intact in children's grammars. Because, in their view, pragmatic knowledge plays no role in children's misinterpretations of pronouns, they are led to hypothesize that children's difficulties lie in another direction. Specifically, they suggest that previous researchers may have overlooked experimental factors that could have contributed to the apparent Principle B violations. In this section, we argue against this suggestion.

First, we should point out that Grimshaw and Rosen's argument does not follow from a modular view of the language faculty. It allows children's poor performance to indicate knowledge of a grammatical principle because competing experimental factors are seen as masking their true grammatical knowledge. (Detailed arguments against this kind of competing factors model can be found in Crain and Thornton 1998 and Crain and Wexler 1999.) Our view is that provided the experiment is not flawed, knowledge of a grammatical principle will be shown by a high level of correct responses, about 90%. Other factors will not impinge on children's performance. If the experiment is sound, and a 90% level is not obtained, there is something else to be explained. This is our approach to the 50% acceptance level of *Mama Bear is washing her.*

Let us return to Grimshaw and Rosen's claim that if children were lacking Principle B, they should respond equally well to the two pictures representing possible interpretations of *Mama Bear is washing her* (see (50a) and (50b)). In our view, there is no expectation that the two pictures should be treated the same. In the picture where Mama Bear is washing Goldilocks, the context unequivocally matches the test sentence, but in the picture where Mama Bear is washing herself, there is a mismatch between what is shown in the picture and the adult interpretation of the test sentence. This raises the possibility that there is another referent for the pronoun; hence, it is much more likely that children do not respond to this picture so consistently.

Given that Grimshaw and Rosen do not allow special pragmatic contexts to make available the local coreference reading of *Mama Bear is washing her*, they are led to assert that any acceptance of coreference between *her* and *Mama Bear* amounts to a violation of Principle B.[25] In an attempt to salvage the large number of children's acceptances of the coreferential interpretation of *Mama Bear is washing her*, Grimshaw and Rosen claim that the illicit acceptances are due to experimental artifacts. One proposal is that in experiments investigating children's knowledge of Principle B, the test sentence should be preceded by an appropriate *linguistic* antecedent for the pronoun. It is not enough, in Grimshaw and Rosen's view, for the referent of the pronoun to have been mentioned in a story or discourse. Rather, it must be prominent in the sentence preceding the test sentence. If this requirement is not satisfied, they claim, children will not know what to do and may assume that the referent for the pronoun is the nearest NP. So, hearing a sentence like *Mama Bear is washing her*, if there is no linguistic antecedent, children will end up being forced to violate the binding theory in order to satisfy the pragmatics. Thus, they will take *her* to refer to *Mama Bear* at chance level, accounting for the 50% result.

We agree with Grimshaw and Rosen that test sentences should be presented following an appropriate linguistic antecedent. In Chien and Wexler's experiment, this was done by introducing the characters as follows: "This is Mama Bear. This is Goldilocks. Is Mama Bear washing her?" Both *Mama Bear* and *Goldilocks* are prominent, and either could be taken to be the antecedent of the pronoun. Because the linguistic-antecedent requirement was fulfilled in Chien and Wexler's experiment, lack of such an antecedent cannot have been responsible for children's nonadult interpretations.

In their paper, Chien and Wexler discuss results from experiments on Principle A, pointing out that children generally do well on Principle A as compared with Principle B. Once again, Grimshaw and Rosen raise the possibility that appearances are deceiving. They suggest that children's success with sentences governed by Principle A may not be due to innate knowledge of the principle. It could be, they say, that children are using a strategy that helps them get the right answer in picture tasks such as Chien and Wexler's. In Wexler and Chien's (1985) experiment, for example, performance on Principle A was tested in a two-choice picture task. Presented with the test sentence in (52), children had to select either a picture of the sister pointing to herself or one of the sister pointing to Cinderella.

(52) Cinderella's sister pointed to herself.

Grimshaw and Rosen's point is that children could get the right answer by choosing the picture depicting a "self-action." This would not entail any knowledge of the binding theory. We agree that this is a logical possibility. According to an experiment reported by Grodzinsky and Kave (1993), however, children do not fall back on such a strategy. Also, in unpublished work, Chien and Wexler have shown that in sentences where the antecedent of the reflexive is a grammatical object and not a subject, children have no problem in taking the object to be the antecedent.

(53) Mary showed Susan a picture of herself.

For example, presented with (53), children do not have any difficulty in taking *Susan* to be the antecedent of *herself*; but if children demanded that *self* indicate a self-action, they would not be able to accept such interpretations. (In fact, if *Mary* is the antecedent, it's not even clear that a self-action is being reported.)

Grimshaw and Rosen also suggest that previous experiments may have used verbs that are inherently reflexive. In addition to a transitive use, a verb like *wash* has an intransitive use in which the subject carries out the action on himself or herself (in this case, a use in which the subject washes himself or herself; e.g., *Mary washes*). It is possible that if test sentences included verbs with this intransitive use, children might have some tendency to ignore the syntactic object and to take a sentence like *Mama Bear is washing her* to be *Mama Bear is washing* (= herself), a tendency that might explain the results. In fact, Wexler and Chien (1985) were concerned that the inherent reflexivity of the verb might be a factor and investigated this possibility. They found no significant difference between the inherently reflexive and noninherently reflexive verbs, a result that held independently for both pronouns and reflexives. In fact, for reflexive sentences, the percentage correct varied by only 7% across the different verbs, and for the pronouns, the percentage correct varied by only 4% across the different verbs. Thus, the responses were in no way influenced by potential inherent reflexivity of the verb.[26]

In addition, empirical evidence in Chien and Wexler's study from several kinds of control sentences not related to Principle B showed that children do not ignore the syntactic object. For example, Chien and

Wexler included controls with objects that were lexical NPs, as in (54), using exactly the same set of verbs as for the pronouns.

(54) Mama Bear is washing Goldilocks.

Children performed almost perfectly on these sentences. Thus, they could not have ignored the syntactic object. Of course, one might suppose that children would be more likely to ignore a pronoun than a name, because the pronoun is in some sense underspecified. But if children ignore the pronoun in *Mama Bear is washing her*, they should also ignore it in *Every bear is washing her*. This was not the case, since children rejected the sentence with the quantificational NP *every bear*. In brief, the inherent reflexivity of the verbs is highly unlikely to have played any part in children's poor performance.

Grimshaw and Rosen also raise concerns about using sentences involving reflexives as controls. Wexler and Chien (1985; also Chien and Wexler 1990) had used reflexives in their experiments for many reasons, including a demonstration that children know Principle A. For example, they tested sentences like (55).

(55) Mama Bear is washing herself.

They also argued that the fact that children did so well on tests of reflexives (they knew they were bound) suggests that the apparent Principle B violations are not merely an artifact due to the children's not understanding the task. If experimental difficulties caused children to do poorly on sentences like *Mama Bear is washing her*, they should also have caused them to do poorly on sentences like (55) since the verbs, sentence length, and other factors were controlled to make sure that stimuli were equally difficult with respect to extraneous factors. Grimshaw and Rosen dispute the logic of this control. They say that the sentences with the pronoun and the reflexive are different and therefore can't necessarily be expected to be equally difficult. It is important to point out that Chien and Wexler's reason for using reflexives as controls was to maintain the one-clause sentence structure of the test sentence, while changing only one variable (pronoun vs. reflexive).

Grimshaw and Rosen also suggest that lack of attention to stress may have induced some of the nonadult acceptances of *Mama Bear is washing her*. This is unlikely to have been the case; this potential drawback was discussed in Chien and Wexler's (1990) paper, and their experimenters were trained to use even intonation.

As part of their exploration of the Principle B findings, Grimshaw and Rosen carried out an experiment that attempted to remedy all the potential confounding factors they had noted. However, the results they reported did not veer from previous findings.[27] Despite their methodological changes, children accepted the equivalent of *Mama Bear is washing her* on the coreferential interpretation 42% of the time, and on the external referent interpretation (where Mama Bear washes Goldilocks) 83.8% of the time. They accepted what looked like Principle C violations 37.5% of the time. Although their methodological changes brought about no changes in experimental results, Grimshaw and Rosen continued to maintain that experimental factors were at work in previous experiments.

2.4.3   Children's Knowledge of Bound Variables
In this section, we review recent studies that show children's competence with bound variable interpretations, a competence that Grimshaw and Rosen's account disputes.

Recall Grimshaw and Rosen's suggestion: "Suppose that children find the distributed reading associated with the quantifier–bound variable pair difficult, and construct this interpretation for pronouns less often than the alternative interpretations" (1990, 214). In other words, Grimshaw and Rosen suggest the existence of a processing difficulty that is particular to children. This view requires assuming that children have very different processing systems from adults and that children's responses are only partly influenced by their grammar. In this assumption, Grimshaw and Rosen are in line with a trend in psycholinguistics emanating from Fodor, Bever, and Garrett 1974 in which linguistics and psycholinguistics do not constrain each other. As noted earlier, Grimshaw and Rosen embrace a competing factors model, not the modular view of the language system expressed in Fodor's more recent work (Fodor 1983) and throughout Chomsky's writings. We put this issue aside, however, and turn to the empirical facts. (See Wexler 1998 for discussion.)

It is clear from Chien and Wexler's (1990) study that children have no difficulty treating reflexives as bound variables. It follows from Grimshaw and Rosen's proposal that reflexives bound by a quantificational NP should give children more trouble than reflexives with an R-expression for an antecedent, and they note a small trend in this direction in Chien and Wexler's results. But the trend is too small to be meaningful: children accepted sentences like *Every bear is washing herself* 89.4% of the time and sentences like *Mama Bear is washing herself* 97% of the time. More important, though, it should be noted that the reflexive sentences were unambiguous controls. Unlike pronouns, reflexives are unambiguous with respect to their referent. For example, if a child sees a picture in which three bears are washing themselves and Goldilocks is watching, and if the experimenter asks, "Is every bear washing herself?", the only possible interpretation requires a "Yes" answer. For this reason, pronouns, which are ambiguous, may be more appropriate for assessing whether or not children experience difficulty with bound variables.

This said, it may well be true that children have difficulty processing linguistic representations that involve bound variables in certain cases. It seems to be true that in certain structures, children prefer to interpret pronouns deictically, instead of as bound variables.[28] However, several studies have shown that children are adept with distributivity and with interpreting pronouns as bound variables.

One such study was conducted by Chien and Wexler (1991). This study aimed at determining whether children, especially those children who accepted coreference in sentences like *Mama Bear is washing her*, could give pronouns (as opposed to reflexives) bound variable interpretations. The study tested 281 children divided into five age groups at 1-year intervals (3 through 7 years of age). The same task was used as in Chien and Wexler's earlier study: children judged whether a sentence matched a picture or not. Because the task used complex pictures showing a character thinking about a scene that was illustrated in a thought bubble over its head, it challenged children's cognitive abilities. Various controls with lexical NPs (e.g., *Goldilocks*) instead of pronouns showed that even 5-year-old children were not perfect at the task. For this reason, the results are illustrated with data from the 6-year-old group.

Children were tested on three kinds of sentences, each accompanied by a match and a mismatch picture ("Yes" or "No" response correct), to yield six different items. The mismatch conditions were all conditions in which an adult would say "No" because saying "Yes" would require a Principle B violation, or an illicit acceptance of coreference. That is, the mismatch pictures demanded an interpretation in which the embedded subject was coreferential with or bound by the object pronoun.

The three sentence types are illustrated in (56)–(58), where $N = name$, $Q = quantifier$, and $P = pronoun$.

(56) Is Goldilocks thinking that Mama Bear is touching her?
     (NNP)

(57) Is every bear thinking that Goldilocks is touching her?
(QNP)

(58) Is Goldilocks thinking that every bear is pointing at her?
(NQP)

The NNP sentences were controls that tested whether children would allow coreference in a configuration where adults do not. In the match condition, Goldilocks is thinking that Mama Bear is touching Goldilocks (i.e., a picture of Mama Bear touching Goldilocks appears in the thought bubble), and in the mismatch condition, Goldilocks is thinking that Mama Bear is touching Mama Bear. The QNP sentences tested whether children could bind a pronoun with a quantifier. In the match condition, three bears are each thinking that Goldilocks is touching that particular bear. In the mismatch condition, the bears are all thinking that Goldilocks is touching Goldilocks. Nonadult acceptances of the mismatch condition were predicted, as cases of illicit coreference. NQP sentences also involve the possibility of binding a pronoun by a quantifier, this time in the embedded clause, but Principle B rules this out. In the match condition, Goldilocks is thinking that every bear is pointing at her, Goldilocks. In the mismatch condition, Goldilocks is thinking that every bear is pointing at herself. Saying "Yes" to the mismatch picture amounts to a Principle B error; therefore, it was predicted that children should say "No."

If children have difficulty accessing bound variable representations, as Grimshaw and Rosen predict, and if Principle B is not responsible for their rejections of sentences like *Every bear is washing her*, then children should find variable binding difficult in both (57) and (58). On the other hand, if Principle B is responsible for their rejections, then children should accept the bound variable reading in (57), where it is legitimate, but reject it in (58), where Principle B rules it out. The results did not support Grimshaw and Rosen's predictions. Children allowed the pronoun to be bound by *every bear* in (57) 76% of the time, but allowed a bound variable interpretation of the pronoun in (58) only 15% of the time.

Grimshaw and Rosen would also expect children to have more difficulty giving a bound variable interpretation to *Is every bear thinking that Mama Bear is touching her?* (with a quantificational NP antecedent) than they would allowing coreference between the pronoun and *Goldilocks* in *Is Goldilocks thinking that Mama Bear is touching her?* There was only a small difference in the acceptance rates, however: 76% versus 88%. In sum, we do not take the results to show that children have difficulty with bound variable interpretations.

Another study, by Miyamoto and Crain (1991), investigated children's knowledge of distributivity in ambiguous sentences like (59),[29] in which the plural pronoun *they* can be given either a collective or a distributive interpretation.

(59) They are lifting four cans.

On the collective interpretation, *they* refers to a group of people, and the total number of cans lifted is four. On the distributive interpretation, however, each person is understood to be lifting four cans. In the syntactic representation corresponding to this interpretation, a distributive D-operator that behaves like a silent *each* is attached to the plural pronoun (Heim, Lasnik, and May 1991). Testing children's responses to such sentences is relevant because the child must be able to distribute across members of a set in order to treat a pronoun bound by a quantificational NP as a bound variable.

The experiment tested 24 children between the ages of 3;0 and 6;0 using a variant of the truth value judgment task. Short scenarios were acted out with toys, and children were asked to judge whether the scenarios matched a puppet's description of them by saying "Yes" or "No." In the experimental trial corresponding to (59), Big Bird and Ernie compete to lift the most cans. In the first part of the story, Big Bird and Ernie each succeed in lifting two cans. This context favors a distributive description of the scene (*They are lifting two cans*), but the puppet describes the situation with *They are lifting four cans.* children rejected the puppet's statement 70% of the time, showing that they were favoring a distributive description. In the next part of the story, Ernie tries to win the contest by lifting even more cans, so he attempts to lift all four cans by himself. But the cans topple over, and Big Bird has to come to the rescue. Together they lift all four cans, and the puppet describes the situation with a variant of (59), *They are holding four cans.* This description is pragmatically appropriate, and children agreed with the puppet's description 89% of the time.

The experiment showed that children were able to access the distributive interpretation 70% of the time, even though this meant rejecting the puppet's statement. When the data were broken down by age, it was found that the younger children actually preferred the distributive interpretation. Children under 5 years of age rejected the puppet's description of the first part of the story 84% of the time, as compared with the 70% figure for all ages, 3 to 6.

It is possible that the children who did not reject *They are lifting four cans* as a description of the first part of the story are children who have difficulty accessing the distributive interpretation. But the by-age results make this conclusion unlikely. As Grimshaw and Rosen say, any difficulty in accessing the distributive interpretation is likely to be due to processing difficulties. In general, such processing difficulties are more likely to affect younger children than older ones. If this is the case, the younger children's preference for the distributive answer over the collective one cannot be explained.

In this context, we should evaluate the results from the experiment by Avrutin and Thornton (1994) discussed in section 2.2.2. This experiment tested Principle B, but incorporated Miyamoto and Crain's (1991) control for children's knowledge of distributivity. Thus, it was possible to see, for the same individual children, whether lack of facility with the concept of distributivity was responsible for the high number of rejections of *Every bear is washing her*.

The test sentences used by Avrutin and Thornton were all like (60). A referential or a quantificational interpretation of the plural NP in subject position was induced by the experimental context in which the sentence was presented.

(60) The Smurf and the Troll dried them. (context: collective or distributive)

By contrast, the items that controlled for knowledge of distributivity were presented in ambiguous contexts that could facilitate either the collective or the distributive interpretation. For example, the sentence/answer pair in (61) was uttered in a context in which four bugs were lined up in front of two turtles.

(61) I know how many bugs they have.
    a. Two. (distributive)
    b. Four. (collective)

To evaluate Grimshaw and Rosen's hypothesis, the children tested by Avrutin and Thornton can be divided into three groups, according to their response to the distributive controls like (61): those children who can access both collective and distributive interpretations (group 1), those children who can access only collective interpretations (group 2), and those children who can access only distributive interpretations (group 3). Grimshaw and Rosen's hypothesis predicts that children should respond to test sentences like (60) presented in both collective and distributive contexts in the same way, regardless of which group they belong to. This prediction is counterintuitive, so let us lay out the logic behind it.

Group 1 children can access both interpretations in the ambiguous control situations, so they should have no difficulty in accessing the relevant interpretation in the unambiguous test contexts. When sentences like *The Smurf and the Troll dried them* are presented in a collective context, children should apply Principle B, rejecting coreference between the pronoun and the plural NP, at whatever the expected levels is for this experiment.[30] When such sentences are presented in a distributive context, these children should be able to access the bound variable interpretation; they will not be left with only the deictic interpretation of the pronoun. Therefore, they should reject the target sentence because it is ruled out by Principle B. In fact, they should reject it at the same level as the sentence presented in the collective context, since Principle B applies equally to both sentences. Therefore, the rejection rate, whatever it turns out to be, should be the same for sentences with referential antecedents and ones with quantificational antecedents.

Next, consider the group 2 children, who accept only collective interpretations for control sentences such as (61). On Grimshaw and Rosen's view, these children would have rejected *Every bear is washing her* at an elevated rate in Chien and Wexler's study because they have difficulty accessing the distributed bound variable reading. Let us suppose that among group 2 children there are those who cannot access the distributive interpretation at all. For these children, plural NPs will never take on quantificational properties. By default, then, plural NPs will always be treated as referential NPs in the syntax. Thus, both distributive and collective contexts will generate the same syntactic representation in which the plural NP has referential properties. Since all the plural NPs in all representations are referential, Principle B will apply in the same way to all target sentences, no matter what the experimental context is.

We can also assume that among group 2 children there are those who are able to access the distributive interpretation only when the experimental context favors this reading.[31] Children like this will behave like group 1 children (and adults) in responding to Principle B sentences. They can access the distributive reading in the specially designed contexts, and so Principle B will apply equally to representations with referential NPs and representations with quantificational NPs. Again, the result is that the rejection rate is the same for both collective and distributive trials in the experiment.

Group 3 children, who accept only the distributive interpretation of the ambiguous control sentences, may or may not be able to access the collective interpretation in the specially designed unambiguous contexts. Either way, since these children do not have any obvious difficulty with bound variables, they should be able to apply Principle B to all of the relevant syntactic representations. Again, the same level of rejection is expected for the target sentences presented in the two experimental contexts.

Of the 16 children tested in Avrutin and Thornton's experiment, 5 fit the group 1 profile, 9 fit the group 2 profile, and 2 fit the group 3 profile. Of the 16 children, the 9 children in group 2 met Grimshaw and Rosen's expectation that the distributive bound variable interpretation would be difficult to access; therefore, this will be our critical group.[32] Our concern will be whether or not the special contexts in which the target sentences were presented were enough to trigger a distributive representation.

Experimental sentences like (60) produced the following results. Group 1 children accepted the collective context 90% of the time and the distributive context 25% of the time. Of the 9 children in group 2, 5 children found the story contexts helpful and managed, for the most part, to access the distributive interpretation in the Principle B target sentences. These 5 children accepted the collective context 95% of the time and the distributive context 30% of the time. The other 4 children in group 2 were unable to access the distributive interpretation even when assisted by pragmatic context. (These are the 4 children identified in the results in section 2.2.2.) These children treated both contexts alike, accepting the collective context 100% of the time and the distributive context at a slightly lower rate, 94% of the time. Finally, the 2 children in group 3 did not have much difficulty accepting sentences like (60) when they were presented in the collective context. They accepted the collective context 88% of the time and the distributive context 25% of the time.

How do the results relate to Grimshaw and Rosen's proposal? The children in groups 1 and 3 do not support it, since they did not accept target sentences presented in the collective and distributive contexts at the same rate. Of the 9 children in group 2, 4 children did support Grimshaw and Rosen's proposal. Overall, then, their prediction accounts for 25% of the data. (Of course, it should be recognized that the behavior of the 4 children mentioned from group 2 is difficult to explain on other accounts.)

The experiment reveals another telling result. Recall that Grimshaw and Rosen claim that the inaccessibility of the bound variable reading causes children to interpret the pronoun deictically. On this view, in interpreting sentences like *Every bear is washing her*, children consider only the interpretation in which every bear is washing Goldilocks. This did not happen in Avrutin and Thornton's experiment. Children who were unable to generate a quantificational NP antecedent for the pronoun in the distributive context accepted the sentence. This means, however, that children did not take the pronoun to refer outside the sentence. Rather, they took *them* in sentences like *The Smurf and the Troll dried them* to be coreferential with *the Smurf and the Troll*; that is, they took it to find its reference *inside* the sentence.

All of the evidence amassed shows that children differentiate the type of antecedent for the purposes of Principle B. Structures with local quantificational antecedents for the pronoun evoke high rejection rates, which can be taken to indicate knowledge of Principle B. Structures with local referential antecedents for the pronoun evoke low rejection rates.

In sum, Grimshaw and Rosen's account has two important drawbacks. First, previous studies did not fall prey to the experimental artifacts they mention. Second, recent studies have found that children can successfully access bound variable interpretations.

2.5 McDaniel and Maxfield 1992

2.5.1 McDaniel and Maxfield's Account
Assuming like other researchers that children have innate knowledge of Principle B, McDaniel and Maxfield (1992) pursued two new angles on children's apparent Principle B violations. One invoked a structural account of binding principles advanced by Varela (1989).[33] We will not pursue this proposal here. The second constitutes a new account of children's nonadult behavior. On this account, children produce nonadult responses to sentences involving Principle B because they are insensitive to contrastive stress. We believe that insensitivity to stress does not on its own explain children's misinterpretation of pronouns. It is, however, a factor associated with incomplete knowledge of pragmatics.

We return to this point following our discussion of McDaniel and Maxfield's account, in section 2.5.3.

McDaniel and Maxfield's first observation is that in the exceptional situations where local coreference is permitted for adults, the pronoun bears stress. They consider the following examples:

(62) a. You'll never guess who I chose. I chose ME.
   b. You need to think about YOU.
   c. When John looks in the mirror, he doesn't see ME, he sees HIM.

The suggestion is that children do not notice the stress in examples like these. Since they do not perceive stress, they do not know that stress is a necessary condition for local coreference in the special circumstances where it is permitted. Once children's perceptual abilities sharpen, they become aware that the pronoun is stressed in sentences like those in (62), and they begin to use stress appropriately. At this point, they start to *disallow* local coreference in sentences lacking pronominal stress. In other words, it is McDaniel and Maxfield's view that children's adherence to Principle B and their knowledge of stress go hand in hand. On the one hand, children who produce nonadult responses to sentences testing Principle B will not be sensitive to contrastive stress; on the other hand, children who are sensitive to contrastive stress will manifest knowledge of Principle B.

It should be made clear the McDaniel and Maxfield are not claiming that knowledge of Principle B entails knowledge of stress. It could be that a child has knowledge of Principle B, but has not experienced enough examples (presumably sentence/meaning pairs) of sentences like those in (62) that reveal the specific circumstances in which adults accept the local coreference interpretation. A child who has not encountered such examples would have no reason to think that local coreference is ever allowed. Since experience with examples like those in (62) is the source of children's understanding of the exceptions to the ban on local coreference, it is conceivable on McDaniel and Maxfield's view that children could show knowledge of Principle B, then "lose" it, then finally show it again.[34]

McDaniel and Maxfield's account handles the fact that children do not allow sentences like *Every bear is washing her* to mean that every bear is washing herself. Assuming that children know the properties of quantificational NPs, they can only interpret the pronoun as being in a variable-binding relationship. Coreference between the two NPs is not possible. In the adult grammar, the pronoun in such examples cannot be stressed (on the meaning that every bear is washing herself). Thus, children's knowledge of the properties of stress (or lack thereof) should have no bearing on their interpretation of examples with quantificational NPs.

This account also explains McKee's (1988, 1992) finding that children do not make apparent Principle B violations when the pronoun is a clitic. Since clitic pronouns are not stressed, children would not encounter the stressed pronouns in the input that lead them to hypothesize incorrectly that local coreference is possible. As McDaniel and Maxfield point out, however, the situation is more complicated if the language has strong pronouns in addition to clitic ones (e.g., in French). In fact, according to Cardinaletti and Starke (1995), the misinterpretations occur in precisely those languages that have strong pronouns, or strong pronouns that are homophonous with weak forms.

The experiment that McDaniel and Maxfield carried out to test children's knowledge of the binding principles used a grammaticality judgment task (see section 2.2.2 for how the stimuli were presented). Included in the experiment were items testing Principle B (with referential and quantificational NP antecedents) and items testing Principle C, giving the opportunity to compare individual children's performance on both principles. Children's knowledge of contrastive stress was tested using materials unrelated to the interpretation of pronouns. The stress test had two parts. In the first part, children were required to answer a question; if they understood how stress functions, they would answer as shown in (63).

(63) (Props: Bert, a big strawberry, a little strawberry, a big tomato, a little tomato, a pear, a carrot, an orange, and a green pepper).
   Experimenter   Bert doesn't want to eat the BIG strawberry. What do you think he wants to eat?
   Child   A LITTLE strawberry.

The second part of the stress test involved pronouns. The experimenter carried out an action with the props and invited the child to carry out an action too. The child's response (i.e., what referent the child assigned to the pronoun) depended on whether or not the child had understood the stress. Children who understood the stress should have responded as shown in (64) and (65).

(64) *Experimenter*   Goofy is whispering to Grover. Now YOU whisper to him.
   Child   [whispers to Grover]

(65) *Experimenter*   Grover is patting Bert. Now YOU pat HIM.
   Child   [pats Grover]

Of the 35 children tested, 17 children demonstrated adult knowledge of Principle B, rejecting both of the items with referential antecedents; 11 children accepted both items; and 7 children accepted one and rejected one. Children did not behave the same on Principles B and C. Of the 35 children, 25 children correctly rejected both items testing Principle C; 7 children rejected one of the two items; and 3 children accepted both. Overall, knowledge of Principle C looked robust compared with knowledge of Principle B.

The two parts of the contrastive stress test were scored together. Children were given 1 point for each correct answer; the maximum score was 10 points. The mean stress test score for the 35 children was 5.5. Stress test scores increased with age; the means for the 3-, 4-, 5- and 6-year-old groups were 4.7, 4.7, 5.8, and 6.7, respectively. Of the 35 children tested, 22 received stress test scores of over 6. None of these children accepted either of the test sentences like *Mama Bear is washing her*, thus disallowing coreference like adults.

The results show a correlation between children's scores on the stress test and their knowledge of Principle B (though age is another factor that also correlates with knowledge of stress). However, as we will show, the correlation is not strong.

2.5.2   Issues for McDaniel and Maxfield's Account

We begin by describing McDaniel and Maxfield's learnability scenario in more detail. This scenario hinges on the assumption that there is a one-to-one correspondence between acceptance of the local coreference interpretation and difficulty in interpreting pronominal stress. Thus, McDaniel and Maxfield assume that when children are able to perceive and understand the function of stress, they use stress correctly in cases of local coreference. Clearly, positive evidence drives this grammatical change. The authors seem to assume as well that when children begin to notice stress in the permissible cases of local coreference, this observation causes them to abandon the local coreference interpretation in the absence of stress. This step is not driven by positive evidence, however. To salvage McDaniel and Maxfield's account, one might suggest that some kind of Uniqueness Principle (Wexler and Culicover 1980) prohibits structures expressing local coreference from being grammatical both with and without stress. The child's linguistic input determines that local coreference goes hand in hand with stress. Thus, the child purges from the grammar the possibility of a local coreference interpretation in the absence of stress.

A problem with McDaniel and Maxfield's account is the assumption that there is a one-to-one correspondence between local coreference and stress on the pronoun. Unquestionably, stressing the pronoun is the usual way of indicating local coreference, as shown in (62), but there are two notable exceptions. For example, (66) illustrates the identity debate case and (67) illustrates the structured-meaning case (both examples are from Heim 1998). In neither case is the pronoun stressed. In (66), no stress is appropriate, and in (67), it is the subject NP *John* that is stressed.

(66) *Speaker A*   Is this speaker Zelda?
     Speaker B   How can you doubt it? She praises her to the sky. No
     competing candidate would do that.

(67) You know what Mary, Sue, and John have in common? Mary
     admires John, Sue admires him, and John admires him too.

As with the Principle B cases, a local coreference interpretation is permitted for Principle C sentences in the adult grammar even when the pronoun is unstressed. Consider the following kind of example, attributed to Higginbotham (1980), where the pronoun cannot receive stress.

(68) That must be John. At least, he is putting John's coat on.

As with all cases of local coreference, these examples may not be frequent; but the fact that they exist means that McDaniel and Maxfield's account does not work. If the adult grammar allows local coreference both with and without stress, the Uniqueness Principle should not be permitted to jettison the illicit cases of a local coreference interpretation. If anything, examples like (66)–(68) would be positive evidence, confirming the child's hypothesis that local coreference is always acceptable for pronouns that are not bound variables.

Another problem with McDaniel and Maxfield's account is that it does not explain the asymmetry they found between children's performance on Principle B and their performance on Principle C. McDaniel and Maxfield explicitly claim that, as in Principle B sentences, the pronoun is also stressed when local coreference is permitted in Principle C sentences. Their example is (69).

(69) You'll never guess who hit John. HE [pointing to John] hit John!

McDaniel and Maxfield point out that examples relevant to Principle C are rarer than those relevant to Principle B because they occur only with third person; therefore, fewer children will make the mistake with Principle C sentences. Nevertheless, because a local coreference interpretation is allowable under stress, it is expected that children will accept some apparent Principle C violations.

Of the 18 children in McDaniel and Maxfield's experiment who either accepted both items testing Principle B or gave mixed responses, 9 children were adultlike in their knowledge of Principle C, and 6 children rejected one of the two items. McDaniel and Maxfield do not discuss the dilemma posed by these results, focusing instead on the responses of the 3 children who performed poorly on both Principle B and Principle C experimental items. They observe that these children do allow the local coreference interpretation, in apparent violation of Principle C.

In sum, McDaniel and Maxfield's stress-based account can explain why 3 of the children they tested accepted both Principle B and Principle C violations and had difficulty with contrastive stress, but this is definitely a minority of their subjects. The account cannot explain why Principle B correlated with contrastive stress for the majority of children, but Principle C did not.

A final point is that the correlation between poor performance on items testing Principle B and contrastive stress is not strong. Although the correlation is significant with 37 subjects, we calculate that, had only 24 children been tested, the result would not have been significant. Another way of understanding the relationship between contrastive stress and Principle B is in terms of the proportion of variance in children's responses to Principle B sentences accounted for by their knowledge of stress. In this case, the coefficient of determination is .161, which means that only 16% of the variance is explained by children's knowledge of stress. The remaining 84% is left unexplained.

In summary, for several reasons the finer details of McDaniel and Maxfield's account are not convincing. However, we are indebted to them for the observation that children's knowledge of stress and their apparent violations of Principle B might be connected, a connection we consider in our own account, presented in chapter 3.

2.5.3 Children's Knowledge of Contrastive Stress

In this section, we review a number of studies related to children's knowledge of contrastive stress. The finding that emerges from the studies testing children's knowledge of prosodic information (which includes knowledge of stress or "word accent") is that children generally use contrastive stress correctly in their own speech. Moreover, they are able to perceive stress-bearing lexical items. But until the age of about 5 or 6 they have difficulty in understanding how prosodic information functions at the sentence level. This gives rise to a puzzling paradox: production outstrips comprehension. We turn next to some of the studies that point to this asymmetry.

In an experiment conducted by Hornby and Hass (1970), 20 preschool children between the ages of 3;8 and 4;6 were shown pairs of pictures in which the members of each pair differed in only one respect; their task was to describe the pictures. In one third of the picture pairs, the agent differed (e.g., a girl or a boy patting a dog); in another third, the action differed (e.g., a man washing or driving a car); and in the final third, the object of the action differed (e.g., a girl patting a cat or a dog). The child was asked to describe the first picture in a pair; then, with the first picture still in view, the second picture was put in front of the child, and a second description was elicited.

Hornby and Hass found that children did not often use stress in describing the first picture of a pair. When they did use stress in this situation, they did so most often in describing the pictures in which the objects differed. By contrast, children frequently used stress in describing the second picture of the pair. They stressed the subject 80% of the time, the verb 56.25% of the time, and the object 43.75% of the time (compared with figures of 11.25%, 3.75%, and 18.75%, respectively, for first-picture descriptions). These results are suggestive of adult knowledge of contrastive stress (although adult controls were not tested in this experiment). In Horby and Hass's view, the results indicate that children as young as 4 are sensitive to the role of word order in marking the topic-comment distinction—"when the new or contrasting element appears toward the end of the utterance, it is less likely to be marked with contrastive stress than when it appears earlier in the utterance" (Hornby and Hass 1970, 398).

In comprehension experiments, children's performance has been weaker. Maratsos (1973) and Solan (1983) found poor comprehension of the function of stressed and unstressed pronouns, respectively. Halbert et al. (1995; also Halbert 1997) found that some children in the 4- and 5-year-old range had difficulty interpreting contrastive stress in certain syntactic structures. These are exactly the ages of the subjects tested in many experiments evaluating children's knowledge of the binding theory.

In Maratsos's study, children responded to coordinate structures with and without stress on the pronoun. The pronoun appeared in either subject or object position, yielding the following four types of sentences:

(70) a. Susie jumped over the old woman, and then Harry jumped over her.

   b. Susie jumped over the old woman, and then Harry jumped over HER.

    c. Susie bumped into the old woman, and then she bumped into Harry.

    d. Susie bumped into the old woman, and then SHE bumped into Harry.

Maratsos observed that when the pronoun is unstressed, there is a kind of parallelism in effect in the adult grammar. In the first clause of (70a), for example, *the old woman* is the grammatical and logical object of *jumped*, and in the second clause, the unstressed *her* has the same properties. Stress on the pronoun cancels the parallelism, however. In (70b), the pronoun no longer refers to the object of the first clause; it refers to the subject, *Susie*. In Maratsos's terms, the simplest interpretive strategy is the one that obtains in the absence of stress, the parallelism interpretation. Because stressing the pronoun marks a departure from this strategy, he hypothesized that children could learn the interpretations associated with stress later than those associated with lack of stress.

To explore this hypothesis, Maratsos tested 106 children between the ages of 3 and 5. Each child was tested on two of the four sentences in (70). The child was given three toy characters (Susie, an old woman, Harry) and asked to act out his or her interpretation of the target sentence. The experimenter produced each clause of the sentence separately, presumably because the sentences were long. So the experimenter uttered the first clause, and the child acted it out; then the experimenter uttered the second clause, and the child acted that one out. (The children were also asked to imitate a number of sentences, to gain another measure of their language sophistication, but we ignore that task here.)

The main finding was that children's understanding of the role of stress increased with age. The 3-, 4-, and 5-year-olds responded correctly to the stressed-pronoun cases 47%, 67%, and 78% of the time, respectively (compared with 87%, 83%, and 93% accuracy, respectively, in responding to the unstressed-pronoun cases).

Solan (1983), who conducted a version of Maratsos's experiment with a wider range of sentences and an older group of children (between 5 and 7 years of age), did not replicate Maratsos's findings. In Solan's experiment, children did better on the sentences that contained stressed pronouns than on those that contained unstressed pronouns. It is unclear why Solan's results were so different from Maratsos's. Both researchers recognized that the task required children to maintain the target sentences in memory (stress pattern intact) while planning how to act them out (see Hamburger and Crain 1984). In Maratsos's task, an attempt was made to relieve this problem by presenting the two clauses separately. In Solan's task, the experimenter acted out the first clause, so that the child had to act out only the second clause. However, it is not obvious that such a procedural change would cause children to better attend to the sentences with stressed pronouns.

Because Maratsos and Solan report group data only, it is not possible to see the extent to which individual children experienced difficulty in understanding the function of stress. In the study by Halbert et al. (1995), the goal was to find out how individual children used stress to resolve ambiguity. The experiment investigated children's understanding of dative constructions with the focus operator *only*. Two experiments were conducted, using the truth value judgment task. Examples of the test sentences used in one experiment are given in (71).

(71) a. Bill only gave a banana to Sue.
     b. Bill only gave A BANANA to Sue.
     c. Bill only gave a banana TO SUE.
     d. Bill only gave Sue A BANANA.
     e. Bill only gave SUE a banana.

In (71b), for example, the focus operator in conjunction with stress on *a banana* conveys a meaning in which Bill gives a banana, but nothing else, to Sue. On the other hand, (71c) communicates that Sue, and no one else, was given a banana. The second experiment included sentences like those in (72a) that were ambiguous between a double object interpretation (here, the interpretation in (72b) on which the cat was given food, not something else, such as milk) and a compound noun interpretation (here, the interpretation in (72c) on which a woman or girl was given cat food, not something else, such as fish food). In the adult grammar, word stress (and presumably a different intonation contour) is used to disambiguate the two possible interpretations.

(72) a. Bill gave her cat food.
     b. Bill gave her cat FOOD.
     c. Bill gave her CAT food.

For the experiment testing the dative constructions in (71), 33 children between the ages of 3;10 and 6;3 were interviewed (but results from 2 children were disregarded because they did not complete the task). A group of adult controls were also interviewed and were found to be extremely proficient at using stress to assign the intended interpretations of the test sentences. Of the children, 13 performed with the same high level of accuracy. The other 18 children were apparently unable to use stress at all. These children invoked a default strategy for interpreting the sentences. Eleven children strongly favored associating *only* with the theme (i.e., *a banana*). These children ignored the stress on (*to*) *Sue* in (71c) and (71e), in order to maintain the default strategy. Another 5 children favored attaching *only* to the recipient (i.e., *Sue*), thus incorrectly interpreting (71b) and (71d). The remaining 2 children associated *only* with the rightmost constituent of the structure.

For the experiment testing the construction in (72), 18 children between the ages of 3;0 and 5;3 were interviewed (as well as a group of adult controls). In this experiment, in addition to the verb *give*, the verb *throw* was used in some stimuli. Children's success with using stress as a cue to disambiguate sentences like (72) depended on the particular verb used. Sixteen of the 18 children tested were able to use stress to disambiguate the two interpretations with the verb *throw*. Only 7 of the 18 children were successful when the verb was *give*. The remaining 11 children reverted to some default interpretation: 6 children always chose the double object interpretation, 4 children always chose the compound noun interpretation, and 1 child invariably said the sentences were ambiguous.

The empirical evidence reviewed thus far illustrates the observation that children are successful in using contrastive stress in their own speech, but poor at using such prosodic information in comprehension (see Cutler and Swinney 1987 for a review of further studies confirming this result). This finding is puzzling because in other aspects of language acquisition, comprehension outstrips production. Seeking to explain this seeming paradox, Cutler and Swinney (1987) suggest that children may have fared poorly in the comprehension tasks because their knowledge was not assessed using "on-line" measures of response time. They hypothesize that an on-line task may be more sensitive and thus better able to detect positive knowledge of stress (word "accent" in their terms).

With adult subjects, phoneme-monitoring tasks have successfully demonstrated their attention to the prosodic information expressed in a target sentence. In a phoneme-monitoring task, the subject listens for a word beginning with a target sound that has been previously specified. Using this task, Cutler and Foss (1977) found that subjects responded much more quickly to accented words beginning with the target sound than to nonaccented ones. That is, when the target sound was the phoneme /k/, subjects responded much faster to *Does John really want to KEEP that old van?* than to *Does John really WANT to keep that old van?* In another task, focus was manipulated independently of word accent; in this task, a question preceding the target sentence provided the focus. Adults again responded more quickly to focused words than unfocused ones (Cutler and Fodor 1979). As Cutler and Swinney note, "Using prosodic cues in order to located accented words ought to be a useful sentence comprehension strategy for the following reason: speakers usually accent the most important parts of their message. Thus, for a listener, locating accented words is equivalent to locating the semantically most central part—the focus—of the utterance" (Cutler and Swinney 1987, 150).

To find out whether children can use prosodic information successfully, Cutler and Swinney (1987) conducted a number of experiments using a variation on the phoneme-monitoring task, in which children listen for a target word instead of a target sound. In one experiment, children hear sentences like (73a–d). In (73a–b), the target word is an open-class content word, *clean*, and in (73c–d), it is a closed-class function word, *at*.

(73) a. The nurse brought a CLEAN towel and took away the dirty one.
     b. The nurse brought a clean TOWEL and took away the dirty one.
     c. The family is already AT the summer cabin.
     d. The family is ALREADY at the summer cabin.

Children heard two prosodic versions, one with the target word accented (i.e., (73a) and (73c)) and one with some other word accented (i.e., (73b) and (73d)). The target word was always presented prior to the sentence. Twenty-one children between 4 and 8 years of age completed the task; 10 adult controls were also tested. As expected, the adults processed accented target words significantly faster than nonaccented ones; whether the word was a content word or a function word made no difference. The children showed a strong effect of age. The 11 children who were over 6 responded faster to accented words, but they also responded significantly faster to open-class words, unlike adults. The 10 younger children who were between 4 and 6 years old showed no significant effect of accent, although they did show an effect of word class.

A second task attempted to find out whether children were having difficulty perceiving stress per se, or whether the difficulty was at the sentence level. In this experiment, the words of the target sentences in (73) were scrambled so that the children were presented with a list of words rather than a meaningful sentence. Children between 5 and 7 years of age were tested in this task, and they processed the accented words significantly faster than the nonaccented ones, leading to the conclusion that children can perceive stress.

A third task manipulated focus independently of accent. As in the adult task described above, the sentence containing the target word was preceded by a question. It was found that the focus effect increases with age. Of the 3- to 6-year-old children tested in this experiment, only the 5-year-old group showed a significant effect of focus.

Overall, the change in methodology to an on-line word-monitoring task failed to show an improvement in children's performance on comprehension tasks, thereby solving the production/comprehension paradox. Children under 5 or 6 years of age still failed either to show an effect of stress or to use prosodic information to locate sentence focus. In an attempt to solve the paradox, Cutler and Swinney conjecture that children's seemingly appropriate use of contrastive stress in production is the result of a physiological reflex—the fact that the accented words contain the emotive interest of the sentence. In our view, this seems an unlikely explanation, and the puzzling asymmetry remains unexplained.

We have reviewed enough evidence to firmly conclude that many (though not all) children as old as 4 or 5, and perhaps even older, experience difficulty in using stress as a cue to sentence interpretation.

2.6 Avrutin 1994

In this section, we introduce Avrutin's (1994) account of children's misinterpretations of pronouns. Avrutin's account is based on Heim's (1982) file change semantics and thus emphasizes principles of discourse in explaining children's nonadult behavior regarding sentences governed by Principle B. We begin by reviewing the essential ingredients of Heim's theory (for related theories, see Kamp 1981; Karttunen 1976).

2.6.1 File Change Semantics (Heim 1982)

Very briefly: In file change semantics (Heim 1982), a discourse is represented by a box of file cards. As the discourse unfolds, new cards are added to the box, and existing cards are updated with new information.

In a conversation, a listener has to keep track of incoming information by organizing it into a system. Heim conceives of the system metaphorically as a box of file cards. The file cards describe properties of entities, such as "is a cat"; they are used by speakers and listeners to document the actions of and relationships among the individuals introduced in a conversation. In Heim's system, each file card has a number, which can also be equated with a referential index. To see how the system works, consider the discourse in (74) (from Heim 1982, 275).

(74) a. A woman was bitten by a dog.
     b. She hit him with a paddle.
     c. It broke in half.
     d. The dog ran away.

Hearing the first sentence of the discourse, the listener sets up two new cards by assigning them numbers and making entries on them. Card 1 represents the woman introduced in the first sentence by the indefinite NP, *a woman*. On card 1, the listener enters "is a woman" and "was bitten by a dog." Card 2 represents the dog introduced in the same sentence. On card 2, the listener enters "is a dog" and "bit 1." When the second sentence is heard, a new card, card 3, is needed for *a paddle*. More importantly, for our purposes, cards 1 and 2 need updating. On card 1 is written "hit 2 with 3"; on card 2, "was hit by 1 with 3." Hearing the third sentence, the listener adds further information to card 3: "broke in half." The last sentence in the discourse contains a definite description, *the dog*. This implies that a card with the entry "is a dog" already exists. One does: card 2.

As this simple example illustrates, Heim's system captures the distinction between definite and indefinite NPs. An indefinite NP is used when the referent of the NP is being introduced for the first time (and therefore constitutes "new information"). In this case, the listener adds a new file card. In general, a definite NP is felicitous only if its referent has already been introduced in the discourse (and therefore constitutes "old information"). The listener also updates existing file cards in response to pronouns. In the discourse above, for example, the pronoun *she* is taken to refer back to card 1. In Heim's terms, the information is "incorporated" on an existing file card. Reflexives necessarily update an already created file card.

Certain pronouns, however, do not require an existing file card. These are deictic pronouns.[35] As an example, suppose that after the speaker uttered the above discourse, a friendly cat came up and nuzzled him on the leg, and the speaker continued the conversation by saying (75).

(75) Now HE's a friendly cat!

In response to (75), the listener would add a new file card, card 4. The speaker might make the referent clear by actually pointing to the cat and stressing the pronoun, as in (75).

A new file card can be added in this fashion only if the entity is salient enough. For example, when the friendly cat wanders up and draws the attention of the speaker and the listener, a new card is created at that moment. Then, when the speaker comments on the nuzzling event, the card is updated with "is friendly." As far as the listener's file is concerned, then, a deictic pronoun refers to something that is already familiar. For Heim, this point unifies deixis and anaphora. Both assume familiarity, that is, an existing file card. Crucially, a deictic pronoun does not introduce a new file card; instead, it causes the entry on an existing file card to be updated.

So far, we have been assuming that the listener starts a conversation with an empty file box. In reality, Heim points out, this would not happen. Both the speaker and the listener come to the conversation presupposing common knowledge, or "common ground." Heim cites Stalnaker (1979, 321) on common knowledge: "Roughly speaking, the presuppositions of a speaker are the propositions whose truth he takes for granted as part of the background of the conversation." This common ground allows speakers to use definite NPs in situations of first mention, that is, as "novel definites." One famous example discussed by Heim is (76) (from Hawkins 1978).

(76) The sun is shining.

There is no need to mention that there is a sun before uttering this statement, because everybody knows there is a sun. (At least, everybody over a certain age knows there is a sun—this is a piece of real-world knowledge that must be acquired.) Likewise, in order to understand the sentence in (77a), listeners invoke the knowledge that books are written by people termed "authors."

(77) a. John read a book about Schubert and wrote to the author.
    b. John read [a book about Schubert]₁ and wrote to the author₂.

Even though *the sun* and *the author* have not been mentioned before, (76) and (77a) are acceptable utterances. Heim suggests there is a process called *accommodation* (cf. Lewis 1979) that deals with these cases. This process allows a new card to be created for "the sun" or "the author," but this card must be connected, or "bridged," to a discourse referent that is already established. It isn't enough to create a card number 2 and the entry "is an author" (see (77b)). Rather, what is required is that the author under consideration wrote the book about Schubert. So the entry would need to be something like "is author of 1."

Cases like (76) and (77) contrast with cases like (78) (cited by Heim from Hawkins 1978).

(78) Watch out, the dog will bite you.

Here, the listener does not share with the speaker the knowledge that there is a dog in the vicinity; however, he or she is able to take that information from the utterance. The dog is being mentioned for the first time, and a file card "is a dog" is created. In this case, the card cannot be bridged to a network of other discourse referents, because there are none. Rather, the connection is directly with the utterance situation. The entry is better stated as "is a dog close to here." One possibility, Heim suggests, is that every time a file is opened for a conversation, it should include a file card that describes the utterance situation. Linking the utterance to this card could then be thought of as a special case of accommodation.

Heim's system can be summarized as follows:

(79) NPs can be introduced into a discourse by
    a. Introducing a new file card
       i. Indefinites
      ii. Novel definites ⟨usually "bridged" to another card⟩
    b. Updating an existing file card
       i. Definites ⟨most uses of pronouns, including deictic ones⟩

2.6.2 Avrutin's Account

Avrutin's (1994) account of children's apparent violations of Principle B depends on an extension of Heim's theory. Avrutin treats deictic pronouns differently than Heim. In Heim's theory, the presence of a highly salient object in the conversational context suffices for the creation of a new file card; subsequent reference to the object, by a deictic pronoun (e.g., *HE's a friendly cat!*), amounts to an entry on the card already created. Avrutin treats certain uses of deictic pronouns as a subcase of accommodation. On his account, a deictic pronoun does not constitute an entry on an existing card; rather, it introduces a new file card. The file card must, however, be bridged to a file card describing the conversational context, what Avrutin terms the *visual situation* file card.[36]

This leads us to Avrutin's account of the Principle B error, which he takes to be characteristic of Broca's aphasics as well as children. Avrutin claims that the problem shows up when children and aphasics are required to make inferences about the state of mind of other participants in a conversation. This happens because, in his view, these populations have limitations on computational resources. Avrutin suggests that it is the general inability to make inferences that is problematic, and this can be applied to inferences about speakers' intentions. In support of this view that children do not take into account the intentions of other speakers, Avrutin reviews literature including Karmiloff-Smith 1981 and Maratsos 1976. See also Kail and Hickmann 1992.

To see how Avrutin's proposal works, consider a typical sentence involving Principle B.

(80) Mama Bear washed her.

Assume that, in the course of an experiment, this sentence is presented to a subject in two contexts. Assume also that the subject is asked to make a truth value judgment regarding the sentence, having witnessed a story (rather than a picture; hence, the test sentence is presented using the past tense). In the first context, Goldilocks asks to be washed, and Mama Bear indeed agrees to wash her. At the end of the story, the file for the discourse should contain the following cards, with the following entries:

(81) Card 1:   is Mama Bear
                washed 2
     Card 2:   is Goldilocks

On hearing the test sentence (80), the subject must interpret the pronoun. Assigning index 1 to the pronoun causes a Principle B violation, so the only alternative is to update card 2. This results in a file that truthfully describes the scenario. Hence, an adult subject accepts the sentence. Children also accept this sentence at a high rate (80% to 90% for 5-year-olds in Chien and Wexler's (1990) experiment).

In the second context, the sentence is introduced following a situation in which Mama Bear does not wash Goldilocks, but washes herself instead.[37] At the end of this story, the file cards should have the following entries:

(82) Card 1:   is Mama Bear
                washed 1
     Card 2:   is Goldilocks
                (is not washed by 1)

Again, when the test sentence (80) is presented, the subject has to interpret the pronoun. Assigning it the same index as *Mama Bear* would violate Principle B. It must be assigned the same index as *Goldilocks*, the only other discourse referent already mentioned. However, this assignment is not compatible with the situation described; in fact, it overtly flouts the entry under card 2, which states that Goldilocks is not washed by Mama Bear. Therefore, the test sentence is taken to be false and is rejected, at least by adults.

To be explained is the finding that some children do not reject (80) as a description of the events recorded in (82). Apparently, they attempt to make the grammatical representation fit the events recorded in the file. Therefore, they do not update card 2, like adults. Avrutin suggests that the only way to update the discourse file without violating grammatical principles is to treat the pronoun as deictic (see note 35). On Avrutin's extension of Heim's theory, upon hearing test sentence (80), these children assign a new file card to the pronoun. As noted earlier, the newly created file card must be bridged (i.e., accommodated) to the visual situation card. Citing Hawkins (1978), Avrutin notes that there is a constraint that applies to NPs that are introduced by bridging: other participants in the conversation must be able to build the same bridge. For deictic pronouns, this is achieved if the pronoun is accompanied by pointing and is stressed. These actions inform the listener that deixis is intended, and the listener is then able to bridge the pronoun to the visual situation card.

At this point, Avrutin's account is not explicit, but his idea seems to be something like this. Children hear (80) and interpret the pronoun deictically. However, limitations in computational resources prevent children from reliably inferring whether the speaker intended this interpretation or whether, in the absence of pointing and stress, the speaker did *not* intend this interpretation. On the occasions when children *can* make the correct inference, they reject the sentence, as adults do; on the occasions when they cannot, they accept the sentence. This accounts for children's roughly 50% acceptance rate in response to sentences like (80).

If the pronoun is treated as a deictic pronoun, a new card, card 3, will be assigned to it, as in (83). Now cards 1 and 3 can be associated without inducing a violation of Principle B.

(83) Card 1: is Mama Bear
      is washing 1
    Card 2: is Goldilocks
      is not washed by 1
    Card 3: is the bear that's right here in front of me

The discourse file looks as if two guises of Mama Bear are under debate. This possibility, if intended, is not made explicit by Avrutin, perhaps because the situation depicted in the story acted out in front of the child does not resemble the typical identity debate contexts discussed by Heim (see section 2.3.2). The approach invoking different guises for the same entity is compatible with Avrutin's proposal and features prominently in our own account in chapter 3.

Avrutin also addresses the Principle B/C asymmetry that has emerged in the experimental results. Let us assume that (84) is the test sentence that follows a context in which some female character, say, Goldilocks, has turned down Mama Bear's request to wash her, because she has to clean herself up. Mama Bear is left to wash herself.

(84) She washed Mama Bear.

As the characters are introduced, file cards are set up in the usual way, and new entries are made as the story unfolds. Let us suppose that in this discourse, cards 1 and 2 are set up when Mama Bear and Goldilocks, respectively, are introduced. At the end of the story, the cards should have the following entries:

(85) Card 1:   is Mama Bear
                is not washed by 2
                washed 1
     Card 2:   is Goldilocks
                washed 2

At this point, the test sentence (84) is presented, and the child subject must interpret the referent of the pronoun. There are two choices: update an existing file card, or make a new one. Avrutin assumes that the child updates a card that is already in the file. Card 1 cannot be updated, since doing so would violate Principle C. Therefore, it must be card 2 that is updated. However, the resulting file would describe an event that is not compatible with the entries on the cards in (85). In fact, that event (in which Goldilocks washed Mama Bear) is explicitly denied in the entry on card 1. Therefore, one option is for the child to reject the sentence in (84) as false, like adults.

Recall Avrutin's suggestion that in the case of *Mama Bear washed her*, some children apparently attempt to find a grammatical representation that fits the context, permitting the test sentence to be a true description of the events in the experimental story. Assuming the same to be true here, one interpretive option for the child who hears (84) is to assign a new card (call it 3) to the pronoun. In Avrutin's words:

In the absence of any specific contextual conditions . . . such a file corresponds to a situation where there are two different Father Bears [= Mama Bear in our text], and one of them washed the other. This, of course, is not the experimental situation simply because there is only one Father Bear in the story, and he does not wash anybody else except himself. Children therefore reject this sentence. (1994, 77)

If assigning a new card to the pronoun is an instance of accommodation, then, as in the Principle B case, the card introduced for the pronoun will have to be bridged to a visual situation card. As listeners, child subjects must make inferences concerning the speaker's intent but, on Avrutin's account, limitations on computational resources should make them unable to do so in response to both sentences governed by Principle B and ones governed by Principle C. Avrutin suggests that children do not attempt to find a grammatical representation that fits the context for (84), however, because of parsing preferences. We take up this point in chapter 3.

There are advantages in viewing children's deficit as a processing deficit. This view enables Avrutin to say that children, like (nonaphasic) adults, have knowledge of the relevant syntactic and pragmatic principles; there is no need to explain how the child's grammar converges on the adult grammar. Moreover, as Avrutin points out, this view provides a way of explaining similar results found with aphasic adults. It follows that Avrutin must claim that the processing system matures. The question raised by Avrutin's account, and also by Grodzinsky and Reinhart's processing limitations account, is exactly what is it about the processing system that matures?

2.7   Cardinaletti and Starke 1995

In all of the accounts we have introduced that discuss children's interpretation of pronouns, the language studied has been English. However, children have been reported to misinterpret pronouns in other languages as well. In a recent paper, Cardinaletti and Starke (1995) attempt to predict in which languages misinterpretations should occur; specifically, they use the inventory of pronouns available in a language as the basis for predicting whether or not children will misinterpret pronouns in Principle B configurations.

Cardinaletti and Starke claim that universally, pronouns fall into three categories: strong, weak, and clitic (Cardinaletti and Starke, in press). Although a particular language may or may not have pronouns from each category, the pronouns that it does have will fit into these three categories.

Each type of pronoun has its own properties. Strong pronouns can take different positions in the clause (in some languages) and, like lexical NPs, can introduce a new referent. In addition, as the following French examples show, they can be stressed (86a), coordinated (86b), modified by an adverb (86c), and used in focus environments (86d).

(86) a. Il craint TOI.
         he fears YOU
     b. Il craint toi et   ton frère.
         he fears you and your brother
     c. Il craint seulement toi.
         he fears only   you
     d. Il craint toi, pas ton frère.
         he fears YOU not your brother

English pronouns can also be used in these syntactic environments, clearly demonstrating that they exhibit the behavior of strong forms.

(87) a. Mama Bear washed HER.
     b. Mama Bear washed him and her.
     c. Mama Bear washed only him.
     d. Mama Bear washed him, not Mary.

Weak pronouns can appear in only one position in the sentence, cannot introduce a new referent, trigger stress shifts in a sentence, and cannot be coordinated, modified, or focused as can strong pronouns. Cardinaletti and Starke point out (following observations in Selkirk 1972) that English pronouns seem to have some of the properties of weak pronouns. (English has no clitic pronouns.) For example, English pronouns allow contraction, but not in environments that trigger the use of strong pronouns. It is not possible to stress a contracted pronoun, as shown in (88a), or coordinate contracted weak pronouns, as shown in (88b). Nor can a weak form of the pronoun be modified by *only*, as shown in (88c), or focused, as shown in (88d).

(88) a. *Mama Bear washed 'ER.
     b. *Mama Bear washed 'm and 'er.

    c. *Mama Bear washed only 'm.

    d. *Mama Bear washed 'm, not Mary.

These facts lead Cardinaletti and Starke to conclude that English pronouns are ambiguous between strong and weak forms. There is one
exception, however. The pronoun *it* appears unable to take on the properties of strong pronouns; indeed, it always behaves like the weak contracted forms of other pronouns.

(89) a. *Mama Bear washed IT.

      b. *Mama Bear washed it and her.

      c. *Mama Bear washed only it.

      d. *Mama Bear washed only it, not Mary.

    Cardinaletti and Starke propose that adults use the weak form of the
pronoun as the default form in situations in which there is a choice
between a weak and a strong form. (They can, of course, use the strong
form if there is some positive reason to, for example, if emphasis is
required.) Unlike adults, however, young children use the strong form as
the default form. In Cardinaletti and Starke's words, "Unless the pronoun
of the target language is unambiguously deficient, children only use it
as a strong form" (1995, 11). If we assume that local coreference interpretations are possible with the strong pronominal forms but not with
weak forms or with clitic pronouns, children's overacceptance of sentences
like *Mama Bear washed her* is explained. Children should also not allow
local coreference interpretations when the pronoun is *it*, since it is unambiguously a weak pronoun.

    According to Cardinaletti and Starke, Padilla's (1990) work on
Romance supports their proposal. Padilla found that children did not
misinterpret clitic pronouns; that is, they did not allow local coreference
interpretations when the pronoun was a clitic. On the other hand, children
did misinterpret strong pronominal forms. This is in accord with McKee's
(1992) finding that Italian-speaking children also did not misinterpret
pronouns when they were tested on Principle-B-governed sentences containing clitic pronouns.

    The proposal predicts that in languages in which particular pronominal
forms display both strong and weak properties, children will misinterpret
pronouns in syntactic configurations relevant for Principle B. This prediction is borne out for Dutch (Koster 1993, 1994; Philip and Coopmans
1996). The syntactic tests demonstrate that Dutch works exactly like

English (data from Carolina Struijke, personal communication). Pronouns can be conjoined, modified, used to focus, and stressed, showing their strong properties, as illustrated in (90a–d). They can also be contracted and act as weak pronouns, as illustrated in (90e).

(90) a. Mamma Beer heeft hem en   haar gewassen.
        Mama Bear   has   him and her   washed
        'Mama Bear washed him and her.'

     b. Mamma Beer heeft alleen maar hem gewassen.
        Mama Bear   has   just   only him washed
        'Mama Bear washed only him.'

     c. Mamma Beer heeft hem gewassen, niet Marie.
        Mama Bear   has   him washed   not Mary
        'Mama Bear washed him, not Mary.'

     d. Mamma Beer heeft HAAR gewassen.
        Mama Bear   has   HER   washed
        'Mama Bear washed HER.'

     e. Mamma Beer heeft 'er gewassen.
        Mama Bear   has   her washed
        'Mama Bear washed 'er.'

Theoretically, pronouns could also be misinterpreted in languages with pronouns that are unambiguously strong, such as French. In French, for example, the strong form is used for emphasis. Consider (91).

(91) Maman Ours lave   elle.
     Mama Bear   washes her

This sentence would be felicitous if the point was to stress that *she (elle)* was the one being washed, not somebody else. Presumably, this use would often be accompanied by pointing—in which case, it is highly unlikely that the child would misinterpret the pronoun. Possibly, then, it is languages like Dutch and English, which have pronouns that are ambiguous between a strong and a weak form, that will be more difficult for children to sort out.

Cardinaletti and Starke focus on the "strength" of the pronominal forms in a language. They propose that children differ from adults in taking a pronoun that is ambiguous between a strong and a weak form as being strong. According to this proposal, children should interpret pronouns as strong until evidence from the language they are learning informs them that this is not the case. Thus, English-speaking children allow the illicit local coreference interpretation of sentences like *Mama Bear washed her*. Conceptually, we might ask why children make the "default" assumption that pronouns are strong. Moreover, the proposal faces a learnability dilemma. Adding the knowledge that pronouns have weak properties in addition to strong ones does not inform the child that local coreference interpretations are illicit except in special pragmatic circumstances. In the absence of negative evidence, how does the child gain this knowledge?

Many details need to be filled in before Cardinaletti and Starke's proposal can provide a full picture. Although the proposal is not fully worked out, it does seem to successfully predict the languages in which misinterpretations occur.

Chapter 3

A New Account

3.1 Introduction

In this chapter, we present our account of children's misinterpretation of pronouns in matrix sentences like *Mama Bear is washing her*. We also extend the domain of inquiry to a different syntactic structure, VP ellipsis, and make a number of predictions concerning children's interpretation of pronouns contained inside elided VPs.

In presenting our account of how children misinterpret pronouns, we make the unequivocal assumption that children's pronominal errors are not violations of Principle B. The account looks outside the computational system to explain why children accept the local coreference interpretation of a pronoun and a name in pragmatic circumstances in which adults do not. At the broadest level, our account agrees with that of Avrutin (1994), who contends that children misinterpret pronouns because, as listeners, they have difficulty understanding the intentions of other speakers. The source of the misinterpretations differs on the two accounts, however. On Avrutin's account, the difficulty arises because children (and agrammatic aphasics) have a general deficiency in computational resources that prevents them from making correct inferences in many domains. On our account, the difficulty lies, not in the general processing system, but in pragmatic/real-world knowledge specifically related to intentions and knowledge of speakers—children have to learn the contexts in which a speaker can intend a local coreference interpretation.

The view that children have difficulty interpreting pronouns because they lack pragmatic/real-world knowledge is compatible with Grice's (1975) work on conversational implicatures. According to Grice, understanding a speaker's intended meaning depends on three factors: (a) the linguistic meaning of the sentence, (b) the assumption that the speaker is being "cooperative" (as defined below), and (c) sufficient background knowledge and knowledge about the current conversational context. In our view, the third factor is the one that causes children difficulty.

It is unlikely that the linguistic meaning of a sentence is the source of breakdowns in communication, because of the assistance the assignment of meaning receives from innate linguistic principles (i.e., from Universal Grammar). It is reasonable to suppose that innately specified semantic principles, like innately specified syntactic ones, are operative early in language development.

We also assume that general conversational principles such as the principle of cooperation are in place early in language development and therefore are not likely implicated in communication failures. As Chierchia et al. (1998, 98) remark,

> It is difficult to imagine how fixing the parameters of the target language or learning its lexicon could proceed unless children implicitly assume that one normally aims at being truthful, relevant, etc.... We do not contend that every principle (or aspect) of pragmatics is present at an early stage. But we do expect this to be true for the maxims responsible for "generalized" conversational impli-catures, which, as Grice himself points out, do not require world knowledge.

The "generalized" conversational implicatures that Chierchia et al. refer to are guidelines or "maxims," summarized in (1), that govern the main-tenance of conversations (see, e.g., Chierchia and McConnell-Ginet 1990, 190). Like Chierchia et al., we assume that these pragmatic principles are innately given and not learned.[1]

(1) a. Relation: Be relevant.
    b. Quantity: Be only as informative as required for current conversational purposes.
    c. Quality: Say only what you believe to be true and adequately supported.
    d. Manner: Be perspicuous: be brief and orderly and avoid obscurity and ambiguity.

In making conversational implicatures, a participant in a conversation must appeal to background knowledge (also called "common ground"), specific knowledge about the context, and inferences about the "mental model" of the individuals and relations among individuals being assumed by the other participants in the conversation. The role played by such contextual assumptions can be illustrated with the following conversation (from Sperber and Wilson 1986):

(2) *Peter*   Do you want some coffee?
    Mary   Coffee would keep me awake.

In this dialogue, Mary's answer is not fully explicit. Peter must figure out the intent of Mary's answer using general knowledge that he has about people's behavior patterns, or specific knowledge about the other participant in the conversation, Mary. Pursuing a line of reasoning based on general knowledge, Peter might be led by the following chain of inferences to interpret Mary's answer as a rejection of his offer: If Mary wanted coffee, she would presumably say so. Moreover, the fact that she mentions that coffee would keep her awake suggests that she does not want to stay awake. Therefore, she does not want coffee. Pursuing a line of reasoning based on specific knowledge, Peter might be led to interpret Mary's answer as an acceptance of his offer: Suppose that Peter knows that Mary is waiting up late for a phone call. Coffee will help her stay awake. Therefore, she does want coffee.

As Crain and Steedman (1985) remark, it is appropriate to think of specific contextual knowledge as a subcase of real-world knowledge. For present purposes, the point is that we believe that children's pragmatic difficulties lie in this area. Children seem to have difficulty in recognizing that the real-world knowledge other conversational participants bring to the conversation may not be the same as their own. This discrepancy in mental models of the conversational context leads children to allow interpretations of sentences that adults would allow only with special contextual support. Children have to acquire those aspects of real-world knowledge that give rise to local coreference interpretations of pronouns, so they are better able to gauge the intentions of other speakers. This real-world knowledge is fairly abstract, but we assume it is acquired through experience. Since this is the kind of pragmatic knowledge that arises through experience, no learnability problem arises. All children should converge on the adult grammar.

Before we can establish the types of real-world or pragmatic knowledge that children lack, we need to spell out the precise conditions and contexts in which local coreference interpretations are possible for adults.

3.2   Local Coreference Interpretations in the Adult Grammar

We are interested in identifying the cases of pronominal reference that violate the usual principles governing coreference relations dictated by the binding theory. The two cases of legitimate local coreference mentioned

by Chien and Wexler (1990) and discussed in detail by Heim (1998) are
(a) structured meaning and (b) identity debates (see chapter 2). First, we
will consider whether the pronoun needs to be stressed in these situations.
Then, we will try to pinpoint what aspects of the context signal that the
speaker intends a local coreference interpretation.

A prototypical identity debate example is (3), from Heim 1998 (see also
section 2.3.2 above).

(3) *Speaker A*   Is this speaker Zelda?
    Speaker B   How can you doubt it? She is praising her to the sky. No
    competing candidate would do that.

Given that Zelda is the only individual introduced, when speaker B uses
she, it must refer back to *Zelda*. The question is who the second pronoun,
her, refers to. As always, it can refer to some individual not mentioned,
although this meaning would be more readily available with some additional context. For example, another speaker, X, could have preceded
speaker A, as follows:

(4) *Speaker X*   Zelda's very fond of Gilda, isn't she, even though they
    are up against each other in the race for governor? She always seems
    to compliment Gilda's achievements, even in her speeches.
    Speaker A   Is this speaker Zelda?
    Speaker B   How can you doubt it? She is praising her to the sky. No
    competing candidate would do that.

With the additional context in (4), *her* could be taken to refer to Gilda.
Without speaker X's introduction of another character, however, it is
more natural to interpret *her* as referring to Zelda.

In identity debate cases, pronominal stress isn't necessary, though stress
on the object pronoun is possible. In example (3), stress on the pronoun in
either subject or object position is not needed in order for the listener to
get the coreference interpretation. This is the paradigm case of local coreference when two guises of the same individual are under consideration.
The two guises of Zelda at issue in (3) are the guise of Zelda on the stage
at the time the conversation takes place, and the guise of Zelda in the
memory of speakers A and B. If the object pronoun *is* stressed, there
should be a set of candidates to contrast Zelda with; that is, the stress
indicates that there is a set of candidates under discussion.

(5) *Speaker A*   I always get Zelda and Rhonda mixed up. Is this speaker
    Zelda?

Speaker B How can you doubt it? She is praising HER to the sky. No competing candidate would do that.

In other words, Zelda, the candidate who is up on the stage speaking, is praising herself, in contrast to the other candidates.

A prototypical structured-meaning example is (6), also from Heim 1998. Here, stress facilitates the intended local coreference, though in this case the stress is not on the pronoun, but on the name.

(6) You know what Mary, Sue, and John have in common? MARY admires John, SUE admires him, and JOHN admires him too.

In fact, the second sentence is odd without stress, presumably because lack of stress would not focus the NPs as is appropriate for the structured-meaning interpretation. Presumably for the same reason, it is not possible to change the stress pattern of (6) by focusing on the pronoun in object position, as in (7).

(7) You know what Mary, Sue, and John have in common? MARY admires John, SUE admires John, ...
   a. *and JOHN admires HIM too.
   b. *and John admires HIM too.
   c. *and he admires HIM too.

Variations of (7) can be constructed in which the relevant binding principle is Principle C, not Principle B (cf. (8b) and (8d)).

(8) You know what Mary, Sue, and John have in common? MARY admires John, SUE admires John, and ...
   a. HE admires John too.
   b. HE admires him too.
   c. *he admires JOHN too.
   d. *he admires him too.

A few observations about (8) are important. First, from the ungrammaticality of (8c), it is clear that the subject pronoun must bear stress, as in (8a) and (8b). The clauses in (8a) and (8b) complete a structured meaning. In our view, what is expressed when (8a) or (8b) completes the discourse is the proposition that John's admiration of himself is unexpected; this aspect of John's behavior is atypical in some way. In a sense, stress on the pronoun has the effect of presenting John in a different guise, in virtue of the unexpected property of self-admiration. Thus there is no Principle B violation.

For some people, the intuition becomes sharper if the verb is changed from *admire* to *vote*. Real-world knowledge informs us that it is not usual (or seemly) to vote for oneself. In (9), therefore, the last sentence in the discourse suggests that for John to vote for himself would be unexpected.

(9) You know what Mary, Sue, and John have in common?
    MARY voted for John, SUE voted for John, and HE voted for John too.

Examples like (6) and (9) are typical of structured-meaning cases of local coreference. In these examples, as in the identity debate examples, it makes sense to claim that two guises of John are under discussion. In (9), for example, there is John in the guise of the individual, in the flesh, who cast his vote, and there is John in the guise of the candidate that everyone voted for, including himself. (Heim (1998) does not consider examples like (6)–(9) to involve two guises of an individual, however.)

As Heim (1998) notes, the so-called run-of-the-mill examples like *Mama Bear is washing her* do not allow a local coreference reading in normal circumstances. When Grodzinsky and Reinhart's Rule I is applied, the coreference reading is usurped by the bound variable interpretation, which is in turn excluded by Principle B. A stressed pronoun in the same sentence, however, is enough to tip the scales and allow the local coreference interpretation, at least for many speakers. The local coreference reading is made more salient if accompanied by deixis (e.g., pointing).

(10) Mama Bear washed HER.

Some mental accommodation is also necessary to imagine an appropriate context for a local coreference interpretation. (Of course, with sufficient context, this could not be considered a run-of-the-mill example.) The circumstances in which the local coreference presentation of the sentence is felicitous are, in fact, very narrow. What is communicated when the pronoun is stressed is not just the idea that Mama Bear washed herself— rather, it is the idea that Mama Bear is not washing someone else, as one might expect, but is washing herself instead, an event that one might not have expected. As in the structured-meaning sentences, then, stress on the pronoun serves to point out that the individual being referred to is engaging in uncharacteristic behavior.[2]

In a sense, the function of pronominal stress in sentences like (10) is to alert the listener to an individual who has already been mentioned under a different guise. One guise is the character present in the visual scene (in the current example, Mama Bear). The second guise, introduced by the pronoun, is the same character—but a time-slice of that character that is engaged in unexpected behavior, (in the current example, behavior that is not usually associated with the Mama Bear in the visual scene, perhaps because the behavior is not expected of bears generally).

From this perspective, then, all cases of local coreference involve different guises of the same individual. There is a natural hierarchy of such cases, however, depending on the amount of context that is used to establish the alternative guises of the individual. The strongest case of contextual support is a debate about someone's identity. In an identity debate, two "manifestations" of a person are explicitly juxtaposed, and the question amounts to whether or not the two presentations pick out the same person. In Heim's example, two guises of Zelda are clearly distinguished, and the discussion between speakers A and B centers on whether one guise of Zelda maps onto the other. The structured-meaning examples also present two guises of a character, but identity is not at issue. The point of the example is that the properties of an individual who has been introduced under one guise are atypical for that individual, in virtue of being unexpected behavior for anyone in the same circumstances. In these circumstances, the speaker must use stress if a local coreference interpretation is intended. Weakest in the hierarchy are the run-of-the-mill cases. Here, the local coreference reading is available only with pronominal stress, possibly accompanied by pointing. Here, too, atypicality is involved: an individual who has been introduced into the conversational context (in one guise) is behaving in a way that is unexpected, either for that particular individual or for all individuals of the same type (e.g., bears).

3.3 Children's Misinterpretations of Pronouns

Our view is that children's knowledge of pragmatics is incomplete. Children appear to have difficulty evaluating the intentions of other participants in a conversational context (see also Avrutin 1994 for this view). This difficulty arises, in part, because children seem to mistakenly assume that other participants share the same model of the conversational context (see Karmiloff-Smith 1981; Maratsos 1976; Kail and Hickmann 1992). This false assumption has ramifications both in children's speech production and in their comprehension of the speech of others. Our interest is in comprehension, especially in how this difficulty on the part of children leads to their misinterpretation of pronouns.

One consequence of children's lack of pragmatic knowledge is that, as listeners, they may assign interpretations that are not intended by the speaker; in particular, they may assign interpretations that normally require special contextual support to be felicitous for adults. More concretely, they may allow a sentence like *Mama Bear is washing her* to have a local coreference interpretation in a run-of-the-mill context, and not just in identity debate situations, structured-meaning contexts, and so on. What children are missing, then, is real-world knowledge about those situations or contexts that license local coreference interpretations. They must also learn how speakers alert hearers to the fact that local coreference is intended, by use of pronominal stress.

The pragmatic knowledge that children lack is, in our view, acquired through experience. The potential advantage to this approach is that no learnability problem arises; there is no need to explain either how the grammar reaches the adult state or how the processing system becomes adultlike. All children simply converge on the adult grammar with some amount of experience in the world and innate Gricean principles.

In order to identify the specific pragmatic factors that contribute to children's misinterpretations of pronouns, let us consider in more detail the experimental contexts in which the nonadult interpretations appear.

In experiments using the truth value judgment methodology, children are asked to judge whether the target sentence (uttered by a puppet) correctly describes a picture or a story that is presented to them. When the child's judgment follows a story, the target sentence is usually presented in the past tense, as in (11).

(11) Mama Bear washed her.

In the dynamic version of the task (described in chapter 4), a story is acted out with toy characters and props. In each story, some problem or event is worked through until a resolution is found, with the toy characters presenting the pros and cons of their actions.[3] Before (11) is presented for judgment, for example, the child watches a story along the following lines. Goldilocks trips and falls in a puddle, so she stops at Mama Bear's house and asks Mama Bear to help her get clean. Mama Bear says that she would love to help, but her baby has just eaten his dinner, and he spilled it all over her. So, unfortunately, Mama Bear is unable to help Goldilocks because she needs to clean herself up.[4] She is able to give Goldilocks a facecloth, however, so Goldilocks can attend to herself. Following the action of Mama Bear and Goldilocks washing, the puppet says:

(12) *Puppet*   That was a story about Goldilocks and Mama Bear. I know one thing that happened in the story. Mama Bear washed her.

For adults, the question at issue is whether Mama Bear washed Goldilocks or not; this is what the story is about. Adults take the pronoun in (12) to refer to Goldilocks and do not find the story line amenable to a local coreference interpretation of the sentence *Mama Bear washed her*.

In the scenario described above, the local coreference interpretation is possible for adults if (and only if) the pronoun bears stress, as in (13).

(13) That was a story about Goldilocks and Mama Bear. I know one thing that happened in the story. Mama Bear washed HER.

When stress is assigned to the pronoun, the feature of the story that is brought into focus is whether Mama Bear ended up washing herself. We underscore the point, however, that adults do not allow a local coreference interpretation in the absence of stress.

Why, then, do children accept the sentence *Mama Bear washed her* in situations like this, in the absence of stress? On our account, insensitivity to stress does not on its own explain children's allowance of the local coreference reading; it is a factor associated with their incomplete knowledge of pragmatics.

Four factors contribute to children's nonadult responses:

1. Children have not fine-tuned their understanding of the situations in which local coreference interpretations are permitted.
2. Children have not learned that stress on the pronoun (possibly accompanied by pointing) is needed to mark the speaker's intention to convey the local coreference interpretation.
3. Listeners tend to interpret a sentence in a way that makes it true. In the experiments with children, the test sentences were true on the local coreference interpretation and false on the adult interpretation.
4. In the relevant experiments, the event corresponding to the local coreference reading is the last event in the story. This makes that event, and therefore the local coreference interpretation, highly salient.

Let us examine these factors in turn, beginning with learning the contexts in which a local coreference interpretation is permitted. As noted, situations in which a local coreference interpretation of sentences like *Mama Bear washed her* is appropriate are narrowly circumscribed and

depend on real-world knowledge. For adults, the local coreference interpretation is permitted only if the event being described is unexpected (and
if the pronoun is stressed, a factor we will treat separately). No doubt,
most adults have formed opinions about what is typical behavior (in and
out of experimental settings) for bears in general, and for mother bears in
particular. It may not strike adults as unexpected that a mother bear
should decide to wash herself. Consequently, *Mama Bear washed her* does
not evoke a local coreference interpretation. Children's knowledge about
the characteristic behavior of different creatures is far less complete than
adults'. In the absence of firm opinions about the behavioral repertoire of
bears (in and out of experiments), children are open to construe the event
of Mama Bear washing herself as the climax of the story. Not knowing
whether or not this is typical or atypical behavior for Mama Bear, or for
bears generally, children accept the local coreference interpretation of
Mama Bear washed her.

Closely tied to the pragmatic contexts in which local coreference interpretations are felicitous is the second factor contributing to children's
misinterpretations: knowledge about the use of stress to bring a particular
interpretation of a sentence into focus. For adults, even if a situation in
which Mama Bear washed herself was extremely unexpected, this fact
alone would not suffice to evoke the local coreference interpretation of
Mama Bear washed her; the pronoun must also be stressed. Once the
pronoun is stressed, however, it becomes possible to induce a local coreference interpretation even for run-of-the-mill situations (with some
mental accommodation), not just in identity debates or in structured-
meaning cases. For children who assign the local coreference interpretation, however, stress is apparently not a necessary ingredient. We contend
that this simply follows from children's imprecise understanding of how
the pragmatics of local coreference interact with focus and use of stress.
This view is supported by the research presented in section 2.5.3, which
reveals that many children (as old as 5) have difficulty using prosodic information to locate the focus of a sentence. They do not seem to know
that the focus generally bears stress and that therefore, as listeners, a
useful comprehension strategy is to locate the lexical items that are
accented.

A third factor in children's acceptance of local coreference interpretations is their innate knowledge of pragmatics, namely, their innate
knowledge of the principles of cooperation and relevance. Children oper-
ate on the assumption that speakers are speaking truthfully, being rele-

vant, and so on. If they did not, it would be difficult to see how they could succeed in converging on the adult grammar. There is also empirical support for the observation that children attempt to understand sentences in a way that makes them true. Experience with the truth value judgment task has shown that children attempt to access an interpretation of a sentence that makes it true, if this is at all possible (Grimshaw and Rosen 1990; Crain and Thornton 1998). In the kinds of experiments in which children were found to produce nonadult responses, overaccepting local coreference, the target sentences were true on the local coreference interpretation and false on the adult interpretation. Of course, this factor does not suffice for adults to accept local coreference. Adults require that the pronoun be stressed, and so forth. But since children are not under such requirements, the fact that the local coreference interpretation makes the sentence true may boost its availability for children.

In short, children's adherence to the principle of cooperation encourages acceptance of the local coreference reading of sentences like *Mama Bear washed her*. To maintain the view that the speaker is being cooperative and is therefore saying something true, children search for the aspect of the context that matches a reading that makes the sentence true. That is, they search the experimental context to see if there is any way in which the sentence *Mama Bear washed her* could be a true description of the story. This search leads them to the final event, in which Mama Bear washed herself. In the absence of a firm conviction that this is typical behavior for bears, children are led to a different conclusion: that the speaker intends to point out that it is uncharacteristic behavior.

Fourth, assuming a strong positive correlation between recency and salience, the local coreference interpretation is made salient for children because Mama Bear's washing of herself is the last event in the story, occurring just before the puppet's assertion. The last event is generally the culminating event, the one that everything else leads up to. In combination with children's incomplete knowledge of what is characteristic behavior for bears, or for Mama Bear, the fact that this is the final event might promote the impression that this event is not characteristic—a situation that is consistent with the local coreference reading. This said, it should be noted that the salience of the last event has no effect in inducing acceptances of the bound variable interpretation of sentences like *Every bear washed her*. When local coreference is not a possible interpretation, because it would violate a grammatical principle, then it cannot be assigned. This is a consequence of the modular architecture of the language apparatus that we ascribe to both children and adults, as outlined in chapter 1.

To underscore this last point, we want to make it clear that the stories associated with the two kinds of sentences in the dynamic version of the task are generally the same (e.g., Avrutin and Wexler 1992; Thornton 1990). Each story has a theme. Usually, the theme involves a problem facing one of the characters, which needs to be resolved. As the story unfolds, the characters discuss the pros and cons of various solutions, and in the end, one is chosen and pursued. In experiments comparing sentences like *Mama Bear washed her* and *Every bear washed her*, the stories are kept as parallel as possible. In both stories, Goldilocks has fallen in a puddle and needs to get cleaned up. In the story for *Mama Bear washed her*, Mama Bear considers whether she can wash Goldilocks. In the story corresponding to *Every bear washed her*, three bears consider doing this. Two of the bears are unable to help at all; one helps a little; but all three bears end up washing themselves. Because the stories are quite similar, the observation that children do not allow a bound variable interpretation of *Every bear washed her* can be chalked up to the application of a grammatical principle, Principle B.

3.4 Children's Extended Creation of Guises

Chapter 2 described several contexts that license a local coreference interpretation. One kind of context involves the same individual in different presentations or guises, as shown in (14) (Heim 1998). In such a context, the pronoun usually receives stress. Such contexts were distinguished from run-of-the-mill contexts, which do not support different guises for the same individual.

(14) Mama Bear washed her

The previous section listed four factors that might contribute to children's over-acceptance of the local coreference interpretation of sentences like (14), in apparent violation of Principle B. These factors are seen to encourage children to assign different guises to the same individual, thereby promoting the local coreference interpretation, even in run-of-the-mill contexts. The present section provides a more detailed account of how the local coreference interpretation arises in children's comprehension of sentences like (14).

Notice that the referent of the object pronoun in (14) is Mama Bear in one of two guises, dubbed P2. We suggest that children interpret P2 as indicated in (15), such that P2 can be paraphrased as *the individual that washed somebody*. The use of a singular pronoun, *her*, in (14) means that the λ-expression in (15) designates a property of a single individual—the set of individuals who washed somebody contains just one member.

(15) Mama Bear washed [$\lambda x \, \exists y \, [x$ washed y]]

In the contexts in experimental studies of Principle B, Mama Bear would have been accurately described as the individual who washed somebody. In (15), it is claimed that Mama Bear washed that individual—the one that washed somebody. When (14) is assigned the representation in (15), then, it is interpreted to mean that Mama Bear washed Mama Bear. It is important to note that the representation in (15) does not yield the same meaning as the corresponding sentence in which the ordinary pronoun is replaced with a bound variable—the meaning of *Mama Bear washed herself*. Thus Rule distinguishes the two representations, and coreference is permitted.

We call the guise described in (15) the *role reversal guise*. For a transitive verb, V, the role-reversal guise for a pronoun in a sentence "x V pronoun" can be defined as property P in (16):

(16) $Px = \lambda x \, \exists y \, [x$ V $y]$

For simplicity, the role-reversal guise is defined only for an object pronoun, but the definition can be generalized to other grammatical positions in an obvious way.

Our hypothesis is that children who make apparent Principle B errors accept the role reversal guise in too wide a set of contexts; they accept it even when the speaker has not laid the groundwork to support it, and when the pronoun is not stressed. Normally it takes a special context for a pronoun to support a guise like "the individual that washed somebody." With such a guise in mind, the speaker of sentence (14), for example, would ordinarily indicate some reason for asserting that Mama Bear washed the individual that is washing somebody—namely, herself. As noted earlier, one reason would be that such a role reversal is surprising, in view of how the individual typically behaves. Some kind of "surprise" at such a role reversal seems to be a prerequisite for establishing the role-reversal guise for adult speakers. In run-of-the-mill contexts, by contrast, speakers would not have established the fact that such a role reversal is surprising.

There are other guises of course. For example, there is the *deictic guise*, which picks out the referent of a pronoun in the conversational context based on its salience. Alternatively, a pointing gesture could support the assignment of the deictic guise to Mama Bear, as in (17).

(17) Mama Bear washed λx [speaker-pointing-to x]

Because the meaning of (17) is different from the meaning of *Mama Bear washed herself*, Rule I allows an interpretation of (17) on which there is coreference between *her* and *Mama Bear*. Of course, the conditions that allow a context to "select" a referent are not part of grammar. We expect, therefore, that children will sometimes allow a deictic guise even when the context (e.g., pointing or some more subtle means of indicating salience) does not support selection of an appropriate referent.

We contend that the interpretation of pronouns under particular guises explains the apparent exceptions to the binding theory in children's behavior. Our hypothesis is that children over-accept certain guises without sufficient contextual support. In particular, children believe that speakers intend to provide contextual support for guises even when this is not, in fact, their intention. For example, children over-accept the role reversal guise because they believe that the speaker intended them to be "surprised" at the fact that the actor was also the acted-upon. We might look upon this as an instance of children's lack of real-world knowledge—namely, when it is surprising that an actor is acted-upon. Of course, whether something is "surprising" or not depends on the beliefs of speakers and listeners—after all, surprise is a psychological state. Thus our hypothesis is that the cause of children's apparent Principle B errors stems from their lack of knowledge concerning the real-world conditions (e.g., actors as acted-upon) that lead to certain psychological states, including the state of "surprise." The fundamental hypothesis can be stated as follows:

(18) *Extended Guise Creation*
    Children create guises in a superset of the contexts in which adults do. Children create guises in contexts in which adults do not, but they do not *fail* to create guises where they are allowed by adults.

The results that we have mentioned, by Karmiloff-Smith (1981) and others, support our hypothesis of extended guise creation. Children who are given a picture book and asked to tell the story of what is going on often begin by using a pronoun even when this is inappropriate. For example, on seeing as the first picture a boy holding a balloon, the child might inappropriately say to a listener who cannot see the picture:

(19) He is holding a balloon.

On the present analysis, the child is using a deictic guise where such a guise is not supported by the context (for adults). The child is unable to calculate that the listener can't figure out who *he* is from the context; therefore the child doesn't appreciate that the deictic guise is unsupported. The child has engaged in an act of extended guise creation.

It remains to show that extended guise creation does not extend to pronouns that are bound variables, as in (20). Because quantified expressions and bound pronouns are not referential, they cannot bear guises. Nevertheless, it is worth demonstrating that the local coreference interpretation that results from extended guise creation does not carry over to sentences like (20). That is, we will show that the meaning of (20) indicated in (21), in which the pronoun *her* is treated as a bound variable, cannot be derived by interpreting the pronoun as referring to the role-reversal guise.

(20) Every bear washed her.

(21) $\forall x$ bear(x) [x washed x]

(22) $\forall x$ bear(x) [x washed [$\lambda y\ \exists z$ [y washed z]]]

The representation in (22), which we have adapted from (15), corresponds to the role-reversal guise reading of the pronoun in (20). However, (22) does not mean that each bear washed itself; rather, it means that every bear washed the individual that washed somebody. The problem with (22) is that the quantificational antecedent, $\forall x$ bear(x), does not bind the variable, y, in the λ-expression. If we take the λ-expression to refer to a single individual, because of the singular pronoun *her* in (20), then (22) means that each bear washed a particular individual, but it does not create the relevant "distribution" such that each bear washed itself. On the other hand, if the λ-expression in (22) is taken to refer to the set of bears that washed somebody, it still fails to yield the right meaning. Although it is true that every member of the set of bears did wash somebody, it is not true that each of the bears washed the entire set of bears.

Another attempt at a guise-creation meaning for (20) is given in (23).

(23) $\forall x$ bear(x) [x washed [λy [y washed x]]]

Example (23) means that each bear washed the bear that washed it. This is not the bound variable meaning either, for the sentence could be true on this reading if, for example, bear 1 washes bear 2, bear 2 washes bear 1, bear 3 washes bear 4, and bear 4 washes bear 3. In short, there is no way to write out a guise interpretation of (20) that results in the bound variable meaning (21). Thus even a child who creates guises that are not supported by context will not be able to accept (20) on the bound variable interpretation. Therefore, the account we propose does not anticipate apparent Principle B errors for sentences with bound pronouns.

Since some children allow local coreference interpretations in more situations than they should, it is reasonable to infer that these children will have no difficulty accepting such interpretations in situations where adults permit them, that is, in identity debates or structured-meaning cases. In general, where the speaker intends local coreference, we expect children to consistently accept this interpretation. This prediction runs counter to the one made by Grodzinsky and Reinhart's (1993) proposal—namely, that children will respond at chance levels on all instances of the sentence structure that allows local coreference in the adult grammar (see also Avrutin and Wexler 1992 for this prediction). All instances of the structure [name verb pronoun] are subject to Grodzinsky and Reinhart's Rule I, and in their view, application of Rule I causes a processing overload and children end up guessing. To date, there are no reports in the literature of experiments testing whether or not children have difficulty with the relevant situations.

Notice, however, that if all the cases in which local coreference is felicitous are circumstances in which the pronoun has a different guise than the antecedent, then Rule I can be dispensed with entirely. We simply have to define *binding* to ensure that a pronoun cannot be bound by an NP if the pronoun and the NP have the same referent, presented in the same guise. This welcome result would follow from a theory in which the acceptance of a local coreference interpretation hinges on guise-creation. Principle B would suffice; Rule I would not be needed. Whether the result holds, of course, depends on demonstrating that all the good cases of coreference between a pronoun and a local c-commanding antecedent are circumstances in which separate guises are being assigned to these linguistic expressions. Further research is needed to substantiate the claim, but it appears to be convincing for the range of standard cases.

The remaining task is to explain how children expunge the local coreference interpretation in run-of-the mill contexts. In the absence of negative evidence, experience should be assigned no role in eliminating the local coreference interpretation where it is not tolerated by adults. For this, innately specified knowledge must suffice. Here, we wish to appeal to children's innate knowledge of generalized conversational implicatures, such as the Cooperative Principle, which is articulated into specific maxims: quality, quantity, relation, and manner. Based on these innately specified pragmatic principles, children count on speakers to make their intended interpretation clear whenever possible, using whatever means are at their disposal. Children learn from experience that specific contextual cues accompany the local coreference interpretation, such as the factor of "surprise," which often accompanies a sentence in which a pronoun is interpreted in the role-reversal guise. Once children have witnessed a sufficient number of examples of the local coreference interpretation in contexts that contain the relevant contextual cues, they will thereafter refrain from assigning this interpretation in the absence of these special markers of the speaker's intended interpretation. In short, the problem of learnability is circumvented by the accrual of real-world knowledge in combination with innate pragmatic principles that govern the assignment of interpretation to sentences in conversational contexts.

It follows from the account we have given that children should misinterpret pronouns only in languages with pronominal systems quite similar to that of English—that is, only in languages in which local coreference interpretations are possible in the adult grammar. In Cardinaletti and Starke's (1995) terms, these will be languages that have strong pronouns (or strong pronouns that are ambiguous between being strong and weak). Strong pronouns can bear stress, can introduce new discourse referents, and are close enough to being lexical NPs that they can introduce a new guise for an individual. Weak or clitic pronouns, by contrast, are in general too "deficient" to introduce a new referent or to be able to represent an individual in another guise (see Avrutin and Wexler 1992).

We differ with Cardinaletti and Starke (1995) on one point, however. Cardinaletti and Starke suggest that in situations where there is a choice between a weak and a strong form of a pronoun that is ambiguous between the two forms, adults use the weak form if possible. In the same situations, they suggest, children use only the strong form. This suggests that the children who produce nonadult responses to sentences governed by Principle B should not use the contracted (weak) form of pronouns, since a contracted form signals a weak use. Whether or not they do so is an empirical question, but we think it unlikely that they do, given that there is generally a parsing preference to reduce forms where possible and that, on the model we are assuming, the null hypothesis is that children and adults share the same parsing preferences. Therefore, the point is not that children have access only to the strong form; rather, it is that they have not yet learned to distinguish all of the contextual situations in which use of a strong pronoun is licensed.

3.5   The Principle B/C Asymmetry

Experimental findings show that children allow local coreference interpretations for sentences like (24a) but not for sentences like (24b).

(24) a. Mama Bear washed her.
        b. She washed Mama Bear.

The critical difference between sentences subject to Principle B and those subject to Principle C is the obvious one: in the former, the pronoun is in object position, and in the latter, the pronoun is in subject position. We agree with Avrutin (1994) that this difference in position is essentially what accounts for the asymmetry in the experimental findings. The asymmetry uncovered in the experimental findings does not follow naturally from any of the accounts reviewed in chapter 2. Most accounts predict that children will make errors in interpreting the pronoun in both Principle B and Principle C configurations. Both Grodzinsky and Reinhart's (1993) Rule I and Chien and Wexler's (1990) Principle P predict that children will allow coreference in (24a) and (24b), for example. Apparently some other factor is conspiring to give rise to the reported asymmetry. In this section, we offer two possible accounts for the asymmetry, both of which depend on the position of the pronoun. The first is a processing account, and the second is a pragmatic account.

3.5.1   A Processing Account

Consider how a matrix sentence like (24b) is presented to children in a truth value judgment task. Usually, the target sentence is preceded by a *linguistic antecedent* that introduces referents for the pronoun, as in (25).

(25) *Puppet*   That was a story about Goldilocks and Mama Bear. And I know one thing that happened. She washed Mama Bear.

In the literature on sentence processing, it is generally agreed that, owing to capacity limitations on verbal working memory, there is pressure on the human sentence-processing system (the parser) to immediately assign a referent to a pronoun as a sentence unfolds in real time. Because the pronoun in a sentence like *She washed Mama Bear* is in subject position, at the time it is encountered there is no proposition currently under consideration (such as that somebody washed Mama Bear). Presumably this is why a local coreference interpretation does not easily become available, even with pronominal stress, as shown in (26).

(26) SHE washed Mama Bear.

In (25), two potential referents for the pronoun have been established in the previous discourse, Goldilocks and Mama Bear. The most economical option from the point of view of the parser, therefore, is to take the pronoun to refer to one of these referents.

Suppose the parser chooses Goldilocks as the referent. In that case, Principle C is irrelevant. The sentence is simply false, given the preceding context. Now suppose the parser chooses Mama Bear as the referent, instead. In this case, it must reject its decision when it encounters the NP *Mama Bear*. At this point, Principle C becomes operative and dictates that the pronoun must refer to Goldilocks; the sentence is therefore rejected, because it is false on that interpretation. In order to compute a two-guises interpretation, the parser would have to recognize that it had previously encountered a pronoun and reconsider its interpretation to allow the possibility that Mama Bear has been presented under two different guises. While computing all this, the parser would have to put off its decision about the applicability of Principle C. Obviously an on-line incremental parser would find this amount of computation burdensome. We believe that backtracking, in order to reconsider the interpretation of the pronoun, is not likely to be within the parser's capacity, either for children or for adults. Thus, on the processing account just sketched, children do not even consider whether or not two guises of Mama Bear have been introduced in sentences like (26) in which the pronoun appears in subject position.

On the other hand, when the pronoun is in object position, as in (24a), it can be interpreted after the earlier portions of the sentence have been interpreted. An assertion is being made—Mama Bear washed somebody —and the child has to decide who Mama Bear washed. Various options that are compatible with the context can be evaluated, including the role reversal guise in which Mama Bear washed herself.

The processing account relies on the fact that interpretation is taking place on-line, incrementally, on a word-by-word basis (see, e.g., Crain and Steedman 1985 for more on this model). Heim's (1982) motivation for introducing a system of file change semantics was similar: namely, to create a dynamic system that can update information as a discourse unfolds in real time. The file card for each discourse referent is continually updated as new information comes in. For Heim's purposes, however, it is sufficient to note the changes in the file at the level of the clause. Models of sentence processing deal with much smaller units of information and, in this sense, are even more on line.

The claim that children attempt to assign reference to a pronoun in subject position immediately is not new (see Hamburger and Crain 1984; Lasnik and Crain 1985). Hamburger and Crain used it to explain the relatively small proportion of backward anaphora responses by children to sentences like (27) in experiments using the figure manipulation, "do what I say" methodology (e.g., Solan 1983).

(27) When she sat down, Mama Bear served some porridge.

Hamburger and Crain reasoned that the act-out task was the source of this response bias, because the meaning representation must be computed in the absence of a preceding discourse: "Interpreting and executing the first clause without waiting to form a complete plan [of response] means assigning a referent to a pronoun before the following noun phrase has become a candidate" (p. 134). In this case, children tend to assign the pronoun a referent that is not mentioned in the sentence (but is presumably present in the workspace).

3.5.2 A Pragmatic Account

Besides the processing account for the asymmetry in children's responses to sentences governed by Principles B and C, an alternative, pragmatic account is available. On this account, too, pronouns in subject position are viewed as having properties that ones in object position do not. Suppose children, unlike adults, assumed the following:

(28) *Pragmatic Principle of Old Information (PPOI)*
An NP in a structural position that favors old information is interpreted as being coindexed with an NP mentioned in the preceding discourse.

Children know that the subject position of a simple one-clause sentence frequently contains an NP whose referent has previously been established (i.e., old information). This contrasts with object position, which is more likely to contain full/lexical NPs. Evidence for this comes from the observation that pronouns appear more frequently in subject position than in object position in children's productions (see Hyams and Wexler 1993; Schütze and Wexler 1996; Schütze 1997).

According to the PPOI, a pronoun in subject position tends to refer back to an NP previously mentioned in the discourse. This means that children will take the pronoun in the target sentence in (25) as referring to Goldilocks or Mama Bear. In either case, they do not conside the interpretation whereby the pronoun refers to Mama Bear in another guise. If children take Goldilocks as the referent of the pronoun, they should reject the sentence as false because she did not wash Mama Bear in the story context. If they take Mama Bear as the referent, Principle C compels them to reject the sentence and not create the role-reversal guise.

The processing account and the pragmatic account make similar predictions for target sentences like the one in (25). It also follows (correctly) from both accounts that children will accept coreference between a pronoun in a subordinate clause and an NP in a main clause in sentences like (29) (following an appropriate discourse).

(29) Before she left, Mama Bear ate the porridge.

Since the pronoun *she* is inside a temporal clause, and such clauses are presupposed to be true, it is in a position associated with old information. Consequently, it can be coindexed with either of the NPs mentioned in the previous discourse. This time, however, Principle C does not rule out coindexation between the pronoun and the NP *Mama Bear*. Assuming that parallel processing makes both interpretations available, as in (30a), until the appropriate referent becomes clear, children should accept either interpretation, (30b) or (30c), in a context that makes the sentence true on that interpretation. The prediction that children should allow either interpretation (in different contexts) is based on the observation that children favor the interpretation of an ambiguous sentence that makes it true in the context, in keeping with Grice's principle of cooperation.

(30) (Appropriate discourse precedes)
    a. Before she_i/she_j left, Mama $Bear_i$ ate the porridge.
    b. Before she_j left, Mama $Bear_i$ ate the porridge.
    c. Before she_i left, Mama $Bear_i$ ate the porridge.

Having shown how the PPOI explains children's responses to sentences involving Principle C, we wish to spell out two other predictions that it makes.

The first prediction concerns sentences in which a pronoun in object position is governed by Principle C, as in (31a).

(31) a. Big Bird told her that Mama Bear was silly.
　　b. She told Big Bird that Mama Bear was silly.

Principle C dictates that the pronoun, *her*, and the name *Mama Bear* must have different indices in (31a). In contrast to the pronoun in (24b) or (31b), *her* in (31a) is not in a position to which old information is relegated. Therefore, the PPOI does not apply. In this case, then, the pronoun is open to a number of interpretations, including the two-guises interpretation. Therefore, the prediction is that children may allow nonadult coreference between *her* and *Mama Bear* in (31a), in contrast to (31b) where coreference between *she* and *Mama Bear* is not expected. Adults, on the other hand, knowing the circumstances that allow local coreference, will not be open to coreference between *her* and *Mama Bear* in (31a).

The second prediction concerns how Principle B operates in subordinate clauses that do not express old information. A case in point is conditional sentences. A temporal clause and the antecedent clause of a conditional statement are both subordinate clauses. However, unlike a temporal clause, which introduces old information, the antecedent clause of a conditional statement introduces new information. Because the antecedent clause of a conditional statement is a subordinate clause, coindexation will be licensed between pronouns contained in the antecedent clause and NPs occurring in the (consequent) main clause. However, since the semantic content of conditionals is not presupposed to be true, the PPOI does not apply to them. It is instructive, therefore, to consider how children might respond to embedded sentences that are governed by the binding theory.

The intriguing case is the one where the subordinate clause contains a sentence governed by Principle B, as in (32). Now the PPOI does not apply. Therefore, misinterpretations of pronouns within the subordinate clause are predicted to return. As always, the sentence will be felicitous only if preceded by an appropriate discourse.[5]

(32) If Mama Bear washes her, Goldilocks will not eat the porridge.
　　a. If Mama Bear$_i$ washes her$_i$/her$_j$/her$_k$, Goldilocks$_j$ will not eat the porridge.
　　b. *If Mama Bear$_i$ washes her$_i$, Goldilocks$_j$ will not eat the porridge.
　　c. If Mama Bear$_i$ washes her$_j$, Goldilocks$_j$ will not eat the porridge.
　　d. If Mama Bear$_i$ washes her$_k$, Goldilocks$_j$ will not eat the porridge.

In (32), the pronoun *her* is not in a position that expresses old information—it is in object position inside a clause whose content is not presupposed to be true. Therefore, speakers' intentions become relevant once again, and nonadult coreference is predicted to occur. Initially, all of the possibilities in (32a) are under consideration. Coreference between the pronoun and an NP in the same clause is subject to all the considerations that govern any Principle B sentence. Children will reject coindexing the pronoun with *Mama Bear*, as in (32b), on the grounds that this coindexation violates Principle B. They should allow the reading in (32c), where the pronoun is linked to *Goldilocks*, but they will also allow the representation in (32d), where the pronoun refers to *Mama Bear* and two guises of Mama Bear are under consideration. In short, children should appear to violate Principle B in response to sentences like (32) some proportion of the time.[6]

Until the predictions made by the PPOI are investigated more thoroughly, it is premature to take a stand on which account of the Principle B/C asymmetry is correct. However, they are both in the same spirit— namely, in the absence of a proposition being under discussion, the subject position will not allow the creation of a guise reading. Accounts of children's misinterpretations of pronouns that locate the source of the problem in the computational system (e.g., Grodzinsky and Reinhart 1993) cannot predict the Principle B/C asymmetry.

3.6   VP Ellipsis

In this section, we turn to VP ellipsis structures and to the predictions tested in the experiments introduced in chapter 4.

3.6.1   Introduction

Much of this chapter has focused on the pragmatic contexts in which it is possible to override Principle B, and on why children allow coreference in a broader range of circumstances than adults. Having established that children allow local coreference too generously in matrix sentences, we next consider whether nonadult interpretations should be expected in other structures as well—in particular, in VP ellipsis structures.

We take as a starting point the familiar asymmetry between (33) and (34). When children are tested on sentences like (33), where the pronoun has a referential NP antecedent, nonadult overacceptance of local coreference interpretations occurs. When children are tested on sentences like

(34), where the antecedent of the pronoun is a quantificational NP, they are not found to allow illicit bound variable interpretations.

(33) Mama Bear washed her.

(34) Every bear washed her.

We expect the observed asymmetry to occur in our experiment also.

Prediction 1
Some children will accept a local coreference interpretation of sentences with a referential NP antecedent, such as *Mama Bear washed her*; others will not.

Prediction 2
All children will adhere to Principle B in sentences with a quantificational antecedent, such as *Every bear washed her*.

Having established the asymmetry for these sentence types in matrix sentences, we will be in a position to explore binding and local coreference relations in VP ellipsis structures. Consider (35) and (36).

(35) Mama Bear washed her and Goldilocks did too.

(36) Every bear washed her and Goldilocks did too.

For (36), with the quantificational NP *every bear*, there is, of course, a deictic interpretation in which every bear and Goldilocks washed some third person. In fact, this is the only interpretation possible for adults. An interpretation in which every bear washed herself and Goldilocks washed herself is ruled out by Principle B. Now, what about (35)? In looking at matrix sentences, we suggested that sentences like (33) in which the pronoun has a referential NP antecedent cannot be used to unambiguously test Principle B. This is because of the alternative two-guises local coreference interpretation that is available for some children. If VP ellipsis sentences like (35) are parallel to these matrix sentences, then we might expect (35) to have an interpretation on which Mama Bear washed herself and Goldilocks also washed herself. As it turns out, this is not the case for adults, because of an additional, independent constraint that guides the permissible interpretations for elided VPs. This constraint prohibits giving the pronoun in each clause of the VP ellipsis structure a local coreference interpretation.

The effect of this constraint, known as the *parallelism constraint*, fueled our original prediction for this study: that an asymmetry should emerge for matrix sentences of the kind in (33) and (34), but not for VP ellipsis structures of the kind in (35) and (36). However, in our pilot work, and in the research of others conducted independently at the same time (Boster 1994; Koster 1993), it was found that some children accept the illicit reading of (35). This leads us to argue that the relevant constraint on interpreting pronouns in elided clauses has two components, one that is syntactic/computational in nature, and another that can be overridden by pragmatics. The syntactic component, we argue, is intact in all children's grammars; however, some children have not yet mastered the pragmatic component.

3.6.2   VP Ellipsis

Before examining our predictions regarding VP ellipsis and parallelism in child grammar, we review some basic properties of VP ellipsis.

The study of VP ellipsis structures has a long and venerable history in the generative literature, and a number of theoretical approaches have been suggested. One school of thought proposes that at some level of representation, either at LF or in the semantics, the elided clause is reconstructed on the basis of the structure in the overt clause (e.g., Fiengo and May 1994; Hornstein 1995; Kitagawa 1991; Reinhart 1983, 1986; Sag 1976; Williams 1977). Another school of thought proposes that VP ellipsis structures are base-generated as coordinate structures and that the second conjunct is deleted at PF (Chomsky 1995; Chomsky and Lasnik 1993; Tancredi 1992). Supporting this view is the observation that the same interpretations are available for VP ellipsis structures as for coordinate structures produced with *downstressing* (i.e., with flat intonation in the second conjunct). Our research does not attempt to claim that one or the other model is superior. To illustrate the interpretations available for the VP ellipsis structures containing pronouns relevant to our inquiry, we will use some of the technology presented by Fiengo and May (1994). In chapter 5, we will interpret our experimental findings within the PF deletion model of VP ellipsis sketched by Chomsky (1995).

VP ellipsis structures take a number of forms, as shown in (37)–(41). They may be coordinate structures, as in (37)–(39), or structures containing a subordinate clause, as in (40)–(41). In (40), the elided VP is in a temporal adjunct, and in (41), it is in an "antecedent-contained deletion" construction. Our experimental study was restricted to coordinate structures of the form in (37).

(37) Clark Kent ripped off his shirt and Superman did too.

(38) Clark Kent ripped off his shirt and so did Superman.

(39) Clark Kent ripped off his shirt but Superman didn't.

(40) Clark Kent ripped off his shirt before Superman did.

(41) Clark Kent bared his chest to everyone that Superman did.

As is well known, the presence of a pronoun in a VP ellipsis structure gives rise to a multiply ambiguous sentence. The terms *strict* and *sloppy* have traditionally been used to describe the different interpretations. To see these interpretations, consider (42).

(42) Perry polished his car and Jimmy did too.

On the typical strict interpretation, the overt pronoun and the elided pronoun are both taken to refer to Perry; the sentence means that Perry polished his car and Jimmy also polished Perry's car. (In chapter 1, we termed this the "coreference" interpretation, and we have sometimes referred to it as the *strict coreference* interpretation.) There is also another strict interpretation, which is obtained if *his* is taken to refer to an individual not mentioned in the sentence. On this reading, the sentence would mean that both Perry and Jimmy polished someone else's car. (Elsewhere, we have called this the *deictic* interpretation.) On the sloppy interpretation of (42), Perry polished his own car, and Jimmy likewise polished his own car. In sloppy interpretations, the pronoun is treated as a bound variable.[7]

3.6.3 The Parallelism Constraint

Ideally, the interpretations that are available for VP ellipsis structures would follow from principles of the grammar, such as the binding principles, that are independently motivated. It appears, however, that these interpretations cannot be accounted for without positing an additional constraint, often referred to as the *parallelism constraint*, or PARR (e.g., Chomsky and Lasnik 1993; Chomsky 1995; Fox 1998; Lasnik 1972). In some form or other, the parallelism constraint applies to all VP ellipsis structures, those containing pronouns and those without. As will be clear from the way we state the constraint, we will consider it only as it relates to the interpretation of VPs containing pronouns. Our initial statement is that of Fiengo and May (1994), who view the constraint as regulating the reconstruction of elided VPs at the level of LF. Later, we will reinterpret their statement as a constraint that applies in the PF component of the grammar.

To see why it is necessary to posit an independent constraint to guide the interpretation of elided VPs, consider (42) again (repeated here).

(43) Perry polished his car and Jimmy did too.

Although (43) is rich in interpretations, allowing both strict and sloppy readings, there is (at least) one logically possible interpretation that is excluded. The sentence cannot mean that Perry polished a third person's car and that Jimmy polished a fourth person's. On this ungrammatical reading, the NPs in each conjunct would be indexed as in (44). The lexical material contained in the elided VP is shown in the angle brackets.

(44) *Perry$_i$ polished his$_j$ car and Jimmy$_k$ $\langle$polished his$_m$ car$\rangle$ too.

The interpretation shown by the indices is not excluded by the binding theory; each pronoun in each conjunct is free in its governing category, as required by Principle B. Yet the interpretation is illicit.

Fiengo and May's (1994) statement of the constraint, which we initially term the *reconstruction rule*, requires some introduction. In Fiengo and May's framework, in addition to indices, NPs bear α or β superscripts. The superscripts define the relationship of an NP to other NPs in the sentence as either *dependent* or *independent*. An index on an NP that is independent of another occurrence is called an α-*occurrence* of an index; an index on an NP that is dependent on another occurrence is called a β-*occurrence*. Independent pronouns and NPs can be accompanied by stress and/or pointing; dependent pronouns cannot. Although this is not strictly true in Fiengo and May's theory for reasons that are not relevant here, for our purposes, it is safe to say that pronouns that have a β-occurrence of an index are interpreted as bound variables, and pronouns that have an α-occurrence of an index are referential pronouns. Thus, we can use Fiengo and May's notation as a graphic to express the referential or bound variable status of the pronoun in each clause of a VP ellipsis structure.

With this as background, we give Fiengo and May's informal statement of the reconstruction rule.[8]

(45) *Fiengo and May's (1994) reconstruction rule*
    If an occurrence of an index is independent, an α-occurrence, "copy" the occurrence itself; if the occurrence is dependent, a β-occurrence, "copy" the dependency. (p. 149)

Let us begin by demonstrating that the strict and sloppy readings of sentences like (43), shown in (46a–c), conform to the reconstruction rule.

(46) a. Perry$_i$ polished his$_i^\alpha$ car and Jimmy$_k$ ⟨polished his$_i^\alpha$ car⟩ too.

b. Perry$_i$ polished his$_m^\alpha$ car and Jimmy$_k$ ⟨polished his$_m^\alpha$ car⟩ too.

c. Perry$_i$ polished his$_i^\beta$ car and Jimmy$_k$ ⟨polished his$_k^\beta$ car⟩ too.

The two strict interpretations (i.e., the strict coreference interpretation and the deictic interpretation) are represented in (46a) and (46b). In Fiengo and May's terms, on the first strict (i.e., strict coreference) reading in (46a), the pronoun in the overt VP has an α-occurrence of an index, so that particular index must be reconstructed in the elided conjunct at LF. This yields the interpretation in which both Jimmy and Perry polish Perry's car. On the other strict (i.e., deictic) interpretation in (46b), the pronoun in the overt VP still bears an α-occurrence of an index, but this time it is index m, indicating a third party. This index is reconstructed in the elided conjunct at LF, yielding the interpretation that both Perry and Jimmy polished someone else's car. Finally, on the sloppy interpretation in (46c), the pronoun in the overt VP bears a β-occurrence of an index. Therefore, the fact that the pronoun is dependent (i.e., a bound variable) is what must be, and is, mirrored in the elided conjunct.

Now consider interpretations excluded by the reconstruction rule. We have already considered one such interpretation in (44), repeated here.

(47) *Perry$_i$ polished his$_j^\alpha$ car and Jimmy$_k$ ⟨polished his$_m^\alpha$ car⟩ too.

In (47), the pronoun in the first conjunct is independent, an α-occurrence. Therefore, according to the reconstruction rule, the same index should be reconstructed on the pronoun in the elided conjunct. However, it has not been, and the representation is ungrammatical. The reconstruction rule also excludes the interpretation shown in (48).

(48) *Perry$_i$ polished his$_i^\beta$ car and Jimmy$_k$ ⟨polished his$_m^\alpha$ car⟩ too.

On this, interpretation, Perry polished his own car and Jimmy polished someone else's. This interpretation is ruled out because the pronoun in the first clause is dependent, and the one in the second clause is independent.

As will be clear when we turn to our experiment, children appear to make errors of coreference in VP ellipsis structures, but they do not make syntactic errors; children know that dependent occurrences are copied as dependencies. This division apparent in children's knowledge led us to "unpack" the reconstruction rule into two parts. First, the pronouns in the two conjuncts must be either both dependent (i.e., bound variables) or both independent (i.e., referential). Second, a reconstructed independent pronoun must bear the same index that appears on the pronoun in the overt conjunct. Thus we propose that the statement of the rule should be modularized as follows:

(49) *Modularized reconstruction rule*
   a. *Dependence matching*
      Copy the dependence value of the index.
   b. *Independent index copying*
      If the dependence value of an index is independent, copy the index.

Although (49) appears to have the same effects as Fiengo and May's statement of the rule in (45), the separation/modularity of the two parts will allow us to capture the acquisition facts in a natural way. To the extent that (49) is correct, then, it is worth pointing out that the acquisition facts pointed up the empirical inadequacy of (45) in a way that was difficult to see from adult data. Fox (1998) gives a statement similar to ours.

(50) *Fox's (1998) statement of the parallelism constraint*
      NPs in the elided and antecedent VP must either
   a. have the same referential value (= referential parallelism) or
   b. be linked by identical dependencies (= structural parallelism).

Referential parallelism appears to be identical to what we term independent index copying in (49). However, the statement of structural parallelism (using Higginbotham's (1983) notion of "linking") handles more complex cases than does our statement of dependence matching.[9] From this point on, we will adopt Fox's terminology, to simplify the discussion. We will also use the terms *referential pronouns* and (pronouns that are) *bound variables*, rather than the terms *dependent* and *independent pronouns*. Our working definition of the parallelism constraint is stated in (51).

(51) *Parallelism constraint*
      NPs in the elided and antecedent VP must
   a. both be bound variables or both be referential pronouns (structural parallelism) and
   b. if the pronouns are referential pronouns, they must have the same referent (referential parallelism).

Our own position is that structural parallelism is part of the syntactic/ computational part of the grammar and is inviolable. Referential parallelism, on the other hand, can be manipulated to some extent by pragmatics and therefore can be overridden in certain circumstances.

3.6.4. Parallelism in Child Grammars

To our knowledge, no previous studies have investigated whether children know that VP ellipsis structures are subject to the parallelism constraint. Controls to test children's knowledge of the constraint were therefore a prerequisite for our study of children's interpretation of VP ellipsis structures containing pronouns.

   With regard to structural parallelism, consider the sentence in (52a).

(52) a. Every reporter combed his hair and Superman did too.
      b. Every reporter$_j$ combed his$_j^\beta$ hair and Superman$_i$ ⟨combed his$_i^\beta$ hair⟩.

This sentence is grammatical on the sloppy reading in which Superman and the reporters all comb their own hair. On this reading, indicated in (52b), the pronouns in each clause are bound variables, and structural parallelism is maintained. Structural parallelism excludes an interpretation in which every reporter combs his own hair but Superman combs someone else's hair (not his own). On such an interpretation, the pronoun in the antecedent clause is a bound pronoun, and the pronoun in the elided clause is a referential pronoun, as the superscripts in (53) indicate.[10]

(53) *Every reporter$_j$ combed his$_j^\beta$ hair and Superman$_i$ ⟨combed his$_k^\alpha$ hair⟩ too.

If structural parallelism is an innate part of the syntactic/computational system, children (and adults) should not allow this "mixed" reading. Let us state this as a prediction.

Prediction 3
Children will not violate structural parallelism.

   Children's adherence to referential parallelism was also tested. This part of the constraint requires that the pronouns in the overt and elided VPs have the same referent. Consider the sentence in (54). Referential parallelism will be satisfied only if the person captured by Superman is the same person captured by Lois Lane.

(54) Superman captured him and Lois Lane did too.

Referential parallelism rules out a "free reference" interpretation in which Superman captured one person and Lois Lane captured another, as shown in (55).

(55) *Superman$_i$ captured him$_j^\alpha$ and Lois Lane$_k$ ⟨captured him$_m^\alpha$⟩ too.

If, as we have suggested, referential parallelism is subject to pragmatic manipulation, then it is likely to be overridden in certain circumstances. If so, the "free reference" interpretation of (54) might be possible. For adults, however, it seems to be virtually *im*possible.

Interestingly, the coordinate structure counterpart of (54), shown in (56), does have the free reference interpretation. For this interpretation to be possible, the pronoun in each conjunct must be stressed, and deixis is necessary.

(56) Superman captured HIM and Lois Lane captured HIM too.

Of course, the pronouns in this coordinate structure are not downstressed, and therefore its interpretation is not governed by the parallelism constraint. We have claimed, however, that children who accept local coreference in sentences like *Mama Bear washed her* have difficulty interpreting the contextual cues associated with the creation of guises. It is possible, then, that these children have the associated difficulty of not knowing which interpretations are eliminated by referential parallelism. This leads to a question we put to the (statistical) test, as reported in chapter 4.

Question 4
Do children who accept local coreference interpretations in matrix sentences override referential parallelism in VP ellipsis structures?

3.7   Interaction of VP Ellipsis and the Binding Theory

In this section, we consider how the binding principles work in VP ellipsis structures.

It has been reported that the binding principles do not always give rise to such sharp violations of grammaticality in VP ellipsis structures as they do in matrix contexts (Fiengo and May 1994). Certain interpretations that might be expected to violate the binding theory are often judged to be acceptable. Although Principle B is usually reported to be untempered in VP ellipsis structures, apparent violations of Principles A and C have been observed to be acceptable in VP ellipsis contexts.[11] Our experiment on children's interpretation of VP ellipsis structures focused on pronouns in configurations relevant to Principle B, but also examined children's interpretations of pronouns governed by Principles A and C. Below, we introduce the structures tested in our experiments.

3.7.1 Principle B

The main motivation for studying VP ellipsis was to test children's interpretation of pronouns inside elided clauses, especially those in syntactic configurations relevant to Principle B. Following Chien and Wexler's (1990) strategy, structures like (57) with a quantificational NP in one clause can be used to ensure that the pronouns in the structure are constrained by Principle B and that the possibility of local coreference is eliminated.

(57) Superman brushed him and every reporter did too.

Principle B should rule out a bound variable reading in which Superman brushes himself, and every reporter brushes himself. Given that the principles and constraints of the grammar are taken to be innate, we would not expect children to allow this reading, whether they accept local coreference interpretations in matrix sentences or not. Principle B should be obeyed in all syntactic structures. This leads to prediction 5.

Prediction 5

All children will adhere to Principle B in VP ellipsis sentences that contain a quantificational NP antecedent.

Unlike in (57), in sentences like (58) the pronoun in both clauses has a referential NP antecedent. This VP ellipsis structure, too, is constrained by Principle B.

(58) Clark Kent brushed him and Perry did too.

For adults, the only possible interpretation of (58) is a strict one in which Clark and Perry brushed some third person. A sloppy, Principle-B-violating interpretation in which Clark brushed himself and Perry brushed himself, as shown in (59), is not allowed. Like adults, children are assumed to rule out this representation.

(59) *Clark Kent$_i$ brushed him$_i^\beta$ and Perry$_k$ $\langle$brushed him$_k^\beta\rangle$ too.

There is, in principle, another way to obtain a reading of (58) that "looks" sloppy (henceforth the *look-sloppy* reading).[12] Suppose the pronoun was given a local coreference interpretation in each conjunct. This would yield a reading in which Clark brushed himself and Perry brushed himself.

(60) *Clark Kent$_i$ brushed him$_j^\alpha$ and Perry$_k$ $\langle$brushed him$_m^\alpha\rangle$ too.
       (Clark$_i$ = him$_j$ and Perry$_k$ = him$_m$)

However, this reading is excluded by referential parallelism, according to which the pronouns in the antecedent and elided conjuncts must have the same referent. This requirement effectively allows only the reading on which Clark and Perry both brushed some other male individual.

We hinted that the effects of referential parallelism may be open to pragmatic manipulation, although we have provided no evidence for this in the adult grammar. It is worth investigating whether the pragmatic conditions that override Principle B in matrix sentences for adults are also at work in VP ellipsis structures. This is the topic of the next section.

3.7.2 Local Coreference in VP Ellipsis Sentences

It is well established that in the adult grammar, local coreference is possible only in narrowly circumscribed situations such as identity debates, circumstances that give rise to a structured meaning, or circumstances pointing out atypicality. Can such circumstances be devised so that local coreference is allowed in (both clauses of) a VP ellipsis structure? Given that, for matrix sentences, local coreference interpretations are most salient in identity debate situations, we begin our investigation with this "strong" case. Consider situations like (61) and (62), which are more or less parallel to Heim's identity debate example discussed in chapter 2.

(61) *Speaker A*   It's hard to tell who's who when everyone is dressed in Halloween costumes. Which are the infamous Smith girls? Is that witch Zelda and that witch over there Gilda?
Speaker B   How can you doubt it? The two of them have exactly the same mannerisms. Zelda is preening her and Gilda is too.

(62) *Speaker A*   I have trouble keeping all the candidates for the Town Council straight. The Smith twins are candidates, aren't they? Is that candidate Zelda and that one Gilda?
Speaker B   How can you doubt it? Both give tons of speeches. Zelda praises her to the sky and Gilda does too. Only the Smith twins would do that.

Local coreference seems to be at least marginally possible in these structures, since the context is heavily biased toward such an interpretation and no other individuals are mentioned for the pronouns to refer to. For example, in (61), *Zelda is preening her and Gilda is too* seems marginally to allow the meaning that Zelda is preening herself and Gilda is preening herself. The fact that these examples are marginal for adults may be related to the presence of the focus particle *too*. Structured-meaning examples are harder to construct, but not impossible.

(63) You know what Mary, Sue, Liz, and John have in common? They all admire John. Mary admires him, Sue admires him, Liz admires him, and John does too.

The reason why this example doesn't work well is probably that the structured meaning depends on the predicate *admire him*. In the VP ellipsis version, this predicate is elided and thus the structured meaning is lost.

In run-of-the-mill examples like (64), it is clear that the adult grammar does not allow a look-sloppy reading with local coreference in both clauses.

(64) *Lois Lane brushed her and Goldilocks did too.

However, even in matrix sentences, heavy stress on the pronoun is generally a condition for local coreference. The next step, then, is to see whether stress is sufficient to trigger a local coreference interpretation in VP ellipsis structures. Suppose someone utters (65), while pointing to Lois Lane.

(65) Lois Lane brushed HER and Goldilocks did too.

Even with stress and pointing, this example does not allow a local coreference interpretation of both clauses. No doubt this is because it is not possible to provide contextual cues for the pronoun in both conjuncts, only for the overt one. Instead, the deixis forces a strict coreference interpretation in which both Lois Lane and Goldilocks brush Lois Lane. Notice that this interpretation is consistent with the parallelism constraint. As the representation in (66) shows, referential parallelism is maintained in (65); the pronouns in both the elided and antecedent conjuncts have the same referential value. Furthermore, in keeping with structural parallelism, both conjuncts contain a referential pronoun.

(66) Lois Lane$_i$ brushed her$_j^\alpha$ and Goldilocks$_k$ ⟨brushed her$_j^\alpha$⟩ too.
    (where Lois Lane$_i$ = her$_j$)

Given that we have proposed that some children have difficulty understanding the set of circumstances that allow local coreference, we might expect that exactly those children who accept local coreference in matrix sentences will accept (64) on a strict reading. Exactly the same pragmatic knowledge is at stake. This constitutes our sixth prediction.

Prediction 6
Only children who accept local coreference interpretations of matrix sentences will allow local coreference in the first conjunct of VP ellipsis sentences (a strict coreference reading).

The next question is whether or not there are children who allow local coreference in both conjuncts of VP ellipsis sentences. As we just noted, such coreference is marginally possible for adults, but only in circumstances in which it is cultivated to the extreme. It could be that children will allow such an interpretation, represented in (67b), more liberally.

(67) a. Clark Kent brushed him and Perry did too.
    b. *Clark Kent$_i$ brushed him$_j^\alpha$ and Perry$_k$ ⟨brushed him$_m^\alpha$⟩ too.
      (where Clark$_i$ = him$_j$ and Perry$_k$ = him$_m$)

Acceptance of the interpretation for (67a) in which Clark Kent and Perry both brush themselves involves giving the pronoun in each conjunct a local coreference interpretation; it also involves overriding referential parallelism. Previously, we suggested that there may be children who are willing to overlook referential parallelism, since it appears to be linked to pragmatic knowledge. If such children exist, then we predict that they may allow the look-sloppy interpretation of (67a).

In the experiment reported in chapter 4, we tested whether (a) acceptance of local coreference interpretations in matrix sentences and (b) willingness to override referential parallelism determine the availability of the look-sloppy reading for sentences like *Clark Kent brushed him and Perry did too*. In other words, we tested the following predictions:

Prediction 7
Children who allow local coreference interpretations in matrix sentences like *Mama Bear washed her* may also accept a look-sloppy interpretation of VP ellipsis sentences with referential NP antecedents in each clause (e.g., (67a)).

Prediction 8
Children who override referential parallelism may accept nonadult interpretations of VP ellipsis sentences with referential NP antecedents in both clauses (e.g., 67a)).

Of course, it is difficult to distinguish the look-sloppy reading of (67a) from the bound variable reading that violates Principle B (see (59)). This is why we included the control structure containing a quantificational NP antecedent, (57). Results from children's performance on this structure were used to assess their knowledge of Principle B. We reasoned that if children behaved in accordance with the binding theory, we would take nonadult interpretations of (67a) to show that they were allowing illicit local coreference in each conjunct.

3.7.3 Principle A and Strict Readings of Reflexives

As a point of interest, we studied whether or not children (and adults) allow strict readings of reflexives in VP ellipsis contexts. Reflexives usually give rise to sloppy interpretations, since they are dependent on an antecedent and are interpreted as bound variables in VP ellipsis. In sentences like (68a), whose structure is given in (68b), Principle A is satisfied in both the overt and elided conjuncts.

(68) a. Perry laughed at himself and Jimmy did too.
     b. Perry$_i$ laughed at himself$_i^\beta$ and Jimmy$_j$ $\langle$laughed at himself$_j^\beta$$\rangle$ too.

The odd fact is that some speakers can give reflexives a strict interpretation in VP ellipsis structures, deviating from treating reflexives as bound variables. Hestvik (1995) argues that the strict reading is much more easily accessed in sentences with a subordinate clause like (69) than in coordinate structures like (68a).

(69) Perry laughed at himself before Jimmy did.

On the strict reading, (69) would mean that Perry laughed at himself before Jimmy laughed at Perry.

Hestvik offers several accounts of why a strict reading is available for (69), but highly dispreferred for (68a). On one account, a strict reading for (68a) is excluded by a principle of Universal Grammar, the Empty Category Principle (ECP). (On the definition Hestvik assumes, a trace of movement must have an appropriate antecedent that binds it.) In somewhat simplified terms, the asymmetry between coordinate and subordinate clauses is explained along the following lines. Reflexives are assumed to move to a higher projection—call it δ—at LF (see, e.g., Lebeaux 1983; Pica 1987; Chomsky 1986, 1993), either before or after reconstruction of the VP. In a coordinate structure, raising the reflexive before reconstruction results in an ECP violation. The raised reflexive does not bind the trace in the reconstructed coordinate clause because it cannot c-command into the conjoined clause. This structure is shown in (70).

(70) a. Perry laughed at himself and Jimmy did too.
     b. *[Perry [$_\delta$ himself$_i$ [$_{VP}$ laughed at t$_i$]]] and Jimmy $\langle$laughed at t$_i$$\rangle$ too

The only alternative is to raise the reflexive after reconstruction. This means the raised reflexive in each clause can only be associated with its own clause; as a result, only the sloppy reading can be generated. Now consider the subordinate-clause VP ellipsis case, illustrated in (71).

(71) a. Perry laughed at himself before Jimmy did.
   b. [Perry [$_\delta$ himself$_i$ [$_{VP}$ laughed at t$_i$]]] before Jimmy ⟨laughed at t$_i$⟩ too

The sloppy reading of (71) is derived in the same way as the sloppy reading of (70). For (71), however, both derivations are available; raising the reflexive before reconstruction is also grammatical. From its raised position, the reflexive is able to bind the trace in the VP of the main clause and the subordinate clause, as shown in (71b).

In brief, on this theory, a strict reading of a reflexive in a coordinate structure cannot be generated. Since the ECP is a "hard" constraint, the strict reading should be ruled out, not "dispreferred," a fact that is problematic. Acknowledging this dilemma, Hestvik offers another account, in which he suggests that

although a VP ellipsis is always syntactically reconstructed, it is possible to reinterpret it "off-line" as a deep anaphor, using a secondary interpretation strategy. This "deep anaphora strategy" thus provides a way to bypass the prohibition against strict reflexives in coordination.... The prediction is that the immediate and preferred reading should be sloppy, but that speakers, typically upon conscious reflection, will accept a strict reading as a secondary interpretation. (1995, 227)

Basically, this statement can be interpreted as suggesting that in this situation, pragmatic knowledge is overriding syntactic knowledge.

A different treatment of reflexives is offered by Fiengo and May (1994). This treatment appeals to the intuition that reflexives are morphologically complex, being composed of [pronoun + self]. The idea is that the pronoun is the argument, and *self* has purely syntactic status, by making the reflexive subject to Principle A. However, on this account, a reflexive can be reconstructed in two ways: either as [pronoun + self] or as a freestanding pronoun. If the reflexive is reconstructed as a pronoun, it will be subject to Principle B, not Principle A, and the strict reading will result.

Although Fiengo and May's account of reflexives differs from Hestvik's, it also rules out a strict reading of a reflexive in a coordinate structure. In order to generate a strict reading, the reflexive in the elided clause needs to be reconstructed as a pronoun (not as [pronoun + self]). This makes it subject to Principle B, and in both (72) and (73) Principle B is not violated—the pronoun is free in the clause.

(72) Perry$_i$ laughed at him$_i^\beta$ + self before Jimmy$_j$ $\langle$laughed at him$_i^\beta\rangle$.

(73) *Perry$_i$ laughed at him$_i^\beta$ + self and Jimmy$_j$ $\langle$laughed at him$_i^\beta\rangle$ too.

The problem is that β-pronouns are dependent on an antecedent. In its subordinate-clause position in (72), the pronoun can take *Perry* as an antecedent. In its coordinate-clause position in (73), it cannot, according to Fiengo and May, because the index is not "resolvable"; that is, there is no NP with the same index in the same conjunct of the VP ellipsis structure for it to depend on.

The data from adult controls in our study shed some light on whether or not the strict reading of reflexives in coordinate structures is readily available. Since the suggestion in the literature is that adults, or at least some adults, can generate the interpretation, we supposed that children would not differ.

Question 9
Do both children and adults allow the strict interpretation of a reflexive in VP ellipsis sentences, irrespective of whether they accept local coreference interpretations in matrix sentences?

3.7.4 Principle C
Just as we expect children to obey Principle B, so we expect them to obey Principle C. Furthermore, we do not expect Principle C effects to be masked by nonadult acceptances of local coreference, given the processing factors or pragmatic factors discussed in sections 3.5.1 and 3.5.2.

Prediction 10
All children should obey Principle C in matrix sentences, irrespective of the status of sentences like *Mama Bear washed her* in their grammar.

Consider the interaction of Principle C with VP ellipsis in a sentence like (74). The parallelism constraint does not apply to (74) because the pronoun is not contained in the elided VP.

(74) Perry brushed Superman and he did too.

The object NP in the elided VP will be reconstructed with the same index as *Superman*. Suppose that *he* is coindexed with *Superman*. This is shown in (75), where *he* and *Superman* share the index i. Principle C is violated in

(75) because the name *Superman* is c-commanded by a coindexed pronoun and therefore is not free.

(75) *Perry$_j$ brushed Superman$_i^x$ and he$_i$ ⟨brushed Superman$_i^x$⟩ too.

Thus, Principle C effects rule out certain instances of coreference within a clause, just as Principle B does. However, there is more to be said. Although Principle C rules out *Perry brushed Superman and he did too* on the indexing indicated in (75), the interpretation on which Superman brushes himself does seem to be possible. Why is this? One avenue to investigate is that Principle C is sidestepped in the elided clause. This can happen, on the theory proposed by Fiengo and May.

In Fiengo and May's theory, names, although normally subject to Principle C, may optionally be reconstructed as [+pronominal]. As the product of this "vehicle change," the "pronominal correlate" of the name becomes subject to Principle B instead of Principle C. This explains why examples such as (76) are grammatical.

(76) Mary loves John and he thinks that Sally does too.
   a. *Mary loves John$_i$ and he$_i$ thinks that Sally ⟨loves John$_i$⟩ too.
   b. Mary loves John$_i$ and he$_i$ thinks that Sally ⟨loves him$_i$⟩ too.

If the VP *loves John* is reconstructed, the sentence is ruled out by Principle C. As shown in (76a), the reconstructed *John* is not free. But if the reconstructed VP is subject to Principle B instead of Principle C, the sentence becomes well formed, as illustrated in (76b). Now, the pronominal correlate of *John* (i.e., *him*) is free in its clause.

Vehicle change does not change the status of example (75), however. In this case, taking the reconstructed VP *brushed Superman* to be subject to Principle B instead of Principle C does not sidestep a binding theory violation. Even if *Superman* was replaced with *him*, by vehicle change, the example would still violate Principle B. So vehicle change cannot explain why the apparently illicit interpretation seems possible.

We would argue that this VP ellipsis structure, in context, presents exactly the kind of situation that is amenable to a local coreference interpretation. To develop this line of reasoning, let us begin by observing "normal" coreference relations in coordinate (not VP ellipsis) structures.

(77) a. John hit Fred and Bill poked him.
    b. John hit Fred and he poked Bill.

It has long been noted that there is some kind of "parallel function strategy" at work in coordinate sentences like these (e.g., Akmajian and

Jackendoff 1970). If the pronoun is in object position, it will refer to an object antecedent, and if the pronoun is in subject position, it will refer to a subject antecedent. When the pronoun is stressed, however, the parallel interpretation no longer holds.

(78) a. John hit Fred and Bill poked HIM.
     b. John hit Fred and HE poked Bill.

In (78a), the pronoun in object position is stressed, and now, contrary to the usual interpretation, it refers to the subject of the first conjunct, *John* (given that there are no other possible antecedents without a richer context). In (78b), instead of referring to the subject, the pronoun refers to the object of the first clause, *Fred*. In this kind of context, stress is being used as a cue for overturned expectations.

In VP ellipsis structures, the effect of stress cannot be seen when the pronoun is in object position for obvious reasons—the VP (containing the object pronoun) is elided. As a result, stress cannot override the effects of Principle B in the same way it can in matrix sentences. However, when the pronoun is in subject position, as in (79), stress has a role to play, and the stressed pronoun becomes immune to the effects of Principle C. In fact, it is virtually impossible to say (79) without stressing the pronoun.

(79) Perry brushed Superman and HE did too.

A pronoun in subject position of a coordinated clause usually takes the subject of the preceding clause as its antecedent. However, in the case of (79) spoken without stress, the result would make no sense. The resulting meaning would be a tautology, which would violate Grice's principle of cooperation. With stress, the pronoun in (79) is interpreted as referring to the object of the first clause, *Superman*.[13] In a truth value judgment experiment testing possible interpretations of sentences like (79), an additional referent for the pronoun would make the sentence ambiguous. That is, experimental subjects would have to choose between taking the pronoun to refer to Superman and taking it to refer to some individual not mentioned in the sentence.

Notice that stress serves to overturn our expectations about the referent of the pronoun. This is reminiscent of the run-of-the-mill context considered for matrix sentences. That is, *Mama Bear is washing HER* expresses the fact that Mama Bear didn't wash the person the listener might expect, but herself instead. The sentence in (79) is similarly felicitous in a context in which it is not out of line for Perry to brush Superman, but unexpected that Superman would brush himself. In this situation, two guises of Superman are presumably under consideration. The subject *he* presents Superman in the role-reversal guise.

(80) Perry$_j$ brushed Superman$_i$ and HE$_k$ ⟨brushed Superman$_i$⟩ too.

The next step is to explain why local coreference is available for a VP ellipsis structure governed by Principle C, but not for a matrix sentence govened by Principle C. Recall that neither children nor adults should allow local coreference in matrix sentences (e.g., *She washed Mama Bear*) because of processing reasons or pragmatic factors (see section 3.5). Let us consider the processing account in more detail.

On the processing account, local coreference is ruled out for sentences like *She washed Mama Bear*, because the pronoun must be interpreted immediately on-line, before a proposition that would give rise to a two-guises interpretation has been encountered. A listener hearing a VP ellipsis sentence like (79), however, hears the proposition concerning who brushed Superman in the first conjunct before the pronoun *he* is encountered in the second conjunct. Therefore, in (79), unlike in a matrix sentence, the pronoun is not interpreted in the absence of a proposition. An assertion is being made (someone is brushing Superman), and a decision has to be made about who is doing it. The various options compatible with the context can be evaluated, and clearly the unexpected result that Superman is brushing himself is one of the possible interpretations. This is much like when the pronoun is in object position, as it is in *Mama Bear is washing her*. The pragmatic account in section 3.5.2 will lead to similar conclusions.

What are the predictions for children who allow local coreference in sentences like *Mama Bear washed her*? Since these children have not mastered the pragmatic knowledge and derivative requirements on pronominal stress that constrain local coreference interpretations, they should allow local coreference in the elided clause of VP ellipsis sentences like (79). Thus, children who lack the pragmatic knowledge will look like adults, disallowing local coreference in *She washed Mama Bear*, but allowing it in the elided VP of sentences like (79). In their case, however, the asymmetry does not reflect adult knowledge. We are led to prediction 11.

Prediction 11
Adults and children, irrespective of the status of their pragmatic knowledge, may allow local coreference in the elided clause of a VP ellipsis structure governed by Principle C.

We finish the chapter by looking at these predictions from the point of view of the accounts presented by Grimshaw and Rosen (1990) and Grodzinsky and Reinhart (1993). Although these researchers do not make any predictions about how children might interpret VP ellipsis structures, we attempt to formulate what their approaches *might* predict.

On Grodzinsky and Reinhart's view, the proposed asymmetry between matrix and VP ellipsis structures is not to be expected. For Grodzinsky and Reinhart, children should respond at chance levels to matrix sentences governed by Principle C because Rule I requires two representations to be compared. We can assume that the elided clause of the VP ellipsis sentence in (79) is also subject to Rule I, and chance performance is again expected. Hence the lack of an asymmetry.

Recall Grimshaw and Rosen's proposal that children find "the distributed reading associated with the quantifier–bound variable pair difficult, and construct this interpretation for pronouns less often than the alternative interpretations" (Grimshaw and Rosen 1990, 214). This suggests that children will find it difficult to construct sloppy readings for VP ellipsis structures. Naturally, sentences containing a quantificational NP, like (81a), will be difficult; but so will VP ellipsis structures with referential NP antecedents in each clause, like (81b). Given that there are two conjuncts, there is a distributed reading associated with the referential NP–bound variable pair even in (81b). Thus, the bound variable interpretations of both (81a) and (81b) should be rejected at a high rate ((81a) probably evoking a slightly higher rate).

(81) a. Superman brushed him and every reporter did too.

     b. Clark Kent brushed him and Perry did too.

Here, Grimshaw and Rosen's account would seem to predict that sentences with referential NP antecedents will cause children difficulty. It is difficult to make precise predictions, because other factors such as the parallelism constraint are relevant. But it is worth pointing out that (81a) and (81b) pattern similarly in Grimshaw and Rosen's account.

Chapter 4

Experimental Investigations

In this chapter, we present our experiments testing children's knowledge of the binding theory in VP ellipsis structures. In sections 4.1–4.4, we discuss experimental methods, introduce the methodology used in our investigation (the truth value judgment task), and present the experimental stimuli and procedures. In sections 4.5–4.8, we report our experimental results, and in section 4.9 we describe a follow-up study.

4.1 Truth Value Judgment Tasks for Children

The underlying assumption from which our methodological considerations follow is that children have an innate module of the brain that is specialized for language, Universal Grammar. A child acquires his or her target grammar, provided some amount of input from the environment is available. Our goal in conducting empirical experiments is to find out what aspects of children's grammars are given by Universal Grammar, and what aspects develop through experience.

In our study of the properties of VP ellipsis structures, we have identified some that are innate and some that may be governed by pragmatic or real-world knowledge. For example, certain interpretations of VP ellipsis structures are ruled out by principles of the binding theory, purportedly innate principles of Universal Grammar (Chomsky 1981, 1986). Other interpretations are ruled out by the parallelism constraint, which we have suggested may be modularized—one part, structural parallelism, being given by the grammar, and the other part, referential parallelism, being subject to pragmatic considerations. Given the Innateness Hypothesis, we predict that children will demonstrate knowledge of those aspects of the grammar that are innate, but may not show complete mastery of those aspects guided by pragmatic or real-world knowledge.

What methods can be used to determine the representation of a sentence in a child's grammar? For adult grammars, theoretical linguists use a variety of empirical methods to determine the status of a representation. Most frequently, linguists seek grammaticality judgments from a native speaker. Often, the judgment is made in the absence of context; sometimes, a context is provided. A theory is constructed that explains as much of the linguistic behavior (including judgments) as possible, under the constraint of learnability and the usual scientific constraints of simplicity, elegance, and so on.

In principle, the same requirements hold for studying the status of a representation in a child's grammar; that is, researchers need to find data (some form of behavior) that allow them to determine the status of a representation (of a sentence, say). However, some of the kinds of evidence that are used to study adult grammars are not available, or not reliable, for studying children's grammars. In particular, children have difficulty making subtle grammaticality judgments. We assume that cognitive factors are at work here, including, for example, an explicit understanding of the notion "grammatical."[1]

Empirical work on grammatical development thus concentrates on finding methods that allow researchers to determine the grammatical status of particular sentences in the child's implicit grammar. Because it is difficult to tap this knowledge directly, researchers must often devise indirect methods. From children's behavior in these tasks, researchers infer their grammatical knowledge. We focus here on the truth value judgment task (Crain and Thornton 1998; see also Gordon 1996). (For a comprehensive summary of other tasks that have been used with children, see McDaniel, McKee, and Cairns 1996.)

The truth value judgment task takes seriously the idea that language consists of "sentence/meaning pairs" (Wexler and Culicover 1980). A picture, or a story acted out with toys, embodies the context equivalent to the "meaning" part of the sentence/meaning pair. Following the presentation of the picture or the acting out of the story, a puppet usually utters a test sentence. This corresponds to the "sentence" part of the sentence/meaning pair. The child's task is to judge whether the puppet's description of the picture or of the events of the story was true or false. From this judgment, an inference is made about the child's grammar. Tasks based on the truth or falsity of a sentence in context are particularly suitable for testing knowledge of constraints on meaning, that is, constraints that limit the range of meanings that can be assigned to utterances. Among the constraints of this kind are the principles of the binding theory and the parallelism constraint.

Truth value judgment tasks vary according to how the context (meaning) part of the equation is presented, either as a picture (the *picture truth value judgment task*) or as a short story that is acted out with toy characters and props (the *dynamic truth value judgment task*). The picture task itself allows several variations. The target sentence can be accompanied by a single picture; in this case, the picture depicting the meaning that conforms to the constraint and the picture depicting the meaning that violates it are shown to the child on separate trials. This was the method used by Chien and Wexler (1990). Alternatively, the child is shown both pictures at once and is asked to choose the one that matches the test sentence. This was the method used by Wexler and Chien (1985) in testing whether children know the c-command property relevant to Principle A in sentences like *Cinderella's sister is pointing to herself*, for example. In the picture context that depicts the illicit meaning, Cinderella's sister points to Cinderella. In the picture context that is compatible with the adult grammar, Cinderella's sister points to herself.

In the dynamic truth value judgment task, it is always the case that two contexts—that is, meanings of a sentence—are under consideration. In this version of the task, the two contexts are incorporated into a single story, which is acted out for the child. The two contexts represent the interpretation under investigation that is ruled out by a particular constraint (e.g., a binding principle) and a meaning that the adult grammar permits for the sentence. The additional meaning ensures that the target sentence is always presented in a felicitous context. Suppose we were testing the c-command requirement relevant to *Cinderella's sister is pointing to herself* using the dynamic version of the task. The relevant events acted out in the story would be something like these. Cinderella asks her sister to point to her, but her sister won't do it and points to herself instead.[2] Thus, both the illicit meaning, in which Cinderella's sister points to her (Cinderella), and the grammatical one, in which Cinderella's sister points to herself, are made available to the child for consideration within the story.

Both variations of the truth value judgment task have advantages and disadvantages. The experimental results from the dynamic task are extremely reliable. Moreover, in this task, the presuppositions and pragmatics of the sentences being tested are satisfied in the story so that grammar and pragmatics go hand in hand (see Crain and Wexler 1999).

By having the characters in the story discuss the pros and cons of their actions, the task achieves a great deal of precision in matching a target sentence with appropriate contexts that support both its assertion and its denial.

The main disadvantage of the dynamic task is that it is very labor-intensive because each story must be acted out individually for each child. Therefore, it is difficult to test a large number of subjects. To some extent, the fact that the careful experimental conditions of the task elicit precise responses from subjects might overcome this problem. However, in practice, an experimenter often wants to look at subgroups of subjects (e.g., to ask whether those who perform well on X perform well on Y), and in this task, the numbers of subjects in particular subgroups are often small enough that it is difficult to get precise results. It is also difficult to investigate large numbers of items with this task. A maximum of four items testing a particular condition is usual. (Sometimes, only two items are tested, in which case it is not easy to look at properties of individual grammars.) Since roughly 10 stories can be acted out in 30 minutes, it can take three or four sessions to get an in-depth look at any particular phenomenon.

The picture task can be conducted relatively quickly. Large numbers of subjects can be tested on large numbers of items. If only group results are needed (e.g., how 4-year-olds perform compared with 5-year-olds), this task may be sufficient. As illustration of what can be accomplished with the picture task, consider the results that have been standardly taken to demonstrate knowledge of Principle A. To investigate children's knowledge of this principle, Wexler and Chien (1985) and Chien and Wexler (1990) each tested at least 120 subjects: eight groups of 15 subjects at 6-month age intervals from 2;6 to 6;6. Smaller numbers of subjects might have produced much less stable results, a familiar possibility in experimental psychology.

When the experimental linguist is studying the kind of property whose existence developmental psycholinguists and linguists may not easily believe in, it may be useful to perform experiments with many subjects and with many items per structure, opting for a simpler experimental method, with less rich contextual control, even if this allows a little more random error in the experiment. In this case, the picture task may be the right choice. On the other hand, once a property has been demonstrated (say, that children really *do* behave in a nonadult way on sentences governed by Principle B), then it may be useful to get a detailed analysis of the phenomenon and a precise picture of how children behave. In this case, the dynamic task is called for.

In the present study, we chose to use the dynamic version of the truth value judgment task. Children's misunderstanding of pronouns had already been well established, so we were in a position to take a closer look at the phenomenon in a different context, namely, VP ellipsis structures. Moreover, the structures are sufficiently complex to necessitate several events, which may be difficult to portray in a single picture. We recognize that our use of this task meant we were able to test fewer children on fewer items. Despite this drawback, we were able to identify different patterns of behavior among different groups of children.

4.2 The Truth Value Judgment Task

4.2.1 An Overview

The truth value judgment task requires two experimenters (for a detailed description of the task, see Crain and Thornton 1998). One experimenter narrates the story and manipulates the toys that participate in the event. The second experimenter takes the role of a puppet (Kermit the Frog or any other favorite character), who watches the stories along with the child. At the end of each story, the puppet's job is to try and say what he thought happened. Sometimes the puppet describes the story correctly (i.e., the "sentence" matches the "meaning"), but sometimes he doesn't pay attention, and he describes the story incorrectly (i.e., the "sentence" does not match the "meaning"). If the puppet says the "right thing," the child feeds him his favorite food. If he says the "wrong thing," the child gives him a bite of something he doesn't like as well, perhaps his second favorite food, or makes him do push-ups or the like. When a child judges the puppet's utterance incorrect, the experimenter playing Kermit the Frog asks, "What really happened?" This question follows up on the child's reason for rejecting the sentence/meaning pair, and it elicits production data that frequently add important insights to children's interpretation of the test sentences.

The experimenter playing the puppet keeps the child involved in the game. The puppet pays close attention to the story, commenting where appropriate and encouraging the child to be observant. The puppet's description immediately follows the end of the story, while the events are still fresh in the child's mind. No matter whether the child judges the puppet's description true or false, the puppet is enthusiastic, so that the child does not develop a bias toward answering one way or the other. Because it is the puppet's performance and not the child's that is being scrutinized, children do not realize that they are being tested. This makes the game much more enjoyable for children.

We have already noted that the story acted out for children incorporates two contexts that correspond to two potential meanings of the test sentence. Which meaning is aligned with the "Yes" response and which meaning is aligned with the "No" response depends on the hypotheses under consideration in the experiment. Following standard terminology, we refer to the experimenter's own hypothesis as the *experimental hypothesis* and to the opposing hypothesis as the *null hypothesis*. For our purposes, the experimental hypothesis will be that children have knowledge of the principles of Universal Grammar, and the null hypothesis will be that children do not necessarily respond in accord with Universal Grammar.

Crain and Thornton (1998) suggest that in experiments testing knowledge of constraints, the "Yes" response should be aligned with the null hypothesis. It is often reported that children tend to respond "Yes" in experimental tasks requiring a "Yes" or "No" judgment. Therefore, if the "Yes" response is equated with the null hypothesis, the experiment is biased toward favoring that hypothesis. This is one way to prevent type I errors (i.e., accepting one's own experimental hypothesis in circumstances that do not support it). If the "No" response is associated with the experimental hypothesis, children must overcome any bias they may have to say "Yes" in order to judge a sentence/meaning pair as false. Therefore, children's "No" response to the experimental stimuli can be taken as strong evidence in favor of the experimental hypothesis and against the null hypothesis.

The events within the story are also ordered so as to favor the null hypothesis, and in so doing to avoid type I errors. The part of the story corresponding to the null hypothesis (i.e., the illicit meaning of the test sentence) is staged last in the story. Given that the event that corresponds to the "Yes" response comes last and is presumably fresh in the child's memory, a "No" judgment leads to the conclusion that the incorrect interpretation is unavailable because it is excluded by the relevant constraint of Universal Grammar.

4.2.2 An Example

Let us suppose that the aim of the experiment is to test Principle C in matrix sentences like (1).

(1) He dusted Superman.

Principle C rules out the interpretation of the sentence in which *Superman* and *he* are coreferential. In other words, the sentence cannot mean that he, Superman, dusted Superman, or, put differently, that Superman dusted himself.[3] The meaning that violates Principle C ('Superman dusted himself') and the meaning that is compatible with the adult grammar ('He [somebody else] dusted Superman') are both incorporated into the story presented to children. One meaning is made to correspond to a "Yes" judgment of the puppet's description of the story and the other is made to correspond to a "No" judgment. This is so that the child's interpretation of the test sentence can be clearly identified.

As usual, the meaning associated with a violation of the principle being tested is set up as the "Yes" response, and the meaning associated with adult linguistic knowledge is set up as the "No" response.[4] The meaning that corresponds to the "Yes" response is made true in the story presented to children; the toy character Superman does in fact dust himself in the story. The meaning that corresponds to the "No" response is made false; it is not the case that he (some male) dusts Superman. Crain and Thornton (1998) call the research strategy of making the sentence false on a particular reading the *condition of falsification*.

A hypothetical story that embodies the two meanings is as follows. Superman has a problem. He has cobwebs on his shoulders and he needs to brush them off. Unfortunately, he can't reach them very well, so he asks his friend Jimmy the cameraman to brush them off for him. However, Jimmy says that although he'd like to help, he can't. He explains that Lois Lane also walked into cobwebs, and she is covered with more cobwebs than Superman and needs his help more. Since Jimmy won't help him, Superman does his best to dust the cobwebs off himself.

The experimental design can be summarized as in (2). The meaning that is ungrammatical but true in the story (i.e., corresponds to a "Yes" response) is represented by *meaning$_1$*, *true*. The meaning that is grammatical but false in the story (i.e., corresponds to a "No" response) is represented by *meaning$_2$*, *false*. This notation will be used throughout the discussion of the experimental stimuli.

(2) Sentence: He dusted Superman
    Characters: Jimmy, Superman, Lois Lane
    *Meaning$_1$, true: Superman dusted himself
    Meaning$_2$, false: Jimmy dusted Superman

Each story has four components according to Crain and Thornton: *background, assertion, possible outcome*, and *actual outcome*. The background can be thought of as a function to which the assertion applies and is represented by an elliptical expression. The assertion fills out the ellipsis. The background can be set up in many different ways, depending on what is taken to be the elliptical expression; in (3), it is the NP in object position and is represented by *so-and-so*. What is stated in the assertion should represent a *possible outcome* of the story—Jimmy does consider dusting Superman, although this is not what eventually transpires. The actual outcome negates the possible outcome; he (Jimmy) didn't dust Superman—Jimmy dusted Lois Lane instead and Superman was left to dust himself.

(3) Background: He dusted *so-and-so*
    Assertion: He (Jimmy) dusted Superman
    Possible outcome: Jimmy dusted Superman
    Actual outcome: Jimmy dusted Lois Lane
                          (Superman dusted himself)

One might ask why it is necessary to incorporate the scenario in which Jimmy considers dusting Superman, but decides to dust Lois Lane instead, given that this part of the story does not test whether children allow *He dusted Superman* to mean that Superman dusted himself. The answer is that if a test sentence is presented in a context in which there is no reason to deny it, it is unlikely that children will do so. They might respond according to Principle C and say "No"; but it is more likely that they will either agree with the puppet's statement because they're confused or say that they don't know how to respond. Associated with judging a sentence as false is a pragmatic condition that Crain and Thornton term the *condition of plausible dissent*; it is felicitous to deny a sentence only if the assertion it makes is under consideration. Thus, in the story Jimmy considers dusting Superman but rejects this possibility.

4.2.3 Realizing the Actual Outcome

In our example story, the possible outcome is represented by the test sentence itself: *He dusted Superman*. The actual outcome is represented by the negation of the test sentence, which indeed is true of the story; that is, he, Jimmy, *didn't* dust Superman.

A complication arises for sentences containing quantificational elements such as the universal quantifier *every*. Take a sentence like *Every reindeer brushed him*, one of the stimuli we used in testing children's knowledge of Principle B. In a story for which this is the test sentence, the possible outcome is that every reindeer does brush *him* (some male). However, the actual outcome entails that the negation of the test sentence must be true. The problem is that the test sentence can be falsified in two ways, depending on whether negation is interpreted inside or outside the sentence. That is, it has to be true either that not every reindeer brushed him (see (4a)) or that none of the reindeer brushed him (every reindeer did not brush him) (see (4b)).

(4) a. NEG S
    b. NP NEG VP

The question is, which possibility should be represented in the actual outcome of the story? Crain and Thornton (1998) suggest that it is more natural to negate the general reading of such a sentence than the specific reading; the former takes less cognitive effort to negate than the latter. This follows from the Principle of Parsimony proposed by Crain and Steedman (1985).

Let us illustrate using the example *Every reindeer brushed him*. In the story acted out for children, there will be several ways to satisfy the truth of the interpretation 'not every reindeer brushed him'. Suppose three reindeer make up the *every reindeer* contingent. Then interpretation (4a) is true if reindeer A didn't brush him, if reindeer B didn't brush him, or if reindeer C didn't brush him (to name some of the possibilities). It is even true if none of the reindeer brushed him. This is the general reading. By contrast, the reading 'every reindeer did not brush him' is true in only one very specific circumstance: namely, when all of the reindeer failed to brush him. This specific reading takes more cognitive effort to construct. It is suggested, therefore, that the actual outcome of the story accompanying the test sentence *Every reindeer brushed him* should be that not every reindeer brushed him (some male).[5]

VP ellipsis sentences introduce further complexities because they involve a conjunction of events. As illustrated in (5), they can be falsified by falsifying the action of the first conjunct only, by falsifying the second conjunct only, or by falsifying both conjuncts.

(5) a. NEG S AND S
    b. S AND NEG S
    c. NEG S AND NEG S

Consider a key VP ellipsis structure that tests Principle B, *Perry trusted him and Clark Kent did too.* In the actual outcome, the negation of this sentence must be true. This can be implemented in several ways: if Perry did not trust him (some male) but Clark Kent did; or if Perry trusted him but Clark Kent did not; or if neither Perry nor Clark Kent trusted him. The question is, which is the most general reading in this case? It seems that the reading in which neither Perry nor Clark Kent trusted him is more specific and would take more cognitive effort to construct. If so, the ideal actual outcome would be one in which either Perry or Clark Kent trusted him. At the time the experiment was carried out, this was not apparent, and our stimuli for these stories fulfilled the condition of falsification by negating both conjuncts. To our knowledge, this topic has not been investigated, and how crucial this manipulation is remains a matter for future research.

If the VP ellipsis test sentences contain quantifiers, there are even more ways to negate them. Our tests of the binding theory sentences containing the universal quantifier *every* were negated using the more general *not every* form of negation.

4.3 Materials

This section introduces the stimuli used in the experiment. Three types of stimuli were used, testing (a) children's knowledge of the binding principles in non-VP-ellipsis structures, (b) children's knowledge of the parallelism constraint in VP ellipsis structures, and (c) the interaction of VP ellipsis and the binding principles.

In designing the materials, we always adopted the experimental hypothesis that children have knowledge of the principles of Universal Grammar. Our stimuli testing Principle B followed this assumption even though we knew from previous literature that some children allow what look like violations of this principle. We have argued extensively that these apparent violations are in fact acceptances of an alternative (nonadult) local coreference interpretation that does not violate Principle B. This being the case, the sentences testing Principle B and Principle C in VP ellipsis structures also may be potentially ambiguous for some children. In the discussion of the stimuli below, we will make clear which items admit, or potentially admit, the extra local coreference option.

4.3.1 Controls for Binding and Local Coreference

We began by evaluating children's knowledge of Principles B and C in matrix sentences. We did so because it was important to identify which of our child subjects would have given the nonadult local coreference response to matrix sentences in previous experiments. These children were tested further on VP ellipsis structures.

Following results reported by Chien and Wexler (1990), we predicted that children would not treat sentences like (6) on a par with sentences like (7). That is, we predicted that children would not treat the pronoun and the quantificational NP in sentences like (6) as anaphorically related, because doing so would violate Principle B. By contrast, we expected that at least some of the children who rejected (6) would accept (7), allowing local coreference between the two NPs. Examples like (8), containing reflexives, were controls to show that children could allow a bound variable interpretation of a pronominal form in a one-clause syntactic configuration.

(6) Every reindeer brushed him.

(7) Bert brushed him.

(8) Every reindeer brushed himself.

Stories were designed that could in principle be used to test both (6) and (7). This step guaranteed that (6) and (7) were tested in the same discourse context, so that a difference in children's responses to the two types of sentences could not readily be attributed to discourse factors.[6] Control items like (8), in which the pronoun was replaced by a reflexive, were tested in the same experimental context.

Let us consider the design of the stories that tested sentences like (6)–(8). A sample design is illustrated in (9).

(9) Sentence: Every reindeer brushed him
    Characters: 3 reindeer, Bert
    *Meaning$_1$, true: Every reindeer brushed himself
    Meaning$_2$, false: Every reindeer brushed Bert

The interpretation that is ungrammatical in the adult grammar is lined up with the grammatical one, within the context of the story presented to the child. The meaning ruled out by Principle B, in which every reindeer brushed himself, meaning$_1$, is made available alongside meaning$_2$, a grammatical reading in which the pronoun refers to a character not mentioned in the test sentence (here, Bert). The illicit meaning$_1$ is true, and is designed to evoke a "Yes" response in order to bias the experiment against our hypothesis that children will obey Principle B.[7] The grammatical meaning$_2$ is false, and is designed to evoke a "No" response from children who have adult grammatical knowledge of Principle B.

The story line that embodies the design features in (9) is roughly as follows. Bert and three reindeer friends have a snowball fight, and they all get covered in snow. When they go inside, Bert is shivering, so he asks the reindeer to brush the snow off him. Two of the reindeer (separately) refuse, saying they have too much snow to deal with, and they brush themselves. The third reindeer helps Bert a little bit, but then brushes the snow off himself. Bert thanks the helpful reindeer for starting to brush him. He says he's sorry he can't reciprocate by helping brush the reindeer; he needs to finish brushing all the snow off himself because he's still very cold. In the story, then, it is true that every reindeer brushed himself. Therefore, a child who allows meaning$_1$ should respond "Yes" to the puppet's description *Every reindeer brushed him*. On the other hand, a child to whom meaning$_1$ is unavailable because it is ruled out by Principle B should take the pronoun to refer to Bert, as in meaning$_2$. This meaning is false, because it isn't the case that every reindeer brushed Bert; only one of the reindeer did. Therefore, a child who interprets the sentence as having meaning$_2$ should say "No."

It is worth checking to see how the story satisfies the truth value judgment task "recipe." The four factors are listed in (10).

(10) Background: Every reindeer brushed *so-and-so*
     Assertion: Every reindeer brushed Bert
     Possible outcome: Every reindeer brushed Bert
     Actual outcome: Only one reindeer brushed Bert
                          (Every reindeer brushed himself)

The background behind the story is that Bert has a problem: he wants the reindeer to brush the snow off him. The assertion that applies to the background is that every reindeer brushed him. In the story, it is possible that all of the reindeer could have brushed Bert. They all consider it, but, as it turns out, two of them say they have too much snow to deal with, and they brush themselves; so only one reindeer brushes Bert. The actual outcome represents the negation of the possible outcome: not every reindeer brushed him. The truth of meaning$_1$ is fulfilled in the final part of the story. The third reindeer brushes himself after helping Bert, so at this point every reindeer has brushed snow off himself.

Now consider how items in which the pronoun has a referential NP antecedent, like (7), were tested. Suppose the same reindeer story was used to test this sentence, *Bert brushed him*, that was used to test *Every reindeer brushed him*. (Recall that the same story pattern could be used to test both sentences like (6) and sentences like (7), though in fact no particular story was ever presented to a child more than once.) The features of the design are given in (11).

(11) Sentence: Bert brushed him
     Characters: Bert, helpful reindeer
     *Meaning$_1$, true: Bert brushed himself
     Meaning$_1$, false: Bert brushed the helpful reindeer

The reading corresponding to meaning$_1$ is the local coreference reading (alternatively, the reading that violates Principle B). On the meaning that is available, meaning$_2$, the pronoun refers to some other character, not mentioned in the test sentence itself (here, the helpful reindeer). Children who understood *Bert brushed him* as having meaning$_1$ would say "Yes" because Bert did in fact brush himself after the helpful reindeer stopped brushing him. Children with the adult grammar would understand the sentence to have meaning$_2$, however. These children should judge the sentence to be false and should respond "No" to it as a description of the story, because Bert did not brush the reindeer who helped him. Bert explicitly says that he can't brush the helpful reindeer, because he's still cold.

It was necessary to verify that trials like (6) were a valid test of Principle B (see Chien and Wexler 1990). This was achieved by checking to see whether the stories did, in fact, allow a bound variable interpretation when it was legitimate. Since reflexives provide a grammatical bound variable reading, a reflexive was substituted for the pronoun in (6), as in (8). The features of this design are shown in (12).

(12) Sentence: Every reindeer brushed himself
     Characters: 3 reindeer, Bert
     Meaning$_1$, true: Every reindeer brushed himself
     *Meaning$_2$, false: Every reindeer brushed Bert

Here, meaning$_1$ corresponded to a grammatical reading, not to a reading ruled out by the grammar, as in (6). In the story, every reindeer did brush himself, so children were expected to respond "Yes" to the description *Every reindeer brushed himself*. Since the "Yes" answer corresponded to a grammatical reading, we did not expect that children would choose meaning$_2$. To interpret the sentence in this way, children would have to allow the reflexive to refer outside the sentence to Bert, which is unlikely, given that this interpretation is not a possible grammatical interpretation. Unlike the target sentences that contain pronouns, this control sentence is unambiguous.

Four trials of each of the sentence types in (6) and (7) were presented to children. The verbs used in these trials were *brush*, *wipe*, *blow on*, and *fan*. We purposely chose verbs that are not inherently reflexive, to safeguard against the possibility that children would interpret the test sentence without interpreting the pronoun in object position (on this issue, see Wexler and Chien 1985; Chien and Wexler 1990; Grimshaw and Rosen 1990). Two trials of sentences like (8) were presented to children.

We also wanted to demonstrate that children who reject bound variable pronouns that are locally bound as in (6) do not do so because they cannot access bound variable interpretations of pronouns, as Grimshaw and Rosen (1990) suggest. To put it the other way around, we wanted to show that children can indeed access bound variable interpretations of pronouns (in addition to bound variable interpretations of reflexives), thus replicating the results of Chien and Wexler's (1991) study. Therefore, we included another control, using test sentences of the form *Every Cabbage Patch boy said Superman likes him*.[8] In such sentences, a bound variable interpretation of the pronoun is grammatical. By demonstrating children's ability to assign bound variable interpretations to pronouns with quantificational antecedents when it is possible, we aimed to lend credence to our test of Principle B in (6), where the bound variable interpretation is ruled out. The test situation is summarized in (13).

(13) Sentence: Every Cabbage Patch boy said Superman likes him

Characters: 3 Cabbage Patch boys, Superman, Pokey the Horse

Meaning$_1$, true: Every Cabbage Patch boy said Superman likes him (Cabbage Patch boy)

Meaning$_2$, false: Every Cabbage Patch boy said Superman likes Pokey

Because the purpose of the control was to demonstrate that children accept bound variable interpretations of pronouns, this interpretation was set up as the "Yes" response. Given that children have a tendency to say "Yes" if their grammar allows the interpretation in question, the availability of the bound variable reading should thereby have been boosted. Thus, meaning$_1$ corresponded to the interpretation in which every Cabbage Patch boy claimed that Superman liked him (i.e., the Cabbage Patch boy). However, the alternative interpretation of the pronoun, expressed by meaning$_2$, was also grammatical. On this reading, the pronoun refers to an individual not mentioned in the test sentence, Pokey the Horse. Because both "Yes" and "No" judgments are admissible, a "No" response to a sentence like (13) is not evidence that children *cannot* assign a bound variable interpretation to pronouns, but it does show a preference for the deictic interpretation. However, an acceptance shows clearly that the pronoun *can* be a bound variable. If a child who accepts sentences like (13) rejects ones like (6), then it is clear that the rejections are due to Principle B and not to any difficulty in treating pronouns as bound variables as suggested by Grimshaw and Rosen.

Insofar as possible, the plots of the stories for testing (6) and (13) were kept parallel. There were three characters who made up the *every* contingent (here, the Cabbage Patch boys), an outside referent for *him* (Pokey the Horse), and the character named in the text sentence (Superman). The story line is as follows. Each Cabbage Patch boy expresses his certainty that Superman likes him, giving a reason. Two of them say they don't think Superman likes Pokey, but the third disagrees, saying Superman would like to go for a ride on Pokey.[9] Taking Pokey as the referent for *him* would therefore cause children to respond "No" to *Every Cabbage Patch boy said Superman likes him* as a description of the story.[10] The requirements for the story can be summarized as follows:

(14) Background: Every Cabbage Patch boy said Superman
                        likes *so-and-so*

    Assertion: Every Cabbage Patch boy said Superman
                        likes Pokey

    Possible outcome: Every Cabbage Patch boy said Superman
                        likes Pokey

    Actual outcome: Only one Cabbage Patch boy said Superman
                        likes Pokey
                        (Every Cabbage Patch boy said Superman
                        likes him)

There were two trials of this type.

The final control testing children's knowledge of the binding principles in matrix sentences investigated their adherence to Principle C. (This item,

Table 4.1
Sentence types used to establish children's knowledge of binding in matrix sentences

Sentence types	Relevant principle
Every reindeer brushed him	B
Bert brushed him	B/Local coreference
Every reindeer brushed himself	Bound variable control
Every Cabbage Patch boy said Superman likes him	Bound variable control
He dusted Superman	C

too, is presumably open to a local coreference reading, though we have argued it does not occur for processing reasons or pragmatic reasons.) This design was discussed as the example at the beginning of section 4.2.2. There were two trials of this type.

The experimental items discussed in this section are summarized in table 4.1.

4.3.2 Recovering Elided Clauses

The trials discussed in this section all tested children's knowledge of the properties of VP ellipsis. As a precursor to testing children's knowledge of the binding theory in VP ellipsis structures, we wanted to investigate whether or not children can recover elided VPs. It was also important to test children's knowledge of both clauses of the parallelism constraint (structural parallelism and referential parallelism).

Let us begin with the trials, carried out in the first experimental session, that probed how children interpret an elided VP. Since it had not been previously established that children reconstruct elided VPs correctly, it was essential to show that children can do this. The items in these trials, examples of which are given in (15) and (16), contained an R-expression in the VP, not a pronoun as in the binding theory trials testing Principle B. Because the ambiguity introduced by the pronoun was eliminated, these trials were unambiguous for adults.

(15) The caveman kissed the dinosaur and Fozzie Bear did too.

(16) Ariel touched the creature and every girl did too.

The story leading up to the test sentence in (15) was this. The caveman has lost his pet dinosaur, so Fozzie Bear agrees to help him find it. Fozzie Bear finds the dinosaur, and the caveman is so happy that he kisses it.

Fozzie Bear considers kissing the dinosaur too, but because he is a bit afraid of the dinosaur, he celebrates their success by kissing his own hand instead.

The question investigated using (15) and (16) was whether children understand that the syntactic structure of the overt VP in the first conjunct must be reconstructed in the elided VP. This was tested by pitting a meaning that recovered the syntax of the VP against one in which only the verb (not the entire VP) was recovered. Consider the experimental design used for (15).

(17) Sentence: The caveman kissed the dinosaur and Fozzie
                             Bear did too
       Characters: caveman, dinosaur, Fozzie Bear
       *Meaning$_1$, true: The caveman kissed dinosaur and Fozzie Bear
                             kissed his own hand
       Meaning$_2$, false: The caveman kissed dinosaur and Fozzie Bear
                             kissed dinosaur

Meaning$_1$ is the interpretation that is ruled out. If a child were to recover only the verb, and not the entire VP—understanding the sentence to mean that the caveman kissed the dinosaur, and Fozzie Bear also did some kissing (because he kissed his own hand)—the child might respond "Yes" to this meaning. Meaning$_2$ is the grammatical meaning licensed in the adult grammar. A child who recovered the entire elided VP—understanding that Fozzie Bear kissed the dinosaur (false in the story)—would respond "No" to this meaning.

The background for the sentence brings into question who Fozzie Bear kissed: *The caveman kissed so-and-so and Fozzie Bear kissed so-and-so too.* The assertion is that the caveman and Fozzie Bear both kissed the dinosaur. The is a possible outcome, but the actual outcome is that Fozzie Bear kissed his own hand.

There were also trials like (15) in which meaning$_2$ was true. In the story corresponding to this meaning, the caveman and Fozzie Bear kissed the same dinosaur. There was no other obvious interpretation that could be given to the sentence, and the expectation was that children would say "Yes." (These trials also doubled as practice for the puppet game associated with the truth value judgment task.)

To check whether children can correctly recover the syntax of the elided VP, we also tested sentences like (16), which contains a quantificational NP instead of a name as the subject of the second conjunct of the VP ellipsis structure.

The story leading up to the test sentence in (16) was this. Ariel and three of her girlfriends are out for a walk when they discover a creature that looks as if it may be dead. Ariel touches it to see if it is alive, despite the fact that it is ugly and has warty skin. The three friends consider touching it, but they are concerned it may give them warty skin too. They decide not to touch the creature; instead, they touch their own skin (their legs), to make sure it is still soft.

(18) Sentence: Ariel touched the creature and every girl did too

Characters: Ariel, 3 girls, creature

*Meaning$_1$, true: Ariel touched the creature and every girl touched herself

Meaning$_2$, false: Ariel touched the creature and every girl touched the creature

Meaning$_1$ is ungrammatical if the entire elided VP is reconstructed, because in the story, every girl did not touch the creature; instead, every girl touched herself. If only the verb and not the entire VP is recovered, however, the meaning is true, because every girl did some touching. Thus, children could say "Yes" to meaning$_1$. Meaning$_2$ is the one that dependents on recovering the exact syntactic structure of the overt VP. Adults take the utterance to mean that Ariel touched the creature and every girl touched the creature. Since this did not happen in the story, children who give the sentence its adult meaning should say "No".

The background for (16) is *Ariel touched so-and-so and every girl touched so-and-so too*. Filling in the background gives the assertion that Ariel and every girl touched the creature. This is a possible outcome, but the actual outcome is that the girls touched themselves instead.

We also conducted trials for (16) in which meaning$_2$ was true and the only possible interpretation for the sentence. We expected children to say "Yes" to these trials. (These trials also served as practice trials.)

There were four control items like (15) and four items like (16). In each case, "Yes" was the correct answer for two of the items and "No" was correct for the other two. The verbs used were *kiss, point to, touch*, and *wipe down*.

Trials testing the parallelism constraint were separated into those testing structural parallelism and those testing referential parallelism. The structural parallelism trials tested whether or not children know that the pronouns in both conjuncts must both be either bound variables or referential pronouns. The referential parallelism trials tested whether or not children know that a referential pronoun must have the same referent as the pronoun in the elided VP. Examples of the sentence types used to test these questions are given in (19) and 20, respectively.

(19) The Incredible Hulk brushed his hair and every Troll did too.

(20) The lizard man lifted him and the ugly guy did too.

The story leading up to test sentence (19) was this. The rock star has a problem: he thinks his hairstyle isn't quite perfect. He asks the Incredible Hulk to brush his hair for him, and the Incredible Hulk agrees. Soon the rock star is worried that his hair is messy again, and this time he asks the Trolls to brush it for him. Although the Trolls consider helping him, they say they can't because they have to get the tangles out of their own long hair.

(21) Sentence:	The Incredible Hulk brushed his hair and every Troll did too
Characters:	Incredible Hulk, rock star, 3 Trolls
*Meaning$_1$, true:	The Incredible Hulk brushed the rock star's hair and every Troll brushed his own hair
Meaning$_2$, false:	The Incredible Hulk brushed the rock star's hair and every Troll brushed the rock star's hair

Meaning$_1$ corresponds to the ungrammatical reading of the utterance, ruled out by structural parallelism.[11] On this reading, the Incredible Hulk brushed the rock star's and every Troll brushed his own hair. This is a mixed reading: the pronoun in the first conjunct is a referential pronoun, and the one in the second conjunct is a bound variable. A child who did not have the structural parallelism constraint could say "Yes" to this meaning, since this was the meaning acted out in the story. Meaning$_2$ corresponds to the grammatical meaning, in which the Incredible Hulk brushed the rock star's hair and so did every Troll. This event did not happen in the story, so children obeying structural parallelism should say "No" in response to the puppet's description, (19).

The background for the story brings into question whose hair is being brushed by the Trolls: *The Incredible Hulk brushed so-and-so's hair and every Troll brushed so-and-so's hair too.* The assertion claims that the Incredible Hulk and every Troll brushed the rock star's hair. Although this is a possible outcome to the story, the actual outcome is different; the Incredible Hulk brushed the rock star's hair, but the trolls did not.[12]

(22) Background: The Incredible Hulk brushed *so-and-so's* hair
                          and every Troll brushed *so-and-so's* hair too
     Assertion: The Incredible Hulk brushed the rock star's
                          hair and every Troll brushed the rock star's
                          hair too
     Possible outcome: The Incredible Hulk and every Troll brushed
                          the rock star's hair
     Actual outcome: Only the Incredible Hulk brushed the rock
                          star's hair
                          (Every Troll brushed his own hair)

The story leading up to test sentence (20) was this. The Smurf and
Mickey Mouse are friends. The Smurf is tried of being smaller than his
friends and of only being able to see at ground level. He longs to see what
things look like from on high. So when he and Mickey Mouse come
across two big weirdoes, an ugly guy and a lizard man, he asks the ugly
guy to lift him up on his shoulders. The ugly guy wants to prove how
strong he is, so rather than lift the Smurf, he decides to lift Mickey
Mouse, who is bigger. The Smurf is disappointed and asks the lizard guy
to lift him, since the ugly guy refused to. The lizard man is happy to
oblige and lifts the Smurf onto his shoulders so that he can see.

The experimental design used to test sentences like (20) is as follows:

(23) Sentence: The lizard man lifted him and the ugly guy did
                          too
     Characters: lizard man, ugly guy, Smurf, Mickey Mouse
     *Meaning$_1$, true: The lizard man lifted the Smurf and the ugly
                          guy lifted Mickey Mouse
     Meaning$_2$, false: The lizard man and the ugly guy lifted the
                          Smurf

Meaning$_1$ is the interpretation for (20) that is excluded by referential
parallelism. The sentence cannot mean that the lizard man lifted one
character and the ugly guy another. However, in the story this indeed
happened: the lizard man lifted the Smurf, and the ugly guy lifted Mickey
Mouse. Therefore, if children are willing to violate referential parallelism,
they might say "Yes" to the illicit interpretation. Meaning$_2$ is the reading
that is grammatical for adults. The sentence mean that both the lizard
man and the ugly guy lifted the same person. This was not true in the
story, so children whose grammar includes referential parallelism will say
"No."

Table 4.2
Sentence types used to test children's recovery of elided clauses and knowledge of the parallelism constraint

Sentence types	Test
The caveman kissed the dinosaur and Fozzie Bear did too	Recovery of elided NP
Ariel touched the creature and every girl did too	Recovery of elided NP
The Incredible Hulk brushed his hair and every Troll did too	Structural parallelism
The lizard man lifted him and the ugly guy did too	Referential parallelism

The four components of the story are summarized in (24).

(24) Background: The lizard man lifted *so-and-so* and the ugly guy lifted *so-and-so* too

   Assertion: The lizard man lifted the Smurf and the ugly guy lifted the Smurf too

   Possible outcome: The lizard man and the ugly guy lifted the Smurf

   Actual outcome: Only the lizard man lifted the Smurf (The ugly guy lifted Mickey Mouse)

Although there were only two trials each to test structural parallelism and referential parallelism, they turn out to be an important part of the puzzle in interpreting our results. Trials like (19) used the verbs *touch* and *brush*; trials like (20) used *capture* and *lift*.

The sentence types discussed in this section are summarized in table 4.2.

4.3.3 VP Ellipsis and the Binding Principles

In this section, we introduce first the stimuli used to test children's knowledge of Principle B in VP ellipsis structures and then the control stimuli. Two sentence types were designed to test Principle B.

(25) Batman cleaned him and every turtle did too.

(26) Gonzo covered him with sunblock and Snuffy did too.

In trials like (25), the NP in the second conjunct was a quantificational NP. In trials like (26), the antecedent of the pronoun in both conjuncts was a referential NP. As mentioned in chapter 3, (25) unambiguously tests Principle B, so we will consider this structure to be the paradigm test of

Principle B. Although examples like (26) are subject to Principle B, they also potentially allow a local coreference interpretation of each conjunct. As explained in chapter 3, this look-sloppy interpretation of the pronoun in each conjunct is possible only if (a) referential parallelism is not maintained and (b) local coreference is permitted in the absence of pronominal stress. Examples like (26), then, are not clear tests of Principle B, but they may shed some light on children's knowledge of the conditions under which local coreference interpretations can be assigned.

The story leading up to test sentence (25) was this. The Smurf has been painting his house and dropped some paint on his hat. Unfortunately, he can't reach it, so he asks Batman to help him get clean. Batman says he'd like to help, but he was just spraypainting glitter on his Batmobile and he got paint on his cape; he can't help the Smurf because he has to get the paint cleaned up. So the Smurf asks his turtle friends to help him get clean. However, the turtles have been making decorations and they are covered with glitter too. Two turtles say they can't help the Smurf because they need to get the glitter off their shell; the other turtle helps the Smurf get the paint off him and then gets his own shell clean.

In examples like (25), the illicit reading that violates Principle B involves treating the pronouns in each clause as bound variables. This illicit interpretation, meaning$_1$, is pitted against the deictic interpretation of the pronoun, meaning$_2$. The design features for (25) are illustrated in (27).

(27) Sentence: Batman cleaned him and every turtle did too
     Characters: Batman, 3 turtles, Smurf
     *Meaning$_1$, true: Batman and every turtle cleaned themselves
     Meaning$_2$, false: Batman and every turtle cleaned the Smurf

Meaning$_1$ is the sloppy meaning that corresponds to Batman cleaning himself and every turtle cleaning himself. Since these events indeed took place in the story, a child lacking knowledge of Principle B should respond "Yes" to the test sentence. However, a child who adheres to Principle B should take the pronoun to refer deictically. This is meaning$_2$. On this interpretation, the sentence means that Batman and every turtle cleaned the Smurf. In the story, however, this event did not take place. Batman did not clean the Smurf, and only one of the turtles did. Therefore, Meaning$_2$ is false, and children who have knowledge of Principle B should respond "No."

The four components of the story are illustrated in (28).

(28) Background: Batman cleaned *so-and-so* and every turtle
                          cleaned *so-and-so* too
     Assertion: Batman cleaned the Smurf and every turtle
                          cleaned the Smurf too
     Possible outcome: Batman and every turtle cleaned the Smurf
     Actual outcome: Only one turtle cleaned the Smurf
                          (Batman cleaned himself and every turtle
                          cleaned himself)

It is clear from the background that what is at issue is who Batman and
the turtles cleaned. The assertion claims that it was the Smurf. This is a
possible outcome; both Batman and the turtles considered helping the
Smurf get clean. However, the actual outcome is that only one turtle
cleaned him. Thus, the test sentence is false on the reading where *him*
refers to the Smurf. Notice that the second conjunct is negated according
to the general reading in which *not every turtle* cleaned the Smurf, thus
satisfying the condition of plausible dissent. In this story, the test sentence
is falsified by making the first conjunct false also; Batman didn't clean the
Smurf either. (This last step was not necessary to fulfill the requirements
of the truth value judgment task.)

The story leading up to test sentence (26) was this. Porky Pig and his
friends Gonzo and Snuffy decide to go to the beach. At the beach, they
decide they need to put on some sunblock so they won't get sunburned.
Porky Pig is very concerned about his fair skin and asks Snuffy to put
sunblock on for him. Snuffy says he'd like to help, but he's concerned
about his large trunk; he has to get sunblock on it right away. Gonzo is
also unable to help because he needs to pay immediate attention to his
large nose.

In examples like (26), the ungrammatical reading that violates Principle B is a sloppy reading of the sentence that takes the pronoun in each
conjunct to be a bound variable. As noted, sentences of this type may
potentially be open to a look-sloppy reading. The ungrammatical interpretation (whether it violates Principle B or whether it is a look-sloppy
reading), meaning$_1$ in (29), was pitted against a grammatical strict reading, meaning$_2$.

(29) Sentence: Gonzo covered him with sunblock and Snuffy
                         did too
     Characters: Gonzo, Snuffy, Porky Pig
     *Meaning$_1$, true: Gonzo and Snuffy covered themselves with
                         sunblock

Meaning$_2$, false: Gonzo and Snuffy covered Porky Pig with sunblock

In the story acted out for children, the sloppy meaning, meaning$_1$, was true because both Gonzo and Snuffy covered themselves with sunblock. On the grammatical adult interpretation, meaning$_2$, the sentence means that Gonzo and Snuffy both covered someone else (Porky Pig) with sunblock. This is false because in the story, both Gonzo and Snuffy refused to help Porky Pig. Children responding as adults should respond "No" to the test sentence. Children who do not have the relevant pragmatic condition and who do not require referential parallelism may interpret the sentence as having meaning$_1$ (which involves a look-sloppy reading) and may respond "Yes."

The four components of the story are outlined in (30). The background calls into question who Gonzo and Snuffy covered with sunblock, and the assertion is that it was Porky Pig. The actual outcome falsifies the assertion; neither Gonzo nor Snuffy helped Porky Pig with his sunblock. The condition of plausible dissent is satisfied by negating both conjuncts of the test sentence. (As in the story for (25), this condition would have been satisfied by negating just the second conjunct.)

(30) Background: Gonzo covered *so-and-so* with sunblock and Snuffy covered *so-and-so* with sunblock too

     Assertion: Gonzo covered Porky Pig with sunblock and Snuffy covered Porky Pig with sunblock too

     Possible Outcome: Gonzo and Snuffy covered Porky Pig with sunblock

     Actual outcome: Neither Gonzo nor Snuffy covered Porky Pig with sunblock
                           (Gonzo covered himself with sunblock and Snuffy covered himself with sunblock)

The experiment included four trials each of types (25) and (26). For both sets of trials, the verbs used were *clean, cover with, serve,* and *squirt.*

Alongside the target sentences (25) and (26) testing Principle B were control sentences in which the pronouns in (25) and (26) were replaced by reflexives. These control sentences were designed to ensure that the particular discourse contexts that were used to test sloppy interpretations of pronouns in VP ellipsis structures did, in fact, allow children to assign bound variable interpretations when grammatical. (Recall that this step was taken in the trials involving matrix sentences, as well.)

With one exception, the structure of the control stories was the same as that of the stories testing (25) and (26). The only difference was that in the cases involving quantificational NPs with *every* (see (32)), the second conjunct was negated by using the more specific reading (in (32), the reading in which every horse didn't tickle someone) rather than the more general reading (here, the reading in which not every horse tickled that person).

(31) Bert covered himself with sand and Snuffy did too.

(32) Spiderman tickled himself and every horse did too.

The story leading up to test sentence (31) was this. Pooh Bear and his friends Bert and Snuffy go to the beach. Pooh Bear wants to get completely covered with sand, but his paws are sticky, so he asks Bert to cover him. Bert considers it, but says he wants to be the first one to get covered. Snuffy won't help Pooh Bear get covered either; he wants to be the first one covered with sand too.

In the story leading up to (32), Snoopy has some feathers and wants someone to tickle his back with one. He asks Spiderman to do it, but Spiderman says he would rather tickle his own back and does so with one of the features. Snoopy asks the horses to do it, but they won't tickle him either; they have itchy backs, and they tickle their own backs with the fronds of a palm tree.

The design for the stories is outlined in (33) and (34).

(33) Sentence: Bert covered himself with sand and Snuffy did
                        too

     Characters: Bert, Snuffy, Pooh Bear

     $Meaning_1$, true: Bert and Snuffy covered themselves with sand

     *$Meaning_2$, false: Bert and Snuffy covered Pooh Bear with sand

(34) Sentence: Spiderman tickled himself and every horse did
                        too

     Characters: Spiderman, 3 horses, Snoopy

     $Meaning_1$, true: Spiderman and every horse tickled themselves

     *$Meaning_2$, false: Spiderman and every horse tickled Snoopy

The expectation was that children should accept these sentences, which (because they contain reflexives rather than pronouns) are unambiguous. An interpretation in which the reflexive *himself* is not treated as a bound variable (i.e., refers to a character not mentioned in the sentence) would be highly unusual and not expected given standard results (e.g., Wexler and Chien 1985) showing that children know Principle A (i.e., that a reflexive must be bound by a c-commanding NP).

As a further test of their ability to assign bound variable inter-pretations, we investigated children's willingness to assign a sloppy inter-pretation to a pronoun, as opposed to a reflexive. The design for these control trials is shown in (35).

(35) Sentence: Mr. Dog brushed his teeth and every dinosaur
                            did too
      Characters: Mr. Dog, 3 dinosaurs, Cookie Monster
      Meaning$_1$, true: Mr. Dog and every dinosaur brushed their own
                            teeth
      Meaning$_2$, false: Mr. Dog and every dinosaur brushed Cookie
                            Monster's teeth

The presence of the pronoun inside the NP *his teeth* in (35) makes the sentence ambiguous between a sloppy and a strict interpretation. Mean-ing$_1$ corresponded to the sloppy reading, that part of the story in which Mr. Dog and every dinosaur brushed their own teeth. This sloppy reading was grammatical, and children were expected to accept it. Meaning$_2$, the deictic interpretation on which Mr. Dog and every dinosaur brushed Cookie Monster's teeth, was also grammatical. Pilot data revealed a preference for this interpretation. To discourage children from inter-preting the sentence this way, since the goal was to see if children would accept the sloppy interpretation, we attempted to block meaning$_2$ by making it infelicitous in the story. This was done by having Cookie Monster be concerned with his fur in the story, not his teeth. Mr. Dog and every dinosaur didn't brush Cookie Monster's fur; his teeth were not mentioned. So although the test sentence was grammatical on meaning$_2$, this interpretation was not supported by the story line.

The experiment included four trials like (31), two with the verb *cover* and two with the verb *clean*; two trials like (32), with the verbs *tickle* and *lick*; and two trials like (35), with the verbs *brush* and *touch*.

We also investigated another VP ellipsis structure containing a pro-noun. This structure, shown in (36), tests a strict coreference reading that involves local coreference between the pronoun and the name in the first conjunct.

(36) Bert lassoed him and the Tin Man did too.

The prediction is that those children who allow local coreference in matrix clauses should also allow local coreference in the first conjunct of sentences like (36). That is, the grammar of these children should permit a reading in which (in the case of (36)) Bert lassoed himself and the Tin Man also lassoed Bert. This interpretation does not violate referential parallelism. Therefore, it should be possible for all children who allow local coreference in matrix sentences, irrespective of the status of the parallelism constraint in their grammar.

The story leading up to test sentence (36) is as follows. The Indian Chief is teaching Bert and the Tin Man to lasso and he says they need to practice by trying to lasso him. But they are reluctant to lasso the Indian Chief: Bert says the Indian Chief is too far away, and the Tin Man thinks the Indian Chief is too important to lasso. So Bert practices by trying to lasso himself, and the Tin Man uses Bert as a target also.

The design features for testing sentence type (36) are shown in (37).

(37) Sentence: Bert lassoed him and the Tin Man did too
     Characters: Bert, Tin Man, Indian Chief
     *Meaning$_1$, true: Bert lassoed himself and the Tin Man lassoed
                            Bert
     Meaning$_2$, false: Bert and the Tin Man lassoed the Indian Chief

The strict local coreference reading in which Bert lassoed himself and the Tin Man lassoed Bert corresponds to meaning$_1$. This interpretation should be allowed by any child who allows local coreference in matrix sentences. Meaning$_2$ is the adult reading available to children who have mastered the pragmatic conditions on local coreference. This meaning, on which the pronoun is taken to refer to the Indian Chief, is false in the story. Bert and the Tin Man did not lasso the Indian Chief.

The components of the story are summarized in (38).

(38) Background: Bert lassoed *so-and-so* and the Tin Man
                            lassoed *so-and-so* too
     Assertion: Bert lassoed the Indian Chief and the Tin
                            Man lassoed the Indian Chief too
     Possible outcome: Bert and the Tin Man lassoed the Indian
                            Chief
     Actual outcome: Neither Bert nor the Tin Man lassoed the
                            Indian Chief (Bert lassoed himself and the
                            Tin Man lassoed Bert)

The experiment included four trials like (36), using the verbs *lasso*, *rub*, *brush*, and *blow on*.

The remaining two structures tested in the experiment are not related to Principle B. One checks whether children allow a strict interpretation of reflexives; the other tests children's knowledge of Principle C in VP ellipsis sentences.

The sentence structure used to test a strict reading of reflexives is shown in (39). The stories leading up to test sentences like (39) followed the same basic plot line as those leading up to test sentences like (36). Here, Robin asks to be fanned, but Hawkman and the baby boy refuse to help him. Hawkman fans himself, and the baby boy fans Hawkman.

(39) Hawkman fanned himself and the baby boy did too.

The design used to test this sentence structure is shown in (40).

(40) Sentence: Hawkman fanned himself and the baby boy
                           did too
     Characters: Hawkman, baby boy, Robin
     ?Meaning$_1$, true: Hawkman fanned himself and the baby boy
                           fanned Hawkman
     Meaning$_2$, false: Hawkman and the baby boy fanned themselves

The only difference between the stories associated with (36) and (39) concerned the way in which the actual outcome differed from the possible outcome. This was to accommodate the reflexive in the sentence. The four components of the story leading up to (39) are outlined in (41).

(41) Background: Hawkman fanned *so-and-so* and the baby boy
                           fanned *so-and-so* too
     Assertion: Hawkman fanned Robin and the baby boy
                           fanned Robin too
     Possible outcome: Hawkman and the baby boy fanned Robin
     Actual outcome: Neither Hawkman nor the baby boy fanned
                           Robin
                           (Hawkman fanned himself and the baby boy
                           fanned Hawkman)

The experiment included two trials testing sentence structures like (39), using *fan* and *wipe*.

The last VP ellipsis target sentence type investigates an interpretation generally considered to be ruled out by Principle C. Consider (42).

(42) The kiwi bird cleaned Flash Gordon and he did too.

The story leading up to test sentence (42) was this. Flash Gordon and his friends the kiwi bird and the lantern man decide to play rugby. The field is very slippery, and they all slip and get muddy. Flash Gordon is afraid his outfit will stain, so he asks the kiwi bird to help him get it clean. The kiwi bird is helpful and does his best to clean Flash Gordon with his beak. Flash Gordon thinks he's still not quite clean, so he asks the lantern man to help out. The lantern man considers helping, but says he needs to clean his own outfit. Flash Gordon is left to get his own outfit completely clean.

The design used to test structures of this type is shown in (43).

(43) Sentence: The kiwi bird cleaned Flash Gordon and he did too

   Characters: kiwi bird, Flash Gordon, lantern man

   *Meaning$_1$, true: The kiwi bird cleaned Flash Gordon and Flash Gordon cleaned himself

   Meaning$_2$, false: The kiwi bird cleaned Flash Gordon and the lantern man cleaned Flash Gordon

The interpretation ruled out by Principle C is that the kiwi bird cleaned Flash Gordon and Flash Gordon cleaned himself. This interpretation is represented by meaning$_1$ in (43); children whose grammar does not follow Principle C should respond "Yes" to test sentence (42). Meaning$_2$ is the grammatical meaning in which the sentence means that both the kiwi bird and some other character (the lantern man) cleaned Flash Gordon. Since this event did not happen in the story, children whose grammar follows Principle C should respond "No" to (42).

The components of the story used to test this sentence structure are shown in (44).

(44) Background: The kiwi bird cleaned *so-and-so* and the lantern man cleaned *so-and-so* too

   Assertion: The kiwi bird cleaned Flash Gordon and lantern man cleaned Flash Gordon too

   Possible outcome: The kiwi bird and the lantern man cleaned Flash Gordon

   Actual outcome: Only the kiwi bird cleaned Flash Gordon (Flash Gordon cleaned himself)

The experiment included four trials that tested this sentence structure, using the verbs *dust*, *dry*, *clean*, and *paint*.

Table 4.3
Sentence types used to test children's knowledge of binding principles and local coreference in VP ellipsis structures

Sentence types	Principle
Conzo covered him with sunblock and Snuffy did too	B/Local coreference in both conjuncts
Batman cleaned him and every turtle did too	B
Bert covered himself with sand and Snuffy did too	B control
Spiderman tickled himself and every horse did too	B control
Mr. Dog brushed his teeth and every dinosaur did too	B control
Bert lassoed him and the Tin Man did too	Local coreference in first conjunct
Hawkman fanned himself and the baby boy did too	A, strict
The kiwi bird cleaned Flash Gordon and he did too	C

The target structures and the relevant constraints reviewed in this section are summarized in table 4.3.

4.4   Procedures

Nineteen children participated in the experiment. They ranged in age from 4;0 to 5;1, with a mean age of 4;8.[13] Two further children were excluded. These two children had difficulty making appropriate judgments in the first session, which comprised training and the trials checking children's knowledge of recovery of elided VPs. The children who participated in the experiment were all native speakers of English. All were enrolled at child care centers in Arlington, Massachusetts, or Storrs, Connecticut.

Each child subject was tested individually, either in a quiet corner of the classroom or in a room adjoining or near the classroom. Children were not invited to play the game until they had interacted with the experimenters in the classroom several times and were comfortable with them. The experiment took four sessions to complete, and each session lasted approximately half an hour. If the child had difficulty paying attention for that long, the session was, on occasion, split into two parts.[14]

A session comprised 12 to 14 separate stories. In the first session, children were trained how to play the game and were tested on items that checked their knowledge of the VP ellipsis structure. Training items were matrix sentences unrelated to VP ellipsis (e.g., *The Ghostbuster dressed*

Table 4.4
Child subject data for binding control sentence types

Subject Age	ST 4;10	TS 4;11	MP 5;1	EX 4;10	BT 4;0	LT 5;1	PC 4;8	OX 4;5	LX 5;0	TF 4;4	EI 4;9	ED 4;2	OS 4;11	NT 4;6	KQ 4;7	JZ 5;0	MT 4;7	TT 4;7	BE 4;3
Binding control sentence types																			
Every reindeer brushed him	0/4	4/4	0/4	1/4	1/4	0/4	0/2	0/4	0/4	0/4	0/4	0/4	0/4	0/2	0/4	0/4	0/4	0/4	0/4
Bert brushed him	2/4	4/4	4/4	3/4	3/4	4/4	2/4	2/4	2/4	2/4	.2/4	4/4	4/4	2/4	3/4	0/4	0/4	1/4	0/4
Every reindeer brushed himself	2/2	2/2	2/2	2/2	2/2	1/2	—	1/2	2/2	2/2	2/2	2/2	2/2	—	1/1	1/2	2/2	1/2	2/2
Every Cabbage Patch boy said Superman likes him	2/2	2/2	1/2	1/2	2/2	2/2	—	0/2	0/2	1/2	0/2	1/2	2/2	—	1/2	1/2	0/2	0/2	1/2
He dusted the skeleton	0/2	0/2	2/2	0/2	0/2	0/2	0/2	0/2	0/2	0/2	0/2	0/2	1/2	0/2	0/2	0/2	0/2	0/1	0/2

Table 4.5
Child subject data for VP ellipsis control sentence types

	Number of acceptances per number of trials																		
Subject Age	ST 4;10	TS 4;11	MP 5;1	EX 4;10	BT 4;0	LT 5;1	PC 4;8	OX 4;5	LX 5;0	TF 4;4	EI 4;9	ED 4;2	OS 4;11	NT 4;6	KQ 4;7	JZ 5;0	MT 4;7	TT 4;7	BE 4;3
VP ellipsis control sentence types																			
The caveman kissed the dinosaur and Fozzie Bear did too (grammatical)	2/2	2/2	2/2	2/2	2/2	2/2	2/2	2/2	2/2	2/2	2/2	2/2	2/2	2/2	2/2	2/2	2/2	2/2	2/2
The caveman kissed the dinosaur and Fozzie Bear did too (ungrammatical)	0/2	0/2	0/2	0/2	0/2	0/2	0/2	0/2	0/2	0/2	0/2	0/2	0/2	0/2	0/2	0/2	0/2	0/2	0/2
Ariel touched the creature and every girl did too (grammatical)	2/2	2/2	2/2	2/2	2/2	2/2	2/2	2/2	2/2	2/2	2/2	2/2	2/2	2/2	2/2	2/2	2/2	2/2	2/2
Ariel touched the creature and every girl did too (ungrammatical)	0/2	1/2	1/2	0/2	1/2	0/2	0/2	0/2	1/2	0/2	0/2	1/2	1/2	1/2	1/2	0/2	0/2	0/2	0/2

Parallelism

The Incredible Hulk brushed his hair and every Troll did too	0/2	0/2	2/2	0/2	0/2	0/2	0/2	0/2	0/2	0/2	0/2	1/2	0/2	0/2	0/2	0/2
The lizard man lifted him and the ugly guy did too	1/2	2/2	2/2	1/2	0/2	0/2	0/2	0/2	0/2	0/2	0/2	1/2	1/2	0/2	0/2	0/2

Robin). During training (but not after), children were corrected if they made an error. In the second, third, and fourth sessions, the stories designed to test binding principles in VP ellipsis structures were introduced. The stories in each session were presented in random order. The sessions were audiotaped on a portable professional-quality Sony Walkman tape recorder. Children's explanations of why the puppet got the trial wrong were transcribed for analysis.

In each session, children's judgments of the test sentences were scored as "Yes" or "No." Percentages of acceptances for particular items were calculated for the group as a whole, and individually. Tables 4.4–4.6 provide the individual subject data for the child subjects.

Six adults who were undergraduate students at MIT or at other universities in the Boston area also were tested. The adults were tested using the truth value judgment task and the same experimental items that were presented to the children. The only difference was that the adults were not tested individually. The experimenter acted out the stories, and the adults wrote their "Yes" or "No" responses on paper, instead of interacting individually with a puppet. Tables 4.7–4.9 give the individual subject data for the adult subjects.

4.5 Overview of the Experimental Findings

The overall results for the 19 children who participated in the study are summarized in table 4.10. The table shows the percentage of "Yes" responses given to each of the experimental items, calculated for the group of 19 subjects as a whole. The interpretation being tested for each structure is glossed below it in smaller type. For those target sentences testing a constraint such as the parallelism constraint or a binding principle, the "Yes" response reflected an ungrammatical interpretation, so the number of "Yes" responses was expected to be small. An x in the column headed "Grammatical" indicates that a "yes" response reflects an ungrammatical interpretation. For items designed as controls, the "Yes" response was generally grammatical, so the number of "Yes" responses was expected to be large. A √ in the column headed "Grammatical" indicates that a "Yes" response reflects a grammatical interpretation.

The table confirms that the results were clear-cut. As a group, children tended to either accept or reject the sentences. Of the 17 sentence types, 8 were accepted at a rate of 22% or less; 4 were accepted at a rate of 82% or more. This result would be extremely improbable on any kind of random guessing model such as a binomial model where most of the percentages cluster around the mean response probability. The distribution of percentages of acceptance is strongly bimodal, with the modes close to 0% and 100%. Many of the cases that do not have a (near) 100% rate of acceptance or rejection are grammatically ambiguous for the child, so that either a "Yes" or a "No'" is appropriate (see the discussion of, e.g., *Bert brushed him* in chapter 3). The results show that children are responding according to determinate patterns, based on their grammatical competence. This is the expected pattern of results given the modular architecture of the language faculty.

Before turning to details of the experimental findings from children, we should mention the results from the 6 adult subjects. The adults behaved nearly perfectly (see tables 4.7–4.9). This indicated to us that our experimental method did not introduce distortions that might have affected the results with children. In the sections that follow, the adults' responses are discussed only when they shed light on children's behavior.

In each of the following sections, we first present the overall results for the experimental items. We then present results based on dividing the children into two groups: those who make adultlike judgments with respect to local coreference and those who do not. Specifically, we test whether the behavior of the two groups differs on various conditions as predicted in chapter 3. The individual subject data for the 19 children are presented in tables 4.4–4.6.

4.6   Results for Principle B and Local Coreference in Matrix Sentences

In this section, we discuss the results of items testing Principle B, items testing children's acceptance of a local coreference interpretation, and the control items. These results are summarized in table 4.11.

Notably, results from the items testing Principle B and local coreference interpretations conformed to the results reported by Chien and Wexler (1990) and replicated since by other researchers. Children were found to adhere to Principle B. That is, on the trials that unambiguously tested knowledge of Principle B, the ones in which the pronoun had a quantificational NP as antecedent, children did not allow a bound variable interpretation. Specifically, children allowed items like *Every reindeer brushed him* to have a bound variable interpretation only 8% of the time. On the trials that were ambiguous between a test of Principle B and a test of allowing a local coreference interpretation, the ones in which the pronoun

Table 4.6
Child subject data for binding in VP ellipsis: target and control sentence types

Number of acceptances per number of trials

Subject / Age	ST 4;10	TS 4;11	MP 5;1	EX 4;10	BT 4;0	LT 5;1	PC 4;8	OX 4;5	LX 5;0	TF 4;4	EI 4;9	ED 4;2	OS 4;11	NT 4;6	KQ 4;7	JZ 5;0	MT 4;7	TT 4;7	BE 4;3
Binding in VP ellipsis: target and control sentence types																			
Gonzo covered him with sunblock and Snuffy did too	0/4	2/4	0/4	2/4	2/4	1/4	0/4	1/4	2/4	0/4	0/4	2/4	1/4	2/4	2/4	0/4	0/4	0/4	0/4
Batman cleaned him and every turtle did too	4/4	2/4	1/4	0/4	1/4	0/4	0/2	1/4	0/4	0/4	0/4	0/4	1/4	0/2	0/4	0/4	0/4	0/4	0/4
Bert covered himself with sand and Snuffy did too	4/4	4/4	4/4	4/4	4/4	4/4	2/2	4/4	4/4	4/4	4/4	4/4	4/4	2/2	4/4	4/4	4/4	4/4	2/4
Spiderman tickled himself and every horse did too	2/2	2/2	2/2	2/2	2/2	2/2	2/2	2/2	2/2	2/2	2/2	2/2	2/2	2/2	2/2	2/2	2/2	2/2	0/2
Mr. Dog brushed his teeth and every dinosaur did too	2/2	2/2	2/2	2/2	2/2	2/2	2/2	1/2	2/2	1/2	0/2	2/2	2/2	2/2	1/2	2/2	2/2	2/2	0/2

Bert lassoed him and the Tin Man did too	0/4	4/4	3/4	2/4	3/4	1/4	0/2	2/4	3/4	0/4	0/4	4/4	2/4	2/2	4/4	0/4	0/4	1/4	0/4
Hawkman fanned himself and the baby boy did too	2/2	2/2	1/2	0/2	2/2	1/2	–	2/2	2/2	1/2	2/2	2/2	–	2/2	1/2	0/2	0/2	0/2
The kiwi bird cleaned Flash Gordon and he did too	2/4	4/4	0/4	1/4	3/4	2/4	2/2	3/4	3/4	0/4	3/4	3/4	0/2	3/4	2/4	2/4	1/4	2/4

Table 4.7
Adult subject data for binding control sentence types

	Number of acceptances per number of trials					
Subject	JM	MI	JW	LZ	ES	JS
Binding control sentence types						
Every reindeer brushed him	0/4	0/4	0/4	0/4	0/4	0/4
Bert brushed him	0/4	0/4	0/4	2/4	0/4	0/4
Every reindeer brushed himself	2/2	2/2	2/2	2/2	2/2	2/2
Every Cabbage Patch boy said Superman likes him	2/2	2/2	1/2	2/2	2/2	2/2
He dusted the skeleton	0/2	0/2	0/2	0/2	0/2	0/2

Table 4.8
Adult subject data for VP ellipsis control sentence types

	Number of acceptances per number of trials					
Subject	JM	MI	JW	LZ	ES	JS
VP ellipsis control sentence types						
The caveman kissed the dinosaur and Fozzie Bear did too (grammatical)	2/2	2/2	2/2	2/2	2/2	2/2
The caveman kissed the dinosaur and Fozzie Bear did too (ungrammatical)	0/2	0/2	0/2	0/2	0/2	0/2
Ariel touched the creature and every girl did too (grammatical)	2/2	2/2	2/2	2/2	2/2	2/2
Ariel touched the creature and every girl did too (ungrammatical)	0/2	0/2	0/2	0/2	0/2	0/2
Parallelism						
The Incredible Hulk brushed his hair and every Troll did too	0/2	0/2	0/2	0/2	0/2	0/2
The lizard man lifted him and the ugly guy did too	0/2	0/2	0/2	0/2	0/2	0/2

Table 4.9
Adult subject data for binding in VP ellipsis: target and control sentence types

	Number of acceptances per number of trials					
Subject	JM	MI	JW	LZ	ES	JS
Binding in VP ellipsis: target and control sentence types						
Gonzo covered him with sunblock and Snuffy did too	0/4	0/4	0/4	0/4	0/4	0/4
Batman cleaned him and every turtle did too	0/4	0/4	0/4	0/4	0/4	0/4
Bert covered himself with sand and Snuffy did too	4/4	4/4	4/4	4/4	4/4	4/4
Spiderman tickled himself and every horse did too	2/2	2/2	2/2	2/2	2/2	2/2
Mr. Dog brushed his teeth and every dinosaur did too	2/2	2/2	2/2	0/2	2/2	2/2
Bert lassoed him and the Tin Man did too	0/4	0/4	0/4	0/4	0/4	0/4
Hawkman fanned himself and the baby boy did too	0/2	0/2	0/2	1/2	1/2	0/2
The kiwi bird cleaned Flash Gordon and he did too	3/4	4/4	2/4	3/4	4/4	4/4

had a referential NP antecedent, many children allowed a nonadult local coreference interpretation on some trials, giving an overall acceptance rate of 58%.

Our experiment replicates Chien and Wexler's (1990) result, but for younger children. In our experiment, the disparity in the acceptance rate for *Every reindeer brushed him* and *Bert brushed him* was very clear for 4-year-old children. In Chien and Wexler's experiment, the disparity was most apparent for 5-year-old children. Children younger than 5 years old were argued to not understand the concept of *every*, as determined by a control item. Our experiment did not separately test children's understanding of the meaning of *every*, but it is clear that children responded the same way adults do to items containing it. We attribute the differing results either to task differences or to the fact that we falsified the sentences with *every* using the general reading of negation (see section 4.2.3).

The transcripts of children's responses to the target sentences make some valuable points. In (45b), we give examples of why children

Table 4.10
Overall experimental findings by group ($N = 19$; interpretation being tested is given in smaller type)

Sentence types	% "Yes"	Grammatical
Binding theory		
Every reindeer brushed him	8	x
(every reindeer brushed self)		
Bert brushed him	58	x
(Bert brushed self)		
Every reindeer brushed himself	88	√
(every reindeer brushed self)		
Every Cabbage Patch boy said Superman likes him	50	√
(him = Cabbage Patch boy)		
He dusted the skeleton	8	x
(skeleton dusted self)		
Recovery of elided VP and parallelism		
The caveman kissed the dinosaur and Fozzie Bear did too	0	x
(caveman kissed dinosaur; Fozzie Bear kissed own hand)		
Ariel touched the creature and every girl did too	21	x
(Ariel touched creature; every girl touched self)		
The Incredible Hulk brushed his hair and every Troll did too	3	x
(Incredible Hulk brushed rock star's hair; every Troll brushed own hair)		
The lizard man lifted him and the ugly guy did too	21	x
(lizard man lifted Smurf; ugly guy lifted Mickey Mouse)		
VP ellipsis binding targets and controls		
Gonzo covered him with sunblock and Snuffy did too	22	x
(Gonzo covered self; Snuffy covered self)		
Batman cleaned him and every turtle did too	14	x
(Batman cleaned self; every turtle cleaned self)		
Bert covered himself with sand and Snuffy did too	100	√
(Bert covered self; Snuffy covered self)		
Spiderman tickled himself and every horse did too	95	√
(Spiderman tickled self; every horse tickled self)		
Mr. Dog brushed his teeth and every dinosaur did too	82	√
(Mr. Dog brushed own teeth; every dinosaur brushed own teeth)		
Bert lassoed him and the Tin Man did too	43	x
(Bert lassoed self; Tin Man lassoed Bert)		
Hawkman fanned himself and the baby boy did too	65	?
(Hawkman fanned self; baby boy fanned Hawkman)		
The kiwi bird cleaned Flash Gordon and he did too	54	x
(kiwi bird cleaned Flash Gordon; Flash Gordon cleaned self)		

Table 4.11
Results for sentence types used to establish children's knowledge of binding in matrix structures ($N = 19$; interpretation being tested is given in smaller type)

Sentence types	% "Yes"	Grammatical
Every reindeer brushed him (every reindeer brushed self)	8	x
Bert brushed him (Bert brushed self)	58	x
Every reindeer brushed himself (every reindeer brushed self)	88	√
Every Cabbage Patch boy said Superman likes him (Cabbage Patch boy = him)	50	√

responded "No" to the sentence *Every reindeer brushed him*. In the story, it wasn't true that every reindeer brushed *him*, Bert; only one of them did. It is clear from children's responses that they were taking the pronoun in the sentence to refer to Bert, and not the reindeer.

(45) a. *Kermit* I know what happened. Every reindeer brushed him.
　　　Child No.
　　　Kermit What really happened?
　　b. *EI (4;9)* What really happened—only one reindeer brushed him, a little.
　　　JZ (5;0) Only one of them helped him.
　　　TT (4;7) This reindeer brushed back of him.
　　　ED (4;2) These reindeer brushed theirselves and this guy brushed him [= Bert].
　　　NT (4;6) Every reindeer brushed himself and one brushed Bert.

The parallel controls testing whether children would allow *Every reindeer brushed himself* in the same context yielded an acceptance rate of 88%, short of the expected 100%. An acceptance rate near 100% was expected because the sentence is unambiguous; the true interpretation is the only interpretation the sentence can have. The reflexive cannot be interpreted as referring deictically to an individual not mentioned in the sentence.

Sixteen of the 19 children were tested on this structure.[15] Of these 16 children, 4 children (OX, JZ, MT, EI) initially responded "No." From their answers to "What really happened?" it appeared that they responded "No" because the statement *Every reindeer brushed himself* did not completely describe the events of the story.[16] These children said that one of the reindeer had also brushed Bert (in addition to all the reindeer brushing themselves). In explaining what they thought had really happened, these children often used a reflexive, explicitly mentioning that the reindeer had brushed themselves. If a child did use a reflexive, the child's original response was counted as acceptance of the bound variable interpretation. If the child did not use a reflexive, the original response was counted as a rejection of that interpretation. For example, OX's original "No" response was counted as "Yes" on the basis of how she explained the story events. The test item was *Every Troll fanned himself.* In the story, it was true that every Troll fanned himself; one Troll also fanned a third character. (The child explains the situation using *wipe* instead of *fan*.)

(46) *Kermit*   What about *Every Troll fanned himself*?
       OX (4;5)   [shakes head]
       Kermit   That didn't happen in the story? What did all the Trolls do?
       OX   They wiped theirself but only this Troll wiped him a little bit and then wiped his own.
       Kermit   So if I say *Every Troll fanned himself*, is that right or wrong?
       OX   Wrong.

An important observation is that in evaluating whether or not a sentence like *Bert brushed him* was true or false, some children quizzed the experimenter about the referent of *him*. This clearly suggests that they were weighing the possible referents before coming to a decision. This kind of considered decision is not predicted by Grodzinsky and Reinhart's (1993) account. On their account, children end up guessing because they are unable to decide the referent of the pronoun, owing to the processing load imposed by Rule I. Our results suggest that children are not having any difficulty comparing representations. Consider the transcript in (47). In this case, the target sentence was *The buffalo wiped him.* The puppet, Kermit, was trying to get the child to decide on the referent for the pronoun without offering an opinion.

(47) *Kermit*   The buffalo wiped him.
       OS (4;11)   Wiped hisself?
       Kermit   I think the buffalo wiped him.
       OS   Him?

Kermit I'm getting mixed up.
Experimenter Tell us one more time.
Kermit I think the buffalo wiped him.
OS Wiped him? The birdie?
Experimenter That's a tough one, isn't it. Do you think that's right or wrong? The buffalo wiped him ...
OS Right, right.
Experimenter If it's right, what does it mean, then?
OS It means the buffalo wiped hisself and he helped him.

For control items like *Every Cabbage Patch boy said Superman likes him*, in which the pronoun could be interpreted either as a bound variable or as a deictic pronoun, children chose the bound variable interpretation 50% of the time. As mentioned earlier, for grammatically ambiguous items, children may choose a reading and respond at a particular rate depending on the discourse context and other aspects of how the item is presented. The 50% "Yes" rate simply reflects the fact that the sentence is ambiguous for the children. Since children tend to say "Yes" if they can, however, one might wonder why the acceptance rate isn't higher. There are two possibilities. Perhaps this sentence construction evokes a preference for the deictic interpretation, though the reason for this is not clear.[17] Or perhaps the contexts in which these items were presented favored the deictic interpretation of the pronoun.

Putting aside the reason for some children's rejection of the bound variable interpretation, the crucial point is that in cases where the bound variable interpretation is permitted, children accepted it for *Every Cabbage Patch boy said Superman likes him* as often as 50% of the time. This can be compared with sentences in which the bound variable interpretation is ruled out by the grammar, as in *Every reindeer brushed him*, which was accepted only 8% of the time. This result is consistent with our hypothesis that children know Principle B as a matter of grammatical representation and consequently will not allow a quantifier to locally bind a pronoun.

Let us now turn to individual subject data and consider whether our first prediction (formulated in chapter 3) was confirmed.

Prediction 1
Some children will accept a local coreference interpretation of sentences with a referential NP antecedent, such as *Bert brushed him*; others will not.

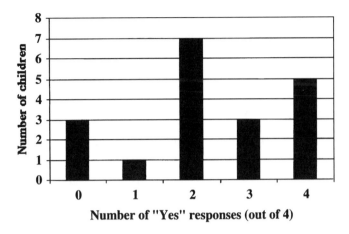

Figure 4.1
Number of acceptances of a local coreference interpretation by children ($N = 19$)

The individual subject data in tables 4.4–4.6 reveal that of the 19 children, 8 children accepted 3/4 or 4/4 trials, 7 children accepted 2/4 trials, 1 child accepted 1/4 trials, and 3 children responded as adults would, accepting 0/4 trials. The histogram of individual responses is shown in figure 4.1.

What can we infer from this response pattern? If children display a single group behavior in their acceptance of the nonadult reading, then this histogram should show a normal (binomial) distribution of responses, with some "balance" point around the mean of 58% "Yes" responses. The scores of individual children should deviate from this balance point with roughly the same frequency in both directions, resulting in the familiar bell-shaped curve associated with normal unimodal distributions. The histogram in figure 4.1 clearly does not fit this pattern. Although the 19 subjects gave "Yes" responses 58% of the time, the histogram reveals a bimodal, and not unimodal, distribution of responses. That is, too many children responded "No" on the majority of trials for a simple binomial model to correctly characterize the children's responses as a group.

To further assess whether these findings fit the binomial model—that is, to determine whether the responses of the children who consistently said "No" differ significantly from the responses of the children considered as a group—we conducted a goodness-of-fit statistical analysis. The procedure is as follows: The probability of saying "No" is $Pr(No) = .42$. This means that the probability of saying "No" on all four trials is $.42^4$, or about .03. Since there are 19 subjects, the binomial model anticipates that

$19 \times .03 = .57$ subjects will respond "No" on all four trials. That is, on the binomial model, not even 1 subject is expected to produce all "No" responses. Yet 3 children actually responded "No" on every trial. Therefore, these children were not responding according to the binomial model; they presumably had adult competence.

Another child accepted the nonadult local coreference interpretation on only one of four trials. If we incorporate this child into our calculations, on the binomial model, the probability that a subject will respond "No" on three or four of the four trials is .1, so about 2 of the 19 children could have been expected to behave in this fashion. Four children do, however. Because only 1 child rejected the illicit interpretation on one out four trials, this child is difficult to classify. It is conceivable that this child had adult competence but was more prone to error than the 3 children who answered "No" on all trials; alternatively, this child may have had the same grammatical competence as the other 15 children but was more successful at the task for some unknown reason.

Unlike the response patterns of these 4 children, those of the other 15 children do appear to be consistent with the binomial model. On this model, the probability that children will give three or four "Yes" responses to the four trials is the probability of giving this response on three trials plus the probability of giving it on all four trials: Pr(3 or 4 yes) = Pr(4 yes) + Pr(3 yes) = $.58^4 + (4 \times .42 \times .58^3) = .11 + .34 = .45$. Therefore, it is expected that $19 \times .45 = 8.6$ subjects will say "Yes" on three or four trials.[18] This is about what was observed. Eight children accepted three or four trials of the type where *Bert brushed him* is taken to mean that Bert brushed himself. The remaining 7 children vacillated equally between "Yes" and "No" responses. Thus, these children responded as they would when confronted with any other ambiguous sentence; they picked a reading and responded, with some tendency toward picking the reading that resulted in a "Yes" response. The latter tendency is not related to their grammatical knowledge, however.[19]

This statistical analysis shows that the responses given by the 19 children considered as a group do not conform to a normal distribution. The distribution is bimodal, with some children manifesting adult knowledge of Principle B and the pragmatic restrictions on local coreference interpretations.

Further statistical analyses of the predictions advanced in chapter 3 were conducted. For these analyses, children were divided into two groups. Group 1 includes the 3 children who responded like adults and accepted no local coreference interpretations and the 1 child who accepted

Table 4.12
Percentage acceptance of local coreference interpretation for matrix sentences by groups 1 ($n = 4$) and 2 ($n = 15$)

Sentence type	Group 1	Group 2
Bert brushed him (Bert brushed self)	6 (1/16)	72 (43/60)

the local coreference interpretation on only one out of four trials. Group 2 includes the remaining 15 children, who allowed local coreference interpretations on at least two of the four trials. The different response patterns by the two groups to sentences like *Bert brushed him* are shown in table 4.12.

In considering other experimental items, we will be interested in whether the difference in the behavior of the two groups persists or not. That is, we will ask whether group 1 children continue to respond "like adults" and whether group 2 children continue to respond in a nonadult manner. Put another way, we will be asking whether or not there are types of sentences for which group 1 children change their behavior, accepting a local coreference interpretation. Similarly, we will be asking whether or not group 2 children change their behavior and start to respond in an adultlike fashion. These changes in group behavior will be examined statistically using McNemar's test for the significance of changes. In some cases, the use of statistics is inappropriate, owing to the small number of children in group 1.

In assessing changes in children's linguistic behavior, we adopted a stringent criterion for considering them to have made a significant change from their earlier pattern of responses. The criterion on the posttest phases of the experiment was adultlike responses on every trial. For example, suppose a child accepted the local coreference interpretation of a structure like *Bert brushed him* on three out of four trials, and—on the posttest phase—accepted an illicit interpretation of some other sentence type on only one out of four trials. This child would not be considered to have undergone a significant change in behavior; he or she did not respond perfectly on the posttest phase.

Let us turn now to prediction 2.

Prediction 2
All children will adhere to Principle B in sentences with a quantificational antecedent, such as *Every reindeer brushed him*.

Table 4.13
Percentage acceptance of Principle B sentences with quantificational NP antecedent by groups 1 ($n = 4$) and 2 ($n = 15$)

Sentence type	Group 1	Group 2
Every reindeer brushed him (every reindeer brushed self)	0 (0/16)	7 (4/56)

Table 4.14
Percentage acceptance of sentences testing recovery of elided VPs and the parallelism constraint ($N = 19$)

Sentence types	% "Yes"	Grammatical
Recovery of elided VP		
The caveman kissed the dinosaur and Fozzie Bear did too (caveman kissed dinosaur; Fozzie Bear kissed own hand)	0	x
Ariel touched the creature and every girl did too (Ariel touched creature; every girl touched self)	21	x
Structural parallelism		
The Incredible Hulk brushed his hair and every Troll did too (Incredible Hulk brushed rock star's hair; every Troll brushed own hair)	3	x
Referential parallelism		
The lizard man lifted him and the ugly guy did too (lizard man lifted Smurf; ugly guy lifted Mickey Mouse)	21	x

Expected results: Children in both groups should produce adultlike responses to the four test sentences with quantificational antecedents. As a consequence, the behavior of group 2 children should exhibit a significant change (but that of group 1 children should exhibit no change).

Table 4.13 reports the percentage of acceptance of the bound variable reading for sentences like *Every reindeer brushed him*. As the table indicates, both groups robustly rejected this illicit interpretation of the test sentences. All 4 children in group 1 rejected it, as did 12 of the 15 children in group 2 who had accepted local coreference interpretations in sentences with a referential antecedent. The remaining 3 children made some number of errors. The change in responses for the children in group 2 was highly significant ($\chi^2 = 10.08$; $p < .005$).

4.7   Results for Recovery of Elided VPs and the Parallelism Constraint

The main results discussed in this section are summarized in table 4.14. The figures are the percentage of acceptance for the entire group of 19 children.

The experimental stimuli included several probes of children's knowledge of the properties of VP ellipsis. The stimuli given in (48) and (49) tested whether children have difficulty recovering the syntactic structure of an elided VP (in this case, a VP that contains no pronouns).

(48) The caveman kissed the dinosaur and Fozzie Bear did too.

(49) Ariel touched the creature and every girl did too.

The results indicate that children did not encounter difficulty in recovering the syntax of the elided VP. In (48), for example, the VP that has been elided is ⟨kissed the dinosaur⟩. Children who correctly recovered this structure should have responded "No," because Fozzie Bear kissed his own hand, not the dinosaur. Children who did not recover the syntactic structure of the entire VP, but just that of the verb, for example, should have responded "Yes," because Fozzie Bear did partake in a kissing event. However, children did not respond according to the latter strategy; they correctly rejected the sentence 100% of the time.

The same sentence, (48), was also tested in a situation in which the grammatical interpretation on which both the caveman and Fozzie Bear kissed the dinosaur was the "Yes" response. As noted, in such cases the sentence was unambiguous, since no other meaning was made available. As expected, children responded "Yes" to this unambiguous situation 100% of the time.

The test sentence in (49) was constructed in a similar manner. Children who correctly recovered the syntactic structure of the VP should have interpreted the sentence as meaning that Ariel touched the creature and every girl touched the creature. In the story, however, it was not the case that every girl touched the creature; the girls all touched themselves instead. Children who recovered only the verb should have interpreted the sentence as meaning that every girl did some touching and should have accepted it. In fact, children rejected the sentence at a rate of 79%.

The results for (49) were not as strong as those for (48), but it is likely that the 21% acceptance rate of the illicit interpretation for (49) is due to experimental factors. Post hoc, it was apparent that the condition of plausible dissent associated with the actual outcome was not satisfied optimally. The girls did not touch the creature because it had warty skin and touched their own legs instead. In retrospect, the girls' alternative action doesn't make a great deal of sense. In addition, the second conjunct should have been falsified by using the more general *not every* form of negation (section 4.2.3). That is, in the story, none of the girls touched the creature but they all touched themselves. Instead, some subset of the girls should have touched the creature and all of them should have touched themselves. With these factors amended, we would expect close to 100% rejection. Note that when (49) followed a version of the story in which Ariel and every girl touched the creature, the children correctly responded "Yes" 100% of the time. The difference in response rates for the two situations—79% versus 0% "No" responses—makes the empirical point.

Overall, the results show quite clearly that children, like adults, recover the syntactic properties of elided VPs. Thus, they demonstrate children's knowledge of some subtle properties of grammar involving the interpretation of empty VPs.

Next, we examine the results from the stimuli designed to test the modularized parallelism constraint. Examples like (50) and (51) tested the requirements on structural parallelism and referential parallelism, respectively.

(50) The Incredible Hulk brushed his hair and every Troll did too.

(51) The lizard man lifted him and the ugly guy did too.

Structural parallelism requires that the pronouns in each conjunct have the same referential value; both must be either bound variables or referential pronouns. For (50), a "Yes" response meant accepting a mixed interpretation, interpreting the pronoun in the first conjunct as referential, and the one in the second conjunct as a bound variable. On this ungrammatical reading, the Incredible Hulk brushed someone else's hair, and the Trolls brushed their own hair. The ungrammatical interpretation was accepted only 3% of the time by the 19 children (in fact, the 3% error rate was accounted for by 2 of the 19 children).

The transcripts showed that children took the pronoun in the first conjunct to be referential; specifically, they took it to refer to the rock star, a character not mentioned in the test sentence but salient in the story presented to children. Children's comments about what really happened (see (52b)) show that they rejected a bound variable interpretation of the elided pronoun, expecting it to be referential, like the overt pronoun.[20]

Assuming both pronouns to be referential, the sentence should have meant that the Incredible Hulk brushed the rock star's hair, and so did the Trolls. Children focused on the fact that the Trolls hadn't also brushed the rock star's hair, in keeping with this interpretation.

(52) a. *Kermit*   The Incredible Hulk brushed his hair and every Troll did too.

   Child   No!

   Experimenter   What really happened?

   b. *ST (4;10)*   The Incredible Hulk brushed his hair and the Trolls didn't.

   OX (4;5)   The Trolls brushed their own hair and the Incredible Hulk brushed the rock star's.

   JZ (5;0)   Only the Terrible Troll [Incredible Hulk] brushed his hair.

   BE (4;3)   Only the 'credible Hulk did.

   ED (4;2)   This guy [Incredible Hulk] only brushed his hair.

   TT (4;7)   His [rock star's] hair got messed up, and he [Incredible Hulk] combed it and these [Trolls] didn't.

The comments from children's transcripts provide evidence that the first conjunct is responsible for deciding how the elided pronoun should be interpreted. Suppose, contrary to the evidence, that the second conjunct decided this, and that children expected that both conjuncts should contain a bound variable pronoun. Then, children would have taken the test sentence (50) to mean that every Troll brushed his (own) hair, and the Incredible Hulk brushed his own hair too. This action did not take place in the story. If children had taken both pronouns to be bound variables, their explanations of why the puppet said the wrong thing would have focused on the fact that the Incredible Hulk didn't brush his own hair. Children did not comment on this fact, however. Children's strong rejection of (50), even though the interpretation that violated structural parallelism was semantically plausible, shows that structural parallelism is a central property of VP ellipsis. Furthermore, their strong rejection of (50) supports our hypothesis that structural parallelism is part of the syntactic/computational system of the grammar and that, as an innate constraint, it cannot be violated.

The second part of the parallelism constraint, referential parallelism, was tested by sentences like (51), *The lizard man lifted him and the ugly guy did too.* (Because both pronouns in the structure are referential, structural parallelism is also maintained.) Referential parallelism requires that an elided pronoun that is referential have the same referent as the overt pronoun in the first conjunct. Thus, in the story presented to children, (51) could only mean that the lizard man lifted the Smurf and the ugly guy also lifted the *same person*. Since the ugly guy lifted Mickey Mouse in the story, we expected that children who know the requirement of referential parallelism would reject (51).

Sentences like (51) were rejected 79% of the time by the group of children. Like adults, many children disallowed the interpretation on which each character lifted a different person, making it clear that they did not think both the lizard man and the ugly guy lifted the same *him* (= the Smurf). The transcripts in (53b) show children interpreting the sentence in an adultlike manner, taking the pronoun in both conjuncts to refer to the same character.

(53) a. *Kermit*   The lizard man lifted him and the ugly guy did too.
       Child   No.
       Kermit   What really happened?
   b. *PC (4;8)*   The monster lifted up Mickey Mouse and lizard man lifted up the Smurf.
       MT (4;7)   He [ugly guy] did lift up Mickey and he [lizard man] lifted up the Smurf.
       LT (5;1)   The lizard guy lifted the Smurf up.

The results for the stimuli testing referential parallelism contrast with the results for those testing structural parallelism. Although children accepted violations of structural parallelism only 3% of the time, they accepted violations of referential parallelism 21% of the time.[21] Although this is not a huge percentage of nonadult interpretations, we generally take errors over 10% to be in need of explanation. Furthermore, in this case, there do not appear to be any experimental factors that could be responsible for the children's acceptances of the illicit interpretation.

One possible explanation for these results is consistent with the discussion of the parallelism constraint in chapter 3. Recall that referential parallelism, unlike structural parallelism, is open to pragmatic manipulation and can be overridden in certain cases. Although adults can override this requirement only in extreme cases, some children may be more willing to do so. This is not a surprise given that it has already been established that children's lack of pragmatic knowledge leads them to allow local coreference interpretations in circumstances where adults would not.

Table 4.15
Percentage acceptance of violations of structural parallelism by groups 1 ($n = 4$)
and 2 ($n = 15$)

Sentence type	Group 1	Group 2
The Incredible Hulk brushed his hair and every Troll did too (Incredible Hulk brushed rock star's hair; every Troll brushed own hair)	0 (0/8)	10 (3/30)

Let us turn now to the behavior of the two groups of children we have defined, the 4 children whose behavior is adultlike on items like *Bert brushed him* (group 1) and the 15 children who allow illicit interpretations of this item, accepting a local coreference reading in which Bert brushed himself (group 2). Does the behavior of the children in the two groups change on the items testing the parallelism constraint? That is, do group 1 children show no changes in behavior and continue to maintain an adultlike pattern of responses? Do group 2 children continue to accept illicit interpretations? Or does their behavior change on the items testing structural parallelism, since this is a purportedly innate (hence inviolable) constraint? Prediction 3 would indeed forecast such a change.

Prediction 3
Children will not violate structural parallelism.

Expected results: Group 1 and group 2 children should both respond correctly to the two test items testing structural parallelism.

The experimental results are shown in table 4.15. The test of significance of changes for the two groups of children was highly significant ($\chi^2 = 11.07$, $p < .0005$). It is clear that the change was due to group 2 children. The 4 children in group 1 continued to respond in an adultlike way, making no errors. Of the 15 children in group 2, however, 13 children changed their behavior and responded in an adultlike way, correctly rejecting both items testing structural parallelism. Only 2 of the 15 children in this group continued to make errors.

We have suggested that knowledge about the situations that sanction local coreference interpretations and knowledge about the requirements of referential parallelism both involve pragmatics in some way. According to referential parallelism, the pronoun in the second conjunct of a VP ellipsis structure should have the same referent as the pronoun in the first conjunct. If children do not adhere to this requirement, therefore, they

Table 4.16

Percentage acceptance of violations of referential parallelism by groups 1 ($n = 4$) and 2 ($n = 15$)

Sentence type	Group 1	Group 2
The lizard man lifted him and the ugly guy did too (lizard man lifted Smurf; ugly guy lifted Mickey Mouse)	0 (0/8)	27 (8/30)

will allow a pronoun in the elided conjunct to pick out an individual other than the one picked out by the overt pronoun. This leads to a question that we sought to examine empirically.

Question 4

Do children who accept local coreference interpretations in matrix sentences override referential parallelism in VP ellipsis structures?

Possible results: A positive answer to question 4 would be the finding that children in group 1 respond correctly to the two test sentences in the present condition, producing adultlike behavior. By contrast, children in group 2 would continue to produce nonadult responses to these sentences. In short, we would expect no significant change in behavior across groups if these two pragmatic factors are both unavailable to children in group 2.

The experimental results bearing on this question are shown in table 4.16. The test of significance of changes reveals a significant change in behavior across groups ($\chi^2 = 7.1$, $p < .005$). The locus of the change can again be readily identified. All 4 of the children in group 1 continued to produce adultlike responses to the target sentences. Moreover, 6 of the 15 children in group 2 continued to respond in a nonadult fashion, as expected. However, 9 children in this group changed their behavior and gave adultlike responses to the test items for referential parallelism. In short, the answer to question 4 was that the majority of group 2 children did not overlook the requirement of referential parallelism but some did.

The results suggest that there is no intimate connection between the processes that give rise to the local coreference interpretations in sentences like *Bert brushed him* and the process of referential parallelism involved in VP ellipsis structures like *The lizard man lifted him and the ugly guy did too*. Although pragmatic knowledge is involved in both cases, our results suggest that children may have access to some pragmatic principles but not others. Apparently, the pragmatic knowledge underlying referential parallelism is in place in child grammar before the pragmatic knowledge

Table 4.17
Percentage acceptance of sentence types testing Principle B, local coreference, and
VP ellipsis by group ($N = 19$)

Sentence types	% "Yes"	Grammatical
Batman cleaned him and every turtle did too (Batman cleaned self; every turtle cleaned self)	14	x
Spiderman tickled himself and every horse did too (Spiderman tickled self; every horse tickled self)	95	√
Mr. Dog brushed his teeth and every dinosaur did too (Mr. Dog brushed own teeth; every dinosaur brushed own teeth)	82	√
Bert lassoed him and the Tin Man did too (Bert lassoed self; Tin Man lassoed Bert)	43	x
Gonzo covered him with sunblock and Snuffy did too (Gonzo covered self; Snuffy covered self)	22	x

needed to rule out the local coreference reading for sentences governed by Principle B.

The results of this section indicate that children understand the basic nature of VP ellipsis and the interpretation of elided clauses. Although this is a rather abstract area of the grammar, in which children have to reconstruct empty VPs and appropriately interpret silence, we have shown that they are adept at this task.

4.8 Results for VP Ellipsis and the Binding Theory

4.8.1 Principle B and Local Coreference
The results for target and control sentences used in testing Principle B and local coreference interpretations in VP ellipsis structures are summarized in table 4.17.

The paradigm case for testing Principle B in VP ellipsis structures was (54).

(54) Batman cleaned him and every turtle did too.

Children rejected this sentence type 86% of the time, or, put the other way, children accepted the illicit bound variable interpretation only 14% of the time. This finding is in keeping with the claim that Principle B is an innate constraint.

The presence of the quantificational NP *every turtle* in (54) serves to rule out the possibility of a local coreference interpretation for this sentence. Thus, acceptance of the interpretation in which Batman cleaned himself and every turtle also cleaned himself can only mean that the child violated Principle B; this nonadult response cannot be interpreted as acceptance of local coreference in each conjunct of the structure. For children with adult knowledge of Principle B, the sentence should have been unambiguous. The overt pronoun should have been given a deictic interpretation in which it referred to some individual not mentioned in the sentence.

According to structural parallelism, the referential pronoun in the first conjunct should have forced an interpretation in which the pronoun in the elided conjunct is also referential; that is, the pronoun should have been taken to refer to another character, not mentioned in the test sentence but present in the story (here, the Smurf). In the story, Batman and two of the three turtles refuse to help the Smurf, because they need to concentrate on getting themselves clean. Thus, it was false that Batman and every turtle cleaned the Smurf, and children should have responded "No." Examples of children's responses to the target sentence follow.

(55) a. *Kermit* Batman cleaned him and every turtle did too.
     Child No!
     Experimenter Tell Kermit what really happened ...
   b. *TS (4;11)* Um, this turtle helped the Smurf and then the turtle helped himself.
     BE (4;3) No, only one turtle did [help the Smurf] and no Batman.
     ED (4;2) This guy [child points to one of the turtles] cleaned this guy [the Smurf] and these turtles cleaned themselves.
     OX (4;5) Batman washed his cape and the turtles cleaned themselves.
     MT (4;7) The turtles hadda wipe the glitter off, but one turtle wiped it off [the Smurf], and Batman couldn't cause he hadda get the glitter off his cape.

Two control conditions were included in the test session, to ensure that children allow bound variable interpretations in the contexts used to test sentences like (54), the target structure. One of the controls involved a reflexive interpreted as a bound variable, and the other involved the pronoun *his*.

(56) Spiderman tickled himself and every horse did too.

(57) Mr. Dog brushed his teeth and every dinosaur did too.

The results showed that the experimental situations we had constructed for test sentences like (54) do in fact allow a bound variable interpretation. This step allowed us to confirm that rejections of the bound variable reading in (54) were due to knowledge of Principle B.

Overall, children accepted sentences like (56) 95% of the time, as compared to a 14% acceptance of the comparable condition, sentences like (54), testing Principle B. These large differences show that children can accept a sloppy bound variable reading when Principle B is not violated. Sentences like (57) check that children know that sloppy readings are available for pronouns as well as reflexives. Children accepted (57) 82% of the time, again a dramatic difference from their low 14% acceptance rate of (54).

Notice that sentences like (57) are ambiguous. The pronoun can be interpreted either as a bound variable or as a referential pronoun. This being the case, we designed the story so that the sloppy bound variable reading would correspond to the "Yes" response, and the referential interpretation of the pronoun would correspond to the "No" response. Although we thereby attempted to encourage a bound variable response, there were two children who favored a referential interpretation of the pronoun, thus accounting for some rejections of (57). These children apparently had a clear structure-specific preference for the deictic interpretation.

Overall, the children demonstrated knowledge of Principle B in VP ellipsis structures. It is worth looking at the behavior of the children in group 2, to see whether there was a significant change in their behavior. Of course, no change in behavior is expected for group 1 children.

Prediction 5
All children will adhere to Principle B in VP ellipsis sentences that contain a quantificational NP antecedent.

Expected results: Group 1 children should not show any change in behavior, since they already respond like adults on items like *Bert brushed him*. Group 2 children should show a change in behavior, however. They should now respond in an adultlike fashion on items testing Principle B.

The results bearing on this prediction are shown in table 4.18. As anticipated, there was a significant change in the pattern of responses for

Table 4.18
Percentage acceptance of Principle B with quantificational NP antecedent in VP ellipsis structures by groups 1 ($n = 4$) and 2 ($n = 15$)

Sentence type	Group 1	Group 2
Batman cleaned him and every turtle did too (Batman cleaned self; every turtle cleaned self)	0 (0/16)	18 (10/56)

the two groups in the relevant experimental condition ($\chi^2 = 7.1$, $p < .005$). As expected, the behavior of the 4 children in group 1 did not change. They continued to respond in keeping with the adult grammar. By contrast, 9 of the 15 children in group 2 responded in an adultlike fashion to Principle B sentences with a quantificational antecedent. The remaining 6 children made occasional errors; only 1 child consistently accepted all four test items of the VP ellipsis condition, in violation of Principle B, elevating the error rate. Apart from the responses of this child, the results agree with prediction 5.

The next topic is whether or not children allow nonadult local coreference interpretations in VP ellipsis structures. Sentences like (58) test whether children allow strict coreference readings, that is, interpretations in which the pronoun in the first conjunct is given a local coreference reading. For (58), then, the question was whether children would allow an interpretation on which Bert lassoed himself and the Tin Man also lassoed Bert.

(58) Bert lassoed him and the Tin Man did too.

An advantage of testing the availability of a local coreference interpretation in structures like (58) is that acceptance of the strict coreference interpretation does not involve violating the parallelism constraint. Even when the pronoun in the first conjunct is given a local coreference interpretation, the pronouns in both conjuncts are treated as referential pronouns and both the overt and elided pronouns pick out the same referent.

As a group, the 19 children accepted a strict coreference interpretation of sentences like (58) 43% of the time. This compares with 58% acceptance of a local coreference interpretation of *Bert brushed him*. Clearly, the strict interpretation is available for VP ellipsis structures. The prediction is that this interpretation is available only for group 2 children, those children who accept illicit local coreference interpretations of matrix sentences. This prediction will be tested shortly.

In (59)–(61), we give sample responses to (58) from our child subjects. A comment from a child who accepted the strict coreference interpretation, in which Bert lassoed himself and the Tin Man also lassoed Bert, is given in (59). By saying that "the Tin Man and hisself" tied them up, the child clearly meant that both the Tin Man and Bert tied up Bert.

(59) *Kermit*   Bert lassoed him and the Tin Man did too.
  OX (4;5)   You're right.
  Kermit   Why was I right?
  OX   Because they tied him up.
  Kermit   Who did?
  OX   The Tin Man and hisself.

The dialogue in (60) shows a child who accepted the nonadult reading and then changed her mind, realizing that the pronoun does not refer to Bert, but to the Indian Chief (the deictic referent for the pronoun not mentioned in the sentence itself).

(60) *Kermit*   Bert lassoed him and the Tin Man did too.
  PC (4;8)   Yes.
  Kermit   Great, I got that right!
  PC   I think I got that wrong.
  Kermit   Want me to say it again? Bert lassoed him and the Tin Man did too.
  PC   Um, lassoed the Indian Chief don't you mean? [feeds food that indicates the puppet was wrong]

The following explanations of what happened in the story are from children who took the pronoun to refer deictically to the Indian Chief, as would adults.

(61) a. *Kermit*   Bert lassoed him and the Tin Man did too.
    Child   No!
    Experimenter   Tell Kermit what really happened.
  b. *MT (4;7)*   Bert lassoed himself and the Tin Man lassoed Bert and no one lassoed the Indian.
    BE (4;3)   No, no one lassoed him.
    TF (4;4)   The Indian didn't get lassoed. Bert lassoed himself and this guy lassoed on Bert.

In chapter 3, we made the following prediction for this condition of the study:

Table 4.19
Percentage acceptance of local coreference in first conjunct of VP ellipsis sentence
by groups 1 ($n = 4$) and 2 ($n = 15$)

Sentence type	Group 1	Group 2
Bert lassoed him and the Tin Man did too (Bert lassoed self; Tin Man lassoed Bert)	6 (1/16)	54 (30/56)

Prediction 6
Only children who accept local coreference interpretations of matrix
sentences will allow local coreference in the first conjunct of VP ellipsis
sentences (a strict coreference reading).

The results bearing on this prediction are given in table 4.19. There was
no statistically significant change in behavior for group 1 and group 2
children in the present condition ($\chi^2 = .8$, $p < .25$). This is the predicted
result. Only 1 of the 4 children in group 1 made an error on one of the
four trials; this group continued to reject nonadult interpretations. More
importantly, group 2 children's behavior did not change significantly on
this item; children in this group continued to accept nonadult local coreference interpretations. Of the 15 children in group 2, 11 children continued to allow local coreference interpretations in the VP ellipsis
structures, whereas 4 children responded like adults.

The final experimental condition to be discussed in this section involved
sentences like (62).

(62) Gonzo covered him with sunblock and Snuffy did too.

Sentences like (62) are governed by Principle B. Principle B rules out a
bound variable interpretation of the pronouns according to which Gonzo
covered himself and Snuffy covered himself. We have already shown,
through children's performance on sentences like *Batman cleaned him and
every turtle did too*, that children reliably adhere to Principle B, rejecting
the bound variable interpretation according to which Batman and every
turtle cleaned themselves. Assuming, then, that children do not violate
Principle B, children's acceptance of test sentences like (62) can be reliably
construed as their permitting some other interpretation.

We have suggested that potentially, a local coreference interpretation of
the pronoun in each conjunct of sentences like (62) is possible, although
this would involve overriding referential parallelism, which we have
argued occurs for some children (see section 4.7). On this reading, Gonzo

and Snuffy both covered themselves with sunblock. On the surface, then, this local coreference interpretation cannot be distinguished from the bound variable one that violates Principle B. The argument that children are not violating Principle B has to be made on logical grounds, by appealing to the results for the condition involving a quantificational NP. We return to this interpretation shortly.

As a group, children rejected the interpretation of (62) in which Gonzo and Snuffy covered themselves with sunblock 78% of the time; put the other way around, children accepted the nonadult interpretation 22% of the time. Boster (1994) (for English) and Koster (1993, 1994) (for Dutch) have also reported some acceptances of the sloppy reading of sentences like (62) in other studies of children's comprehension. However, these authors' explanations of the results take different directions from ours; neither attributes acceptance of the ungrammatical reading, as we have, to a lack of pragmatic/real-world knowledge.[22]

In the beach story preceding test sentence (62), Gonzo refuses to cover Porky Pig (i.e., *him*) with sunblock, and so does Snuffy. Children who took the pronoun *him* to refer to Porky Pig should have rejected the sentence, explaining that Porky Pig's friends didn't help him put sunblock on. The comments in (63b) show that many children did interpret the sentence in this adultlike fashion; that is, they took it to mean that Gonzo and Snuffy both covered some other character with sunblock. Some of them focused on the fact that Porky Pig was left to put his own sunblock on.

(63) a. *Kermit*   Gonzo covered him with sunblock and Snuffy did too.
        Child   No!
        Experimenter   Oh, tell Kermit what really happened ...
    b. *EX (4;10)*   No one!
       BE (4;3)   The pig covered hisself.
       ED (4;2)   These guys covered theirselves with sunblock and this guy covered himself, right.
       OS (4;11)   Porky Pig put sunscreen on hisself.

A control sentence for (62) was (64), in which the pronoun is replaced by a reflexive.

(64) Bert covered himself with sand and Snuffy did too.

This condition was designed to ensure that children can accept a bound variable reading, in the same situation where they rejected it for sentences

Table 4.20
Percentage acceptance of look-sloppy interpretation by groups 1 ($n = 4$) and 2 ($n = 15$)

Sentence type	Group 1	Group 2
Gonzo covered him with sunblock and Snuffy did too (Gonzo covered self; Snuffy covered self)	0 (0/16)	28 (17/60)

like (62). The sentences containing reflexives were accepted 100% of the time. The dramatic difference of 22% acceptance for sentences with ordinary pronouns, such as (62), and 100% acceptance for sentences with reflexives, such as (64), indicates that Principle B or pragmatic factors are responsible for adult interpretations of (62).

Let us return to sentences like (62). Children's acceptance of (62), on the reading where Gonzo and Snuffy both cover themselves with sunblock, hinges on two factors: the ability to override the referential parallelism part of the parallelism constraint, and the ability to allow a local coreference interpretation in each conjunct. In the experimental predictions that follow, we examine these two factors independently.

We begin by testing whether children who accept a local coreference interpretation of *Bert brushed him* are more likely to accept a nonadult interpretation of (62). Recall prediction 7, from chapter 3.

Prediction 7
Children who allow local coreference interpretations in matrix sentences like *Bert brushed him* may also accept a look-sloppy interpretation of VP ellipsis sentences with referential NP antecedents in both clauses, such as *Gonzo covered him with sunblock and Snuffy did too.*

Expected results: Children in group 1 should continue to reject nonadult interpretations of sentences like (62), whereas children in group 2 should continue to allow nonadult interpretations of such sentences. If so, then there should not be a significant change in children's responses.

The results bearing on this prediction are given in table 4.20. As usual, the 4 children in group 1 responded like adults, making no errors on experimental items like (62). By contrast, of the 15 children in group 2, 10 children gave nonadult responses, and 5 children made no errors, responding like adults. The statistical analysis yielded a moderately significant result ($\chi^2 = 3.2$, $p < .05$). It is clear that the 5 children in group 2 who for some reason gave adultlike responses were responsible for the

Table 4.21
Percentage acceptance of reading violating referential parallelism and look-sloppy
local coreference reading by groups 3 ($n = 13$) and 4 ($n = 6$)

Sentence types	Group 3	Group 4
The lizard man lifted him and the ugly guy did too	75 (8/12)	0 (0/26)
(lizard man lifted Mickey Mouse; ugly guy lifted Smurf)		
Gonzo covered him with sunblock and Snuffy did too	17 (9/52)	33 (8/24)
(Gonzo covered self; Snuffy covered self)		

significant statistical finding; the behavior of the majority of children in
group 2 did not change, however.

Next, we looked at the source of children's nonadult acceptances of
sentences like (62). We wanted to find out whether these acceptances
originated mainly from the group of children who overrode referential
parallelism. To test this, we divided the 19 children differently than in
previous analyses. The criterion for division into groups 1 and 2, used for
testing predictions 1–7, was whether or not children accepted local coreference interpretations of sentences like *Bert brushed him*. In order to
test prediction 8, we partitioned the 19 children into a group that allowed
violations of referential parallelism (group 4) and a group that did not
(group 3). Group 3 contained the 13 children who rejected the nonadult
interpretation of sentences like (51), *The lizard man lifted him and the ugly
guy did too* (in this case, the interpretation in which the lizard man and the
ugly guy each lifted a different person). Group 4 contained the 6 children
who accepted the nonadult interpretation of sentences like (51), on at least
one of the two trials.

Prediction 8
Children who override referential parallelism may accept nonadult
interpretations of VP ellipsis sentences with referential NP antecedents in
both clauses, such as *Gonzo covered him with sunblock and Snuffy did too*.

Expected results: Group 3 children should not accept sentences like (62),
whereas group 4 children should.

The results bearing on prediction 8 are given in table 4.21. Of the 13
children in group 3, 7 children made at least one error on items like (62).
In addition, of the 6 children in group 4, who were expected to allow illicit
interpretations of (62), 2 children changed their behavior and responded
like adults. The result was not significant ($\chi^2 = 1.1$, $p < .15$). However,

we had expected that a nonsignificant result would be obtained because children in groups 3 and 4 would show no change in behavior. In this sense, the prediction was not fulfilled: some children in each group did change their behavior.

Let us look at these data in another way. Group 4 children accepted the look-sloppy reading of sentences like (62) eight times overall, an average of $8/6 = 1.33$ acceptances (out of 4). Group 3 children accepted this reading of such sentences nine times overall, an average of $9/13 = .69$ acceptances. That is, there were about twice as many acceptances of sentences like (62) by the children who also accepted sentences like (51). This can readily be seen from the percentages in table 4.21: group 4 children accepted (62) 33% of the time, and group 3 children accepted it 17% of the times. The probability that a group 4 subject will accept a sentence like (62) on any given trial is $8/24 = .33$. The probability that a group 3 subject will accept the same sentence on any given trial is $9/52 = .19$.

The data suggest that the predictions are on the right track, but they are not perfect. This may be because the experiment included only two trials testing referential parallelism. Had there been four trials, we may have found more children who made errors, and who also accepted the non-adult interpretation of (62). More thorough testing of prediction 8 remains for future research. Nevertheless, the results across structures indicate that children's acceptances of the look-sloppy interpretation of (62) are not violations of Principle B but rather reflect a lack of pragmatic knowledge. The fact that overall acceptance to (62) is smaller than acceptance of sentences like *Bert brushed him* shows that many children who allow local coreference in matrix sentences do not violate referential parallelism.

4.8.2 Results for the Strict Reading of a Reflexive in VP Ellipsis Sentences

Syntactic theory suggests that a reflexive cannot be given a strict reading in VP ellipsis structures with coordinate clauses. However, some informants' intuitions do not match this suggestion. Given this, it is possible that adults may accept a strict reading of sentences like (65), one in which both Hawkman and the baby boy fanned Hawkman.

(65) Hawkman fanned himself and the baby boy did too.

Indeed, the adult control data included some acceptances of (65). Overall, the acceptance rate among the 6 adult controls was 17%. This acceptance rate was accounted for by 2 adults, who accepted one of the two trials.

Although adults accepted such sentences some of the time, children did so considerably more often: 65% of the time. The transcript in (66) illustrates a child accepting the strict reading of the reflexive.

(66) *Kermit* So, in this story, Hawkman fanned himself and the baby boy did too.
OS (4;11) Fanned who? They both fanned him.
Kermit What I think happened was this. Hawkman fanned himself and the baby boy did too.
OS Right.

Those children who did not allow a strict reading rejected the trial because the sloppy reading was false in the story—that is, Hawkman and the baby didn't both fan themselves. The comments in (67b) illustrate two children's reasons for rejecting the strict interpretation of the reflexive.

(67) a. *Kermit* Hawkman fanned himself and the baby boy did too.
   Child No!
   Experimenter Tell Kermit what really happened.
   b. *BE (4;3)* The baby boy didn't fan hisself.
   EI (4;9) No, the baby boy didn't. He didn't fan himself.

The dialogue in (68) illustrates another child rejecting the strict reading of the reflexive. This child allows local coreference in his utterances with the focus operator *only*. Although we have not considered such cases, they are discussed in Grodzinsky and Reinhart 1993 as legitimate cases of coreference and further evaluated in Heim 1998.

(68) *Kermit* Hawkman fanned himself and the baby boy did too.
   EI (4;9) Only this guy [Hawkman] fanned him [himself] and this guy [baby boy] fanned that guy [Hawkman]. None of them fanned him [Robin].
   Experimenter [echoes child] This guy fanned him ... You mean Hawkman fanned himself?
   EI Yeah!
   Kermit So what I said was "Hawkman fanned himself and the baby boy did too."
   EI No, the baby boy didn't. He didn't fan himself. Only this guy fanned him [himself].

In discussing the syntactic literature in chapter 3, we noted that the consensus is that a strict reading of reflexives is possible in two-clause structures with a subordinate clause, but that whether it is grammatical in coordinate structures like the one in (65) is a matter of debate. The findings from our experiment show that children, and adults to some extent, allow the strict reading of reflexives in coordinate structures. Even though the strict reading is dispreferred, apparently its availability can be heightened by context. These results do not support most syntactic analyses of this construction, which rule out strict readings in coordinate structures as violations of the syntax (e.g., Hestvik's (1995) analysis, under which the ECP precludes such readings). They favor an alternative suggestion also offered by Hestvik: that it is possible to interpret the pronoun off-line, as a deep anaphor (see Hankamer and Sag 1976). In our terms, this means that a strict interpretation of a reflexive is subject to pragmatic manipulation.

Next, we question whether children who accept local coreference interpretations of matrix sentences are more likely to accept the strict reading of reflexives in VP ellipsis sentences than children who do not. Given that adults seem to accept the strict reading at least some proportion of the time, children's acceptance of this reading should not be contingent on their acceptance of local coreference in sentences like *Bert brushed him*.

Question 9
Do both children and adults allow the strict interpretation of a reflexive in VP ellipsis sentences, irrespective of whether they accept local coreference interpretations in matrix sentences?

Possible results: Group 1 and group 2 children will both accept (65) on the reading in which Hawkman and the baby both fanned Hawkman.

Unfortunately, only 17 of the 19 children were tested on this condition, and the population was too small for statistical tests. However, examination of table 4.22 shows that the 4 children in group 1 accepted the strict reading of (65) only once. For the most part, group 2 children (who accepted local coreference interpretations in matrix clauses) were much more likely to accept the strict reading of a reflexive. This is perhaps not

Table 4.22
Percentage acceptance of strict reflexive reading by groups 1 ($n = 4$) and 2 ($n = 13$)

Sentence type	Group 1	Group 2
Hawkman fanned himself and the baby boy did too (Hawkman fanned self; baby boy fanned Hawkman)	13 (1/8)	81 (21/26)

surprising, given that group 2 children were in general more tolerant of infelicitous pragmatic circumstances.

4.8.3 Results for Principle C

The final results concern Principle C. Matrix sentences subject to Principle C, like (69) evoked a very robust 92% rejection rate from the children. That is, children did not allow (69) to mean that the skeleton dusted himself.

(69) He dusted the skeleton.

Earlier, we concluded that although sentences like *Bert brushed him* test Principle B, they are also open to a local coreference interpretation. Similarly, it might be said that (69) is ambiguous between a test of Principle C and a test of local coreference. However, the results clearly show that children did not allow a local coreference interpretation of sentences like *He dusted the skeleton.* They did not treat it like its Principle B counterpart.

In the story leading up to test sentence (69), a scarecrow does not help dust the skeleton because he has to attend to his own cobwebs, and so the skeleton ends up dusting himself. It was clear from the transcripts that children interpreted the pronoun in (69) as referring not to the skeleton, but to the scarecrow. This choice of referent is consistent with knowledge of Principle C.

The following comments show that children rejected the sentence because *he*, the scarecrow, didn't help dust the skeleton. Many of the children explained that the scarecrow didn't help the skeleton but dusted himself instead. (This left the skeleton having to dust himself also.)

(70) a. *Kermit* So in this story, I think he dusted the skeleton.
      Child No!
      Kermit What really happened?
   b. *LX (5;0)* Well, he dusted hisself, and he dusted hisself too.
      MT (5;7) The skeleton hadda clean hisself and the scarecrow hadda clean hisself so they would be OK for Halloween because he was just as dusty as him.

(71) *ED (4;2)* This guy [scarecrow] dusted hisself like this "dust, dust dust."
   Experimenter And the skeleton?
   ED He dusted himself "dust, dust, dust."

The experimental results support the idea that knowledge of Principle C is innate. Why don't children entertain a local coreference interpretation of these sentences? We discussed two possibilities in chapter 3. One possibility is that there is immediate processing pressure to assign the pronoun a referent before the proposition expressed by the sentence is encountered. The other possibility is that a pragmatic principle (the PPOI) applies specifically to the subject position, in virtue of its role as the bearer of old information. This forces the listener to take the pronoun to refer back to an NP already mentioned in the discourse. The previously mentioned NP cannot be *the skeleton*; if it were, the pronoun and the NP, *the skeleton*, would end up coindexed, violating Principle C. Therefore, the pronoun must refer to the scarecrow, and the child must judge the sentence false. Our experimental results with child subjects are exactly as either of these two possibilities would suggest.

On the other hand, the experimental results do not support the predictions of Grodzinsky and Reinhart's (1993) account. On their account, sentences like (69) are subject to Rule I. Since, on their view, children are unable to perform the calculations required by Rule I, children should perform at chance on the Principle C condition.

Let us turn to the individual subject data.

Prediction 10
All children should obey Principle C in matrix sentences irrespective of the status of sentences like *Bert brushed him* in their grammar.

Expected results: Group 1 and group 2 children should all adhere to Principle C.

The results bearing on this prediction are given in table 4.23. Examining the data from groups 1 and 2, we note that children in group 1 continued to respond in an adultlike fashion. The children in group 2, however, showed a highly significant change from their previous response pattern ($\chi^2 = 11.07$, $p < .0005$). Whereas all 15 children in group 2

Table 4.23
Percentage acceptance of matrix Principle C items by groups 1 ($n = 4$) and 2 ($n = 15$)

Sentence type	Group 1	Group 2
He dusted the skeleton (skeleton dusted self)	0 (0/7)	10 (3/30)

Table 4.24
Percentage acceptance of interpretations that apparently violate Principle C by
group ($N = 19$)

Sentence types	% "Yes"	Grammatical
He dusted the skeleton	8	x
(skeleton dusted self)		
The kiwi bird cleaned Flash Gordon and he did too	54	x
(kiwi bird cleaned Flash Gordon; Flash Gordon cleaned self)		

allowed some local coreference interpretations of *Bert brushed him*, only
2 of the 15 children made errors on the two trials testing Principle C in
sentences like *He dusted the skeleton*.

Principle C was also tested in VP ellipsis sentences like (72).

(72) The kiwi bird cleaned Flash Gordon and he did too.

The results for the matrix control structure and the VP ellipsis target
structure are summarized in table 4.24. Although children adhered to
Principle C 92% of the time for matrix sentences, rejecting an interpretation it prohibited, they behaved differently with respect to the VP ellipsis
sentences. The 19 children accepted VP ellipsis sentences like (72) 54% of
the time. The pattern of findings was quite similar for the control group of
adults. Adults adhered to Principle C in responding to the matrix sentences but accepted the VP ellipsis sentences at a rate of 83%. Every adult
accepted at least two out of the four VP ellipsis sentences.

Before we analyze the pattern of responses by children and adults, let us
take a closer look at the story context and see how the child subjects
responded to it. In the story, the kiwi bird is teaching Flash Gordon and
the lantern man to play rugby. They all fall down in the mud and get
dirty, and Flash Gordon asks the lantern man to clean him. The kiwi bird
helps, but the lantern man says he has to get his own mud off and won't
help, so Flash Gordon ends up cleaning himself. Some comments elicited
from the children who rejected the test sentence are given in (73).

(73) a. *Kermit*   The kiwi bird cleaned Flash Gordon and he did too.
         Child   No!
         Experimenter   Tell Kermit what really happened.
     b. *EI (4;9)*   But this guy [the lantern man] didn't and this guy [kiwi
         bird] did.

> *LT (5;1)*   Because he [the lantern man] didn't clean him but he [kiwi bird] cleans him.
> *EX (4;10)*   The kiwi bird cleaned him, but this [the lantern man] didn't, he cleaned himself.

In the following dialogue, a child accepts the interpretation in which the pronoun is taken to refer to Flash Gordon:

(74) *Kermit*   The kiwi bird cleaned Flash Gordon and he did too.
   BE (4;3)   Flash Gordon cleaned hisself too? [questions experimenter]
   Experimenter   That's a tricky one. You seem a bit mixed up, Kermit. Tell us one more time and [BE] will tell us if you're right or wrong.
   Kermit   The kiwi bird cleaned Flash Gordon and he did too.
   BE   I think you were right.

Given that the pronoun could refer to the lantern man or Flash Gordon, it is not surprising that some children vacillated before giving a judgment. This point is illustrated by the comments of one sophisticated subject who saw the ambiguity of the pronoun.

(75) *Kermit*   So in this story, the kiwi bird cleaned Flash Gordon and he did too.
   JZ (5;0)   [repeats to herself] *The kiwi bird cleaned Flash Gordon and he did too.* Right... Say it again!
   Kermit   OK. The kiwi bird cleaned Flash Gordon and he did too.
   JZ   Hisself or him?
   Kermit   This is hard. Let me think. I think that the kiwi bird cleaned Flash Gordon and he did too.
   JZ   Let's make that a "Yes."
   Kermit   Why is that a "Yes"? What do you think really happened?
   JZ   Well, this bird cleaned Flash Gordon and he [points to Flash Gordon] cleaned him too.[23]

In conducting the experiment, every effort was made to present the target sentences with natural intonation, without stress. But, as we have pointed out, it is unnatural to utter VP ellipsis sentences like (72) without stressing the pronoun in the second conjunct. Assuming, then, that the pronoun in the puppet's target sentence was stressed to some extent, it is not surprising that some adults may have allowed local coreference interpretations of pronoun and name in the elided VP of *The kiwi bird cleaned*

Flash Gordon and he did too. For adults, the presence of stress helps facilitate a local coreference interpretation. The elided clause expresses the idea that getting himself clean is unexpected or atypical behavior for Flash Gordon.

Given that adults sanction local coreference interpretations in this experimental context, children should do so also. Those children who do not accept local coreference interpretations in sentences like *Bert brushed him* may allow them here, for the same reasons that adults do. Those children who do allow local coreference interpretations in sentences like *Bert brushed him* may accept them here, but for a different reason—as the result of their nonadult pragmatic/real-world knowledge. One result of this is that they are unsure of how to interpret stress, and they have not figured out how it interfaces with the pragmatics of local coreference.

Notice that whether or not children allow local coreference interpretations in VP ellipsis structures governed by Principle C is not related to their knowledge of the parallelism constraint. The parallelism constraint governs how elided pronouns (and other NPs) are interpreted. In (72), however, the pronoun is not elided but overt, in subject position of the second conjunct. Thus, the parallelism constraint is not relevant.

We can now address our final prediction.

Prediction 11
Adults and children, irrespective of the status of their pragmatic knowledge, may allow local coreference in the elided clause of a VP ellipsis structure governed by Principle C.

Expected results: Group 1 children may change their behavior and allow a local coreference interpretation; group 2 children should continue to allow local coreference interpretations.

The results that bear on this prediction are given in table 4.25. There is no significant change in behavior ($\chi^2 = 0$). All 4 children in group 1

Table 4.25
Percentage acceptance of interpretations that apparently violate Principle C in VP ellipsis items by groups 1 ($n = 4$) and 2 ($n = 15$)

Sentence type	Group 1	Group 2
The kiwi bird cleaned Flash Gordon and he did too (kiwi bird cleaned Flash Gordon; Flash Gordon cleaned self)	44 (7/16)	57 (32/56)

allowed local coreference interpretations of the VP ellipsis items, thus changing their behavior, as predicted. Although the predicted change in behavior is clearly present, the number of children in group 1 is small enough that this cannot be shown statistically. Of the 15 children in group 2, 12 children continued to allow local coreference interpretations; 3 children changed their behavior and responded like adults.

The data gathered from studying Principle C effects in VP ellipsis structures resolve another question. On our account, an asymmetry between the results for matrix sentences and those for VP ellipsis sentences is expected. Local coreference in matrix sentences like *He dusted the skeleton* is expected to be rejected at a high rate, owing to processing effects or the PPOI. On the other hand, the VP ellipsis sentence is expected to be accepted on these alternative accounts. By contrast, on Grodzinsky and Reinhart's (1993) account, child subjects should respond to both sentence types at chance, because of difficulties with applying Rule I.[24] This did not happen. Although the results for the VP ellipsis sentences could be taken to reflect chance performance, because the children as a group accepted the stimuli 58% of the time, the results for the matrix sentences cannot be interpreted in this way. Matrix sentences like *He dusted the skeleton* were accepted only 8% of the time on the illicit local coreference reading. Thus, Grodzinsky and Reinhart's account cannot be correct in its present form.

In summary, the statistical tests have confirmed that the group of children responded to the experimental test items in a consistent manner. Children's behavior was strongly bimodal. Those children whose pragmatic knowledge is adultlike consistently responded to all of the test items as adults. Those children whose pragmatic knowledge is not complete (according to our criterion of whether or not they accept local coreference interpretations of *Mama Bear washed her*) responded as adults on tests of syntactic knowledge, but gave nonadult responses on items testing their allowance of local coreference interpretations and referential parallelism.

4.9 A Follow-up Study

In our study, VP ellipsis examples like (76) provided one test of children's knowledge of Principle B.

(76) Gonzo covered him with sunblock and Snuffy did too.
   a. *Gonzo$_i$ covered him$_i^\beta$ with sunblock and Snuffy$_j$ ⟨covered him$_j^\beta$ with sunblock⟩ too.

b.   Gonzo$_i$ covered him$_j^\alpha$ with sunblock and Snuffy$_k$ $\langle$covered him$_l^\alpha$ with sunblock$\rangle$ too.

A complicating factor was that these sentences have two representations that result in the same truth conditions: the sloppy, bound variable reading ruled out by Principle B, and the local coreference, look-sloppy reading. For adults, the latter reading is ruled out by pragmatic knowledge and the referential part of the parallelism constraint, which we have suggested can also be manipulated by pragmatic knowledge. However, we hypothesized that children whose pragmatic knowledge is nonadult may have the associated problem of not knowing how pronominal stress is used.

The net result was that our study included no "pure" test of Principle B in VP ellipsis cases where the antecedent of the pronoun in each clause is a referential NP. A "Yes" response to (76) entailed that the child was allowing the sentence to mean something like 'Gonzo covered himself with sunblock and Snuffy covered himself with sunblock'. This "Yes" response could not tell us whether the child was generating the representation in (76a) or the one in (76b). Of course, all was not lost, because a number of other structures showed us that children were not violating Principle B. Examples like (77), for example, controlled for this complicating factor because the presence of the quantifier *every* excluded the possibility of a local coreference reading.

(77) Batman cleaned him and every turtle did too.

It occurred to us post hoc, however, that there is a structure *without* a quantifier that can disentangle the ambiguity inherent in examples like (76). Consider (78).

(78) Kermit's friend wiped him and Big Bird did too.

For adults, this sentence has two interpretations: a deictic one in which Kermit's friend and Big Bird wiped some individual not mentioned in the sentence, and a strict one in which Kermit's friend and Big Bird wiped Kermit. However, children with nonadult pragmatic knowledge might allow the sentence to mean that Kermit's friend wiped Kermit, and Big Bird wiped himself. Children would thereby be allowing local coreference between the elided pronoun and *Big Bird*. If so, children would be generating the structure in (79). In this structure, the pronouns in each clause are referential pronouns. Like (76), this interpretation would entail overriding referential parallelism.

(79) Kermit$_i$'s friend wiped him$_i^\alpha$ and Big Bird$_j$ ⟨wiped him$_k^\alpha$⟩ too.

On Fiengo and May's (1994) theory, a bound variable interpretation of the pronouns in (78) is excluded because the two conjuncts do not have equivalent syntactic structures; the possessive DP subject of the first conjunct is more complex than the subject of the second conjunct. In addition, a sloppy bound variable interpretation of the sentence is ruled out because the pronoun in the first conjunct is not c-commanded by its antecedent, *Kermit*. The only way to get a reading that looks sloppy is to generate (79). If children allow a look-sloppy reading for this structure, then they are clearly allowing a local coreference interpretation and not violating Principle B.

We carried out a pilot study to pursue this possibility. Simple matrix sentences like *Gumby brushed him* were included to identify children who accepted local coreference in matrix clauses.[25] We predicted that these children would allow the local coreference interpretation of (78). We used the same procedures and the same task (the truth value judgment task) as in the main experiment. Sixteen children aged 3;9–5;10 (mean age 4;5) participated in this follow-up study. Only 1 of the children was also a subject in the main experiment.[26] Like the children who participated in the main study, the children all attended child care centers in Arlington, Massachusetts, or Storrs, Connecticut.

In the story leading up to the test sentence *Kermit's friend wiped him and Big Bird did too*, Kermit, Miss Piggy (his friend), and Big Bird go for a walk. Kermit is so busy talking he doesn't notice a pile of peas on the sidewalk, and he slips and falls. He is very upset and asks his friends for help. Miss Piggy comes to the rescue and wipes him up. Big Bird is so busy laughing at the scene that he doesn't notice where the peas are, and he slips and falls himself. After that, he says he certainly won't help wipe Kermit up, because he has to get the squashed peas off his feathers. Big Bird finishes by wiping his own feathers.[27]

The follow-up study included two matrix controls (to identify the relevant children), using the verbs *brush* and *blow on*, and four trials of the crucial VP ellipsis structure, using the verbs *brush*, *wipe*, *paint*, and *cover*. All these verbs had been found to be reliable in the main study.

The children accepted matrix control sentences like *Bert brushed him* 41% of the time and target sentences like *Kermit's friend wiped him and Bib Bird did too* 28% (18/64 trials) of the time. Of the 16 children tested in this follow-up study, 8 children accepted either one or both of the trials testing local coreference in matrix sentences. These are the children who

Table 4.26
Acceptances of local coreference interpretations by individual subjects ($N = 8$)

	Subject							
	NO	LS	UM	NE	LQ	OX	LP	FQ
Sentence types	3;10	3;11	4;1	4;2	4;2	4;2	4;3	4;7
Local coreference								
Gumby brushed him	2/2	1/2	2/2	2/2	2/2	1/2	2/2	1/2
Local coreference in each VP								
Kermit's friend wiped him and Big Bird did too	2/4	4/4	4/4	1/4	2/4	0/4	0/4	0/4

are potential accepters of the local coreference reading of the VP ellipsis sentences. Of course, accepting the local coreference interpretation also involves overriding referential parallelism, and the results of the main experiment showed that not all children who accept the local coreference interpretation of *Gumby brushed him* will override referential parallelism. Therefore, we could not necessarily expect that all of these children would accept the VP ellipsis sentence. The results for the 8 children are shown in table 4.26.

Of the 8 children, 5 children accepted the look-sloppy, local coreference interpretation of the VP ellipsis sentences on some number of trials, 13/32 in total. Three children interpreted these sentences as adults would, as their rejections indicate. This is, of course, a legitimate option, even for children who have not mastered the relevant pragmatic knowledge, because the sentences were ambiguous. Notice that 2 of the 3 children who did not accept the local coreference interpretation for the VP ellipsis sentence accepted a local coreference interpretation for only 1/2 of the matrix controls. It is also possible that the latter acceptances represented performance errors and did not reflect the children's grammars. If this explanation is correct, these children would not have been expected to accept the look-sloppy reading.

The pilot study gives suggestive support to our claim that children who accept look-sloppy readings in VP ellipsis sentences are not violating Principle B. Rather, their acceptances of the local coreference reading reflect developing pragmatic knowledge that becomes adultlike only with experience. Tests of this and similar structures are a rich area for future research.

Chapter 5

Conclusion

5.1   Children's Interpretation of Pronouns in VP Ellipsis Structures

Our account of children's interpretation of pronouns inside VP ellipsis structures builds on our account of children's interpretation of pronouns in matrix sentences. The hearer of a matrix sentence like *Mama Bear washed her* encounters the proposition that Mama Bear washed someone (*her*), and the task is to determine whether the pronoun refers to someone other than Mama Bear or whether it indicates another guise of Mama Bear. For adults, of course, the pronoun unambiguously refers to someone other than Mama Bear. For some children, as we have shown, it does not. Children have more difficulty in understanding what the speaker intended.

The reason that children allow local coreference interpretations is that they create guises that are not supported by the context. Four factors contribute to children's misinterpretation of pronouns in matrix Principle B contexts (see section 3.3). First, children need to fine-tune their understanding of the situations in which local coreference interpretations are permitted. Children's real-world knowledge is incomplete; they have to learn from experience about the situations in which the same individual can be under discussion under different guises. Once this is accomplished, they will be better able to interpret other speakers' utterances.

Second, children must acquire the associated knowledge that stress on the pronoun in sentences like *Mama Bear washed HER* marks the speaker's intention to convey the local coreference interpretation by bringing it into focus. The contexts that permit coreference without violating Principle B are often accompanied by stress on the pronoun, and it is reasonably well documented that children have difficulty interpreting the pragmatic information correlated with prosodic information. Children are reported to acquire this ability around age 6 (Cutler and Swinney 1987), roughly the same age at which they stop overaccepting local coreference interpretations. On our account, this deficit is not perceptual or grammatical in nature—rather, it follows from children's lack of pragmatic knowledge. If children don't understand the contextual requirements for guise creation, they will be slow to learn that stress is an indication that a speaker intends local coreference.

The first two factors contributing to children's nonadult acceptance of sentences, then, result from the fact that children are in the throes of learning pragmatics. The two remaining factors are ones that children have in common with adults. The third factor is the tendency for listeners to interpret a sentence in a way that makes it true. The fourth factor is that, as a feature of experimental design, the event corresponding to the local coreference reading is the last event in the story; this makes the event, and therefore the coreference interpretation, highly salient. Although we assume that the last two factors are operative for adults as well as children, they are clearly not sufficient to cause adults to assign local coreference (a) in run-of-the-mill contexts and (b) in the absence of pronominal stress. The first two associated factors, then, make the difference in causing children to misinterpret pronouns. These factors are also instrumental in understanding how children interpret VP ellipsis structures.

The central VP ellipsis structures that we examined experimentally were ones in which the pronoun or name in the elided VP is subject to Principle B or C of the binding theory, as shown in (1). In (1a), the pronoun in the elided VP is in a configuration relevant to Principle B; in (1b), the name in the elided VP is governed by Principle C.

(1) a. Papa Bear licked him and Brother Bear ~~licked him~~ too

$$\downarrow$$

did

b. Papa Bear licked Brother Bear and he ~~licked Brother Bear~~ too

$$\downarrow$$

did

Although both children and adults were found not to allow apparent violations of Principle C in matrix control sentences (i.e., they did not allow local coreference interpretations of sentences like *She washed Mama Bear*), they did allow apparent violations in VP ellipsis sentences like (1b) (i.e., they allowed the local coreference interpretation in which Papa Bear licked Brother Bear and Brother Bear also licked himself). To explain this finding, we appeal to the architecture of the language system. When the pronoun in the second conjunct is encountered in VP ellipsis sentences like (1b), a proposition, introduced in the first conjunct, is already under discussion. Therefore, the referent of the pronoun is evaluated against this proposition. This allows children and adults alike to consider whether an individual is being presented in two different guises. And adults and children alike apparently judge this to be possible.

This is not the case for matrix sentences governed by Principle C like *She washed Mama Bear*, however. Neither children nor adults allow apparent Principle C violations; that is, neither group accepted local coreference interpretations. In this case, at the point at which the pronoun *she* is encountered, no relevant proposition (that someone washed Mama Bear) has been advanced. Therefore, it is not possible for children or adults to consider whether an additional guise of Mama Bear is being introduced into the discourse. Instead, the pronoun is immediately taken to refer to one of the possible antecedents in the context, *Goldilocks* or *Mama Bear*, in whatever guise she was introduced before. If the pronoun is taken to refer to Mama Bear in whatever guise she was introduced before, an interpretation that presumably involves coindexing *she* and *Mama Bear*, Principle C is violated. In effect, then, the pronoun must be taken to refer to Goldilocks, and the test sentence is judged as false.

In the VP ellipsis experiments testing Principle B, some children were found to entertain interpretive options that are not available to adults. As noted in chapter 1, VP ellipsis sentences like *Papa Bear licked him and Brother Bear did too* offer a complex inventory of potential interpretations, reviewed in (2). The experiments were designed to see which of these interpretations children entertain.

(2) Papa Bear licked him and Brother Bear did too.

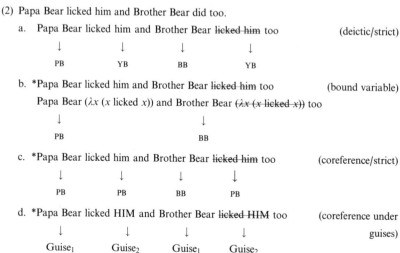

a. Papa Bear licked him and Brother Bear ~~licked him~~ too   (deictic/strict)

    ↓   ↓   ↓   ↓

   PB   YB   BB   YB

b. *Papa Bear licked him and Brother Bear ~~licked him~~ too   (bound variable)

    Papa Bear (λx (x licked x)) and Brother Bear ~~(λx (x licked x))~~ too

   ↓   ↓

   PB   BB

c. *Papa Bear licked him and Brother Bear ~~licked him~~ too   (coreference/strict)

    ↓   ↓   ↓   ↓

   PB   PB   BB   PB

d. *Papa Bear licked HIM and Brother Bear ~~licked HIM~~ too   (coreference under

    ↓   ↓   ↓   ↓   guises)

   Guise₁   Guise₂   Guise₁   Guise₂

    ↓   ↓   ↓   ↓

   PB   PB   BB   BB

For adults, the only possible interpretation is (2a); that is, this sentence can only mean that Papa Bear and Brother Bear licked someone else, say, Yogi Bear (YB). The bound variable (sloppy) interpretation illustrated in (2b) is disallowed by Principle B. The strict coreference interpretation (2c) is ruled out by Principle B and/or some type of pragmatic rule, depending on the version of the binding theory adopted. The impossibility of (2d) requires some discussion.

On the interpretation in (2d), one individual in two guises is under discussion in the first conjunct, and another individual in two guises is under discussion in the second conjunct. As observed in chapter 3, it is quite difficult to imagine a context in which a speaker might want to express the thought represented by (2d), but it can be done. This suggests that to some extent the interpretation of the pronoun in such structures depends on pragmatic factors. Special pragmatic contexts aside, in general, the two-guises interpretation represented in (2d) is excluded for two reasons in the adult grammar: (a) this local coreference interpretation is possible only with a stress-bearing pronoun (except in some identity debate situations), but inside an elided VP, a pronoun obviously cannot be stressed, and (b) the parallelism constraint applies in these structures. As we have characterized it (see also Fox 1998), the parallelism constraint has two parts: (a) structural parallelism and (b) referential parallelism. Our experimental results suggest that structural parallelism belongs to the syntactic, computational part of the grammar and is an inviolable constraint, much like Principles B and C of the binding theory. By contrast, referential parallelism—the part of the constraint at issue in interpreting sentences like (2d)—appears to be more open to pragmatic manipulation. Referential parallelism has the effect of forcing referential pronouns (i.e., pronouns that are not bound variables) to pick out the same referent in each clause. For adults, this eliminates from contention the two-guises interpretation of a VP ellipsis sentence like (2d), in which each pronoun finds its referent within the clause, even though such a local coreference interpretation is possible for pronouns in matrix sentences like *Mama Bear washed her*.

How do children differ from adults in interpreting sentences like (2)? In experimental contexts, we have found that some children allow the strict coreference interpretation shown in (2c) and the look-sloppy interpretation represented in (2d), where two guises of individuals are under discussion.

Interestingly, the two interpretations permitted by some children have a common property: in coordinate structures with two overt conjuncts, the interpretations that are excluded in the grammars of adults are possible. Consider the coordinate structures in (3). (The interpretations under discussion for the sentences in (3) are possible for coordinate structures only if the relevant pronoun in each clause bears heavy stress; deixis (pointing) may also be needed).

(3) Papa Bear licked him and Brother Bear licked him too.

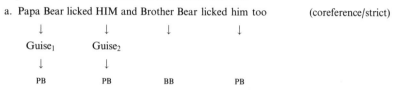

a. Papa Bear licked HIM and Brother Bear licked him too   (coreference/strict)

b. Papa Bear licked HIM and Brother Bear licked HIM too   (coreference under guises in each conjunct)

The fact that coordinate structures can allow the interpretations in (2c) and (2d) is interesting because current views of the parallelism constraint—in particular, the PF deletion model of VP ellipsis that we turn to in section 5.2—views its domain of application as extending over VP ellipsis structures and also those coordinate structures with a "down-stressed" second conjunct (i.e., a second conjunct that has flat intonation, with no stressed elements).

Now we are in position to address children's misinterpretations of the pronouns in VP ellipsis sentences like *Papa Bear licked him and Brother Bear did too*, namely, the ones in (2c) and (2d). The same factors that lead to children's misinterpretation of sentences like *Mama Bear washed her* are relevant here as well: their lack of pragmatic knowledge about the situations that sanction local coreference interpretations (i.e., guise creation), and their associated difficulty in interpreting contrastive stress.

It remains to explain how these factors conspire to cause children to appear to violate the parallelism constraint, however. This constraint should prohibit any interpretation in which the pronoun assumes a different referential value in each clause. We have suggested that the referential part of the parallelism constraint is not a "hard" syntactic constraint; it is subject to pragmatic manipulation. Thus, in accepting interpretations like the one illustrated in (3b), children are overriding referential parallelism, again because they lack pragmatic knowledge, not because their grammar lacks Principle B. Until this pragmatic knowledge is in place, they will be unable to interpret how speakers alert listeners to local coreference interpretations using stress.

In the next section, by appealing to the PF deletion model of VP ellipsis, we will attempt to narrow the differences between children and adults even more. We will suggest that to explain the VP ellipsis results, we needn't make the additional assumption that children override referential parallelism—the results instead follow from the factors we have already identified for children's misinterpretations of matrix sentences like *Mama Bear washed her*.

5.2   The PF Deletion Model

In this section, we interpret our findings within the Minimalist Program, which revives the idea that VP ellipsis structures are derived from coordinate structures (Chomsky 1995; Chomsky and Lasnik 1993; Tancredi 1992). On this view, which we will call the *PF deletion model of VP ellipsis*, the VP of the second conjunct undergoes deletion at PF, instead of reconstruction at LF, as in alternative theories. We will use this model to explain the difficulty some children experience in interpreting VP ellipsis structures.

Part of the motivation for returning to a PF deletion model of VP ellipsis in recent syntactic theory is the desire to eliminate reconstruction. In earlier versions of the principles-and-parameters approach, the operation of reconstruction required that a moved element be lowered back into its original position at LF, or after LF, in order to achieve the correct interpretation. In the Minimalist Program, the effect of reconstruction is obtained by the copy theory of movement. Specifically, a copy of the moved element remains in the base position after movement. The copy is retained in the computational system at LF, but it is deleted at PF. Thus, in the speech output, the moved element is produced in only one position.

In the Minimalist Program, VP ellipsis structures are derived in a way that is analogous to (though not quite the same as) movement. VP ellipsis structures begin life as coordinate structures. The VP of the second conjunct is treated as if it were a "copy," the difference being that in this case, the copy is not actually created by movement. The entire coordinate structure, with copy intact, is sent to LF, where the parallelism constraint applies to it. At PF, the copy in the second conjunct deletes, under identity with the VP in the first conjunct, and a VP ellipsis structure is born.

In order to shed light on what might be taking place in children's grammars, we need to spell out the mechanics of the PF deletion model (Chomsky 1995) in more detail and consider a range of related sentence types. We consider VP ellipsis structures, as in (4a), and coordinate structures, as in (4b–d). It should be noted that our discussion of the derivation of VP ellipsis structures abstracts away from the fact that an auxiliary verb, here *did*, replaces the elided VP in sentences like (4a).

(4) a. Superman polished his shoes and Perry did too.
    b. Superman polished his shoes and Perry polished his shoes too.
    c. Superman polished his shoes and Perry polished HIS shoes too.
    d. Superman polished HIS shoes and Perry polished HIS shoes too.

As noted earlier, coordinate structures may have a flat downstressed intonation in the second conjunct, as in (4b). This intonation pattern is not obligatory, however. It is possible to stress the pronoun in the second conjunct, as in (4c), or to stress the pronouns in both conjuncts, as in (4d) (although admittedly the circumstances in which a speaker might do this are limited). The significant point is that VP ellipsis structures (e.g., (4a)) and coordinate structures with downstressing (e.g., (4b)) are subject to the parallelism constraint whereas coordinate structures with some degree of pronominal stress in the second conjunct (e.g., (4c–d)) are not. We will exploit this difference in our explanation of why children allow more interpretations for certain VP ellipsis structures than adults do. Since Chomsky does not distinguish referential and structural parallelism as we have defined them, we will simply assume that there is a parallelism constraint that incorporates them both, and that it applies at the level of LF.

How does the grammar, as conceived of in the Minimalist Program, generate the structures in (4a–d)? First, consider the consequences of saying the following: In a conjoined structure, if the VP in the second conjunct has the same lexical array of words as the VP in the first conjunct, then the VP in the second conjunct is the copy. If this were true, then the VP in the second conjunct in (4b–d) would be identical to the first and would obligatorily delete at PF. However, only the VP of (4a) has actually been elided. This means that the VPs in the second conjuncts of (4a–d) need to be distinguished from each other in some way. Let us consider them one at a time, beginning with (4c) and (4d).

Chomsky (1995) does not discuss these cases, but the general idea seems clear. Given that the second conjunct in (4c) and (4d) is not downstressed, it is safe to infer that the VP in the second conjunct is not a copy of the first. This explains why it does not delete at PF and, presumably, why it is not subject to parallelism at LF.

Consider next examples like (4b), where the second conjunct has downstressed intonation. At first glance, the VP in the second conjunct of (4b) looks like it might be a copy of the VP in the first conjunct. But since the second conjunct does not delete in this sentence, something must distinguish the two VPs. Moreover, something must distinguish the VP in the second conjunct of (4b) from the VP in the second conjunct of (4a). (We can think of the VP in (4a) as having an intonation that is downstressed to the extent that it is not audible.)

Chomsky (1995) proposes the following solution. A sentence derivation begins with a numeration, essentially a list of lexical items each of which is marked in some way (e.g., with an index or a number). The computational system for human language selects words from the array of lexical items in the numeration and builds up a sentence structure by merging them. If the system is to generate a coordinate structure like (4b), (4c), or (4d), the array must contain two instances of certain lexical items (the ones that will be merged to form the VPs). However, since each lexical item in the array is marked, it will never be possible for a VP to delete under identity; the two VPs may contain the same lexical items, but corresponding items in the two VPs will always have different markings. To make deletion possible, Chomsky suggests that the markings on the lexical items in the VP in the second conjunct of VP ellipsis sentences like (4a) are changed to those of the lexical items in the antecedent VP. The entire structure of such sentences is sent to LF, where it is subject to parallelism, and to PF, where the VP in the second conjunct deletes under identity.

Now, how are coordinate structures like (4b) generated? Chomsky suggests that the markings on the lexical items of the second conjunct of sentences like (4b) are erased. This makes these lexical items nondistinct from (though not identical to) those in the VP in the first conjunct. Nondistinctness suffices to ensure that the lexical items in the two VPs do not conflict; nonidentity ensures that the second conjunct does not delete as in (4a). The markings on the words in the second VP in sentences like (4b) must be erased before Spell-Out, because the nondistinctness of these VPs has consequences at both LF and PF. At LF, the fact that the second VP

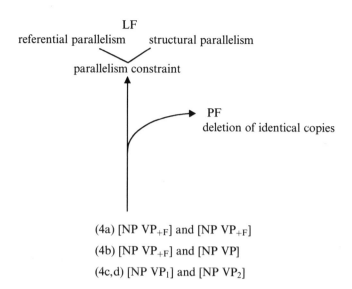

(4a) [NP VP$_{+F}$] and [NP VP$_{+F}$]

(4b) [NP VP$_{+F}$] and [NP VP]

(4c,d) [NP VP$_1$] and [NP VP$_2$]

Figure 5.1
The PF deletion model of VP ellipsis

lacks markings makes it subject to the parallelism constraint; at PF, the removal of features is interpreted as an instruction to "assign down-stressed intonation" to the second VP. The proposal is illustrated in figure 5.1.

Although not all languages have VP ellipsis constructions of the kind found in English, presumably the ellipsis process appeals to mechanisms of Universal Grammar (to be identified by the child). These mechanisms must be in place for all language learners, whether their particular language makes use of them or not. In short, it is reasonable to assume that the computation involved in VP ellipsis is innately specified—in other words, that children have the grammatical wherewithal to generate coordinate structures, identify VPs as copies or nondistinct copies, delete identical copies, and so on. Moreover, children know, as a consequence of their innate grammatical knowledge, that coordinate structures with the markings shown in (4a) and (4b) are subject to parallelism at LF. The difficulty in interpreting pronouns does not arise in the computational system.

Where, then, does the difficulty arise? We propose that the difficulty experienced by some children lies in identifying the output of the parallelism constraint. In particular, children have trouble identifying the output of what we have termed referential parallelism. As noted earlier, the parallelism constraint applies at LF and rules out certain interpretations of sentences like (4a) and (4b), repeated here in (5a) and (5b). We will compare these with (4d), repeated in (5c).

(5) a. Superman polished his shoes and Perry did too.
    b. Superman polished his shoes ánd Perry polished his shoes too.
    c. Superman polished HIS shoes and Perry polished HIS shoes too.

Without context, sentences (5a) and (5b) are ambiguous between a bound variable reading, a strict coreference reading, and a strict deictic reading. For (5a–b), the interpretations that are banned by the parallelism constraint are the interpretations that arise when the pronoun in both conjuncts is stressed. Assuming that pronominal stress forces a pronoun to be referential, the possible readings of (5c) that are not possible for (5a–b) are (a) a coreference reading on which Superman polished his own shoes and Perry polished his own shoes and (b) a reading on which Superman polished a third person's shoes and Perry polished a fourth person's.

Identifying which interpretations of (5a) and (5b) are eliminated as the result of the parallelism constraint draws on pragmatic knowledge, focus, and the associated problem of interpreting contrastive stress. As we have observed, however, this is precisely what children are in the process of figuring out. They often seem to fail to identify a speaker's intended interpretation as signaled to the hearer by use of pronominal stress. Some amount of real-world experience is required to determine which interpretations are excluded for VP ellipsis and coordinate structures with downstressing, but possible for coordinate structures with stress-bearing pronouns. More concretely, experience is required to distinguish the interpretations that are allowed for sentence type (5c), but excluded for sentence types (5a) and (5b).

Recall that one of the findings of our study was that children do not make errors with structural parallelism. Structural parallelism ensures that the pronouns in both conjuncts of structures like (5a) and (5b) are both bound variables or both referential pronouns. "Mixed" readings, in which the pronoun in one conjunct is a bound variable and the pronoun in the other conjunct is a referential pronoun, are not permissible. Here is where structural parallelism differs from referential parallelism: even if the pronouns are stressed, the mixed reading ruled out by structural parallelism does not become available. This is simply due to the fact that bound variable pronouns can never bear stress. To see this, consider the downstressed coordinate structure in (6). In the absence of context, (6a) is ambiguous between a bound variable reading, a strict coreference reading, and a strict deictic reading,

(6) a. The Incredible Hulk didn't brush his hair and no rock star brushed his hair.

b. *The Incredible Hulk$_i$ didn't brush HIS$_j$ hair and no rock star$_k$ brushed HIS$_k$ hair.

Structural parallelism rules out the interpretation in (6b) in which the Incredible Hulk doesn't brush someone else's hair and no rock star brushes his own hair.[1] But notice that even under stress, this reading should not be possible, because it is not generally possible to stress a pronoun that is a bound variable. Hence, children have no difficulty reconciling the output of the parallelism constraint with the range of interpretations that are possible in the adult grammar.

The interpretation that emerges from our experimental findings, then, is not that children "override" or "don't obey" the parallelism constraint. The apparent violations of parallelism come about because some children have difficulty *identifying* the interpretations that are excluded by referential parallelism because their pragmatic knowledge is incomplete. Until this knowledge is in place, children will have difficulty grasping that certain interpretations only become available with pronominal stress. When children learn from experience what constitutes an atypical or surprise context, a "role reversal" context, a "deictic" context and so on, they will easily learn from positive evidence that stress tends to be associated with these contexts. The main conclusion is that children's lack of knowledge in interpreting pronouns lies outside the syntax. Thus, the experimental findings provide no reason to suppose that children violate linguistic principles given by Universal Grammar; the findings are in fact consistent with the basic tenets of the theory of Universal Grammar, including its assumptions about innateness. By contrast, there are aspects of language that are mastered on the basis of experience and take time to acquire. When confronted with nonadult responses in studies of child language, it pays to ask whether the data could derive from these sources. We have argued for the viability of such an account in this book.

Much more needs to be done to confirm and extend this account. For example, the PF deletion model of VP ellipsis predicts, and in fact rests on, the premise that coordinate structures with downstressing and VP ellipsis structures allow the same range of interpretations. This has not been tested empirically, however. A natural extension of the present study would be to investigate both kinds of structures in children's grammars and to see how they interact with pronominal stress.

This book is, in one sense, the culmination of a long line of experimental and theoretical research on the status of the binding principles in child grammar. The original hypothesis of Wexler and Chien (1985)—that children have full competence in the representational/computational aspects of binding but have pragmatic/referential difficulties—seems to be upheld as more evidence is amassed from different languages and across different sentence types. We recognize that this book does not provide all the answers, and we confidently expect that future research will bring new challenges to what has been an exciting scientific adventure.

Notes

Chapter 1

1. Even if this kind of information were available to children, whether they would make use of it remains unclear. In this regard, we should distinguish input from intake. Anecdotal evidence suggests that even when parents attempt to correct children's ungrammatical speech, children may have difficulty identifying the intent of the input (see, e.g., Pinker 1989).

2. Many people find the intuition less clear for *every bear*, but technically the two examples are identical.

Chapter 2

1. The truth value judgment task is discussed in detail in chapter 4.

2. To our knowledge, only two studies have reported a lower error rate for (1): Kaufman 1988 and McKee 1988.

McKee (1988) studied Italian children's acquisition of Principle B using target sentences with clitic pronouns. Avrutin and Wexler (1992) argue that Italian clitic pronouns require a discourse antecedent; in other words, they must be coindexed. If the local subject is the antecedent, then Principle B is violated. Thus, another NP must be taken to be the antecedent, and McKee's result that children do not misinterpret pronouns follows. Thus, Avrutin and Wexler point out that no errors would be expected for clitic pronouns.

Kaufman (1988) reports mixed results in her experiments with English-speaking children. On some types of (complex) sentences, she found the usual misinterpretations of pronouns in Principle B configurations. On other types of (simple) sentences, she found a lower error rate. Chien and Wexler (1990) argue that Kaufman's rejection rate on (some) sentences—88%—was higher than in other experiments because the discourse pragmatics were biased toward rejection.

3. This contrasts with Reinhart's (1983, 1986) version of the binding theory, where Principle B applies only to pronouns that are bound variables.

4. Wexler and Chien (1985) also argued against a maturational account of Principle B, although at about that time maturation was being suggested as a general possibility in linguistic development (Borer and Wexler 1987). The general line of argument against maturation had to do with the similarity of the structural

conditions and relationships of referential dependence underlying Principle A (which Wexler and Chien demonstrated was known to young children) and Principle B as well as with the intuition that it was problems with reference/interpretation/pragmatics, not with syntax, that caused children to respond incorrectly to (1). Of course, at the time, the predictions of their theory had not yet been tested, as Wexler and Chien pointed out.

5. Although it is not always explicitly stated, something like Principle P is fairly standardly assumed in the binding theory. For example, Chomsky and Lasnik (1993) conclude that the standard binding theory framework must include interpretive principles in addition to the binding principles. They propose the interpretive principle in (i) (their (189)).

(i) If the index of α is distinct from the index of β, then α and β are noncoreferential.

Clearly, this is Principle P, without the caveat "unless the context explicitly forces coreference." However, Chomsky and Lasnik do not consider the cases introduced by Evans (1980), Reinhart (1983, 1986), and Chien and Wexler (1990).

Notice that Chomsky and Lasnik call (i) (their version of Principle P) an "interpretive" principle. We take no stance on whether it is interpretive or pragmatic. We have tended to call Principle P pragmatic, because it seems to be influenced by pragmatic conditions. If it is an interpretive principle, then one might wonder how it is possible that children do not know it, but still have full knowledge of Universal Grammar. One possibility is that in fact the principle is not universal. There are a number of reports of pronouns that may be coreferential with local c-commanding NPs, for example, in Middle English (see, e.g., Keenan 1994). It would be useful to know whether in such cases the pronouns were clearly not coindexed with the NPs. For example, in Middle English, could a quantifier locally bind a pronoun? The view expressed here would imply that it could not, if Principle B is in fact universal, but Principle P is not.

6. There is also some debate about how individual subjects respond. Note that Chien and Wexler's (1990) model allows for inconsistent responses on some sentences, but not on others. On sentences for which children have only one grammatical interpretation, they should behave consistently. The sentences on which children might give varying responses are those the model takes to be ambiguous for them. Sentence (1) is just such a sentence, since the child, it is assumed, can allow the pronoun either to refer deictically or to refer with its antecedent in subject position, so long as it is not coindexed with it, because this would violate Principle B.

Chien and Wexler (1990) provide statistical analyses showing that many children who do not respond perfectly on (1) sometimes accept and sometimes reject it. This is pretty much the standard result, and it is what we found in the study reported here. A glance ahead at table 4.4 shows that of 19 children, responding to four trials each on sentences like (1), 5 children consistently said "Yes," allowing coreference, and 3 children consistently said "No." (We expect some children to always say "No" to (1), because they have achieved adult knowledge, so the behavior of the latter group is not surprising.) Thus, the majority of the children (11 of 19) exhibited "inconsistent" behavior, with some tendency for some subjects to consistently say "Yes" more often than a binomial model would allow, in line with standard results (e.g., Chien and Wexler 1990; see the appendix of that paper for a demonstration of how the consistency results can be precisely evaluated). However, Avrutin and Thornton (1994) found that individual children were fairly consistent in either accepting or rejecting sentences like (1) (although no comparison with the binomial model was made). This result is probably due to the different kinds of contexts used in that experiment.

7. In the last two studies, the rejection rate for pronouns with the quantificational NP was not as high as in Chien and Wexler's study. In both cases, the authors argue that this is because the quantifier corresponding to *every* has different properties in different languages. For example, Avrutin and Wexler argue that the Russian word *každyj* is ambiguous between two different representations, depending on whether it is treated as a quantifier or a definite NP. When it is treated as a definite NP, it presupposes a specific set. When it is treated as a definite NP, then when it antecedes a pronoun in the same clause, the pronoun is not a bound variable. Thus, coreference might be expected.

8. It seems to us that three or more objects must be present in order to make the use of the universal quantifier appropriate; if only two objects are present, the appropriate quantifier is *both*. In one experiment reported by Crain et al. (1996), some children prohibited *every* from referring to sets with three or fewer members. This said, we appreciate the practical difficulties of having a single experimenter demonstrate three (or more) camels washing themselves.

9. This result is sometimes claimed to be puzzling. The reason is this. In understanding the discourse in (15a), the child presumably has to reconstruct, at LF, the VP following the subject NP *Bert and Ernie*. Suppose the child filled in *scratched them* from the preceding sentence. Now, in the reconstructed sentence, the pronoun has a referential NP antecedent, and the reconstructed sentence looks exactly like (15b), which allows local coreference. We suggest that at the time the first sentence in the discourse (*I know who scratched them*) is computed on-line, it is clear that the discourse entities that are linked to the operator *who* cannot be *them*, because such a link would violate Principle B. This decision has already been made on-line by the time the VP *scratched them* is reconstructed in the second sentence. This kind of factor comes up again when we discuss why children do not allow local coreference in sentences like *He dusted the skeleton*.

10. The design of these controls is borrowed from a study by Miyamoto and Crain (1991), reported later in this chapter.

11. One might ask why children accepted the distributive context of *The Smurf and the Troll dried them* as much as 27% of the time, since this context is supposed to trigger a Principle B violation. The answer is probably that the context that was acted out was not sufficient to initiate a distributive representation of the sentence for all children. If a distributive representation of the plural NP is not generated, then children would treat it as collective, and in that case, they would be expected to accept the sentence.

12. Using the truth value judgment task to test children's interpretation of *it* involves acting out a story in which some object that is inanimate yet capable of

action (e.g., a robot) doesn't carry out some action on something else (that can be described by *it*) and ends up doing it to itself. In Savarese's story for the test sentence *The fire engine sprayed it*, for example, a fire engine attempts to spray a ferris wheel with water, but fails and ends up spraying itself. It is difficult to come up with suitable objects and associated verbs for stories such as these. In addition, it is often difficult to know, without conducting a pretest, whether children refer to objects such as robots and trucks as *it*.

13. We will ignore the question of whether or not the quantificational element *every* c-commands the pronoun in the examples we introduce (e.g., (21c)).

14. The statement of Rule I excludes coreference for examples like (22), but a restatement of the rule is given in a footnote in Grodzinsky and Reinhart (1993) to allow it, since the coreference option is needed to obtain the strict reading of similar VP ellipsis sentences like *Mama Bear is washing her face and Brother Bear is too* (on the reading on which Brother Bear is washing Mama Bear's face.)

15. In Chien and Wexler's (1990) experiment, the sentence *Mama Bear is washing her* was presented in two contexts. In one picture, Mama Bear was washing herself and Goldilocks was watching. Children judged this sentence/meaning pair correctly about 50% of the time. In the second picture, Mama Bear was washing Goldilocks. In this context, children interpreted the pronoun correctly 80% to 90% of the time. How does Grodzinsky and Reinhart's account explain why children fare badly on the first case, but not on the second? Grodzinsky and Reinhart do not address this point, but the difference can probably be explained in terms of experimental context. In the first case, the picture allows Mama Bear to be under consideration as the referent of the pronoun. In the second case, however, the picture matches the sentence, and children take the pronoun to be deictic. The picture does not raise the possibility of viewing Mama Bear as the referent for the pronoun, so, presumably, children do not need to call upon Rule I at all. In other words, the assumption is that children only consider derivations that allow a "Yes" answer. This is not always the case, however.

16. In our view, the rate at which children accept the illicit interpretation depends on the experimental context. In some contexts, it may be higher; in others, lower. Note, however, that according to Grodzinsky and Reinhart's explanation, the figure will always be around 50%, since it represents guessing on the part of the child.

17. The other examples discussed by Heim are argued to involve bound variables. These examples have led Reinhart (1997) to revise her theory in terms of binding and *covaluation*, rather than binding and *coreference*. Coreference was available only for pronouns with referential antecedents. Covaluation is not sensitive to the semantic status of the antecedent, however.

18. We use Reinhart's LF representations here to keep the formalism consistent.

19. It might be easier to get a coreference interpretation with a verb other than *wash*.

20. Heim also discusses cases with *only*, as in (i), and cases noted by Lakoff (1972), as in (ii).

(i) Everybody hates Lucifer. Only he himself pities him.

(ii) I dreamt I was Brigitte Bardot and I kissed me.

In examples like (i), Heim points out, the pronoun is really a bound variable, yet "coreference" is possible. This difficulty leads Heim to reformulate the theory. Since the revisions are not important for our discussion, however, we do not present them here.

21. This is a simplification. The experiment actually included a number of controls. For example, children's knowledge of bound variable interpretations was tested with single-sentence examples like *No mouse at Simba's party said he wore a hat*. See Conway and Crain 1995a,b and Conway 1997 for details.

22. Since it is easy to make children fail in an experiment, and much harder to design an experiment that shows them succeeding, it seems that if success can be demonstrated, this should be taken as the legitimate result.

23. In crossover structures, the *wh*-phrase moves over the pronoun, leaving a trace. The structure is well formed if the pronoun is deictic, as in (i), where it picks out a singular, male individual. The structure is not well formed if the pronoun has the same index as the *wh*-phrase and its trace, as in (ii); such a structure violates Principle C. In other words, the pronoun cannot be bound by the *wh*-phrase. If it could be, (ii) could mean that the speaker knows which individual, out of a set of people, said he has the best food. This meaning, in which the pronoun is a bound variable, is indicated by the representation in (iii).

(i)   I know who$_i$ he$_j$ said t$_i$ has the best food.

(ii)   *I know who$_i$ he$_i$ said t$_i$ has the best food.

(iii)   I know who$_i$ t$_i$ said he$_i$ has the best food.

24. See Roeper et al. 1985 and McDaniel and McKee 1993 for other experiments on strong crossover.

25. Grimshaw and Rosen do note that stress can encourage local coreference in adult grammars, however.

26. See Chien and Wexler 1990, app. 4, for a discussion of how inherent reflexivity may have affected the results reported in Kaufman 1988.

27. Grimshaw and Rosen did not use bound variables in any of their materials, so nothing can be said about children's responses to sentences like *Every bear is washing her* in their experiment.

28. This effect has been found in structures like *Who thinks he is the best candidate?* (Roeper et al. 1985; Thornton 1990). For reasons that are not fully understood, some children show a strong preference for the deictic interpretation of the pronoun.

29. See Avrutin et al. 1992, Crain et al. 1996, and Miyamoto 1992 for more studies related to children's knowledge of distributivity.

30. According to Grimshaw and Rosen, children's level of adherence to Principle B depends on the experimental factors intertwined with the particular experiment. Performance is expected to vary across experiments.

31. Recall that although group 2 children are defined as those who allow only collective interpretations, this definition comes from their performance on the ambiguous controls. It is quite possible that when the distributive interpretation is presented in the appropriate context, it becomes accessible to them.

32. A point of clarification. Section 2.2.2 reports 4 children as being unable to access the distributive interpretation on the control sentences. These 4 children failed the ambiguous control test and also failed to access the distributive reading even on the test sentences whose contexts facilitated it.

33. The idea is that binding domains differ crosslinguistically. Children begin by choosing the narrowest binding domain; positive evidence from their language causes them to expand it if necessary. This scenario is advanced so that children can converge on the adult grammar in the absence of negative evidence.

34. The proposed acquisition scenario is slightly simplified here, but this does not take away from the basic point.

35. In Heim's terms, deictic pronouns are "novel definite" NPs. They are novel in the sense that they do not have an antecedent in the previous discourse, yet they presuppose familiarity with the referent (perhaps because the referent is present, as in the case described in the text surrounding (75)). However, unlike novel definite NPs that create a new file card (that is bridged to another card), technically, deictic pronouns do not create a new card; they update a card that was created at the point when the referent became salient. Notice that *deictic* is used differently here than elsewhere in the book, where it indicates referential pronouns that do not have an antecedent in the same sentence.

36. This is not very different from saying that a deictic pronoun updates an existing file card, if the card is one that is newly created to describe a salient object. The key difference for Avrutin is that if accommodation is the mechanism by which deictic pronouns are introduced, then bridging is necessary—and making the inferences necessary for bridging is what gives rise to children's difficulty in interpreting pronouns, in his view.

37. A story that conforms to the truth value judgment task described by Crain and Thornton (1998) would be slightly different. Goldilocks would request that Mama Bear wash her. Mama Bear would fail to comply with the request and wash herself instead. This is probably what Avrutin intended. If so, the fact that Mama Bear does not wash Goldilocks needs to be encoded on the file cards, as shown in parentheses in (82).

Chapter 3

1. Another possibility is that innate pragmatic principles mature. See Chierchia et al. 1998 for a study that attempts to tease apart the contributions of the grammar and pragmatics.

2. With stress, (10) also has the meaning that Mama Bear is washing some other female character, one particular member out of a set of females.

3. The event takes this form in order to fulfill the felicity conditions associated with both affirming and denying the test sentence. This is discussed in chapter 4.

4. In narrating the story, the experimenter is careful not to use any reflexive pronouns.

5. In this case, the subordinate clause isn't presupposed to be true, so the target sentence needn't follow the discourse. A different experimental technique is needed for studying these clauses than for studying temporal clauses. The characters are introduced, and the puppet makes a prediction, which is the conditional sentence. A story is then acted out for the child, and the child determines whether or not the prediction was fulfilled. See Conway and Crain 1995a,b for details of the methodology.

6. As we have pointed out, it is not the case that the apparent Principle B violations are always expected to appear 50% of the time. The exact proportion of misinterpretations will depend on the experimental situation and the structure being tested.

7. Whether a sloppy reading entails binding or not is a matter of debate. For Reinhart (1983), it does; for the sloppy reading to obtain, the pronoun must be c-commanded by its antecedent. Fiengo and May (1994) disagree, pointing to the existence of examples like (i), in which the pronoun is not c-commanded by *Max*, yet the sloppy interpretation (in which Max's mother loves Max, and Oscar's mother loves Oscar) is readily available.

(i) Max's mother loves him and Oscar's mother does too.

We will follow Reinhart and others and reserve the term *sloppy* for cases in which the pronoun is a bound variable; for cases in which coreference is relevant, we will use the term *look-sloppy*.

8. This statement of the generalization is buried in chapter 4 of Fiengo and May's book and is probably not meant to be taken as a complete formal statement. We take the liberty of using it as an illustration of how such a rule or constraint might be formulated.

9. Fox is concerned with Dahl's puzzle—that is, the interpretations possible for sentences like *John said he likes his dog and Bill did too*, where each clause contains two pronouns.

10. In our study, we tested the two clauses in reverse order; that is, the test sentence was (i).

(i) Superman combed his hair and every reporter did too.

It may have been better to reverse the clauses, so that the first clause clearly contained a bound variable.

11. Hestvik (1995) cites Hans Kamp as not sharing this view.

Although Principle B seems to constrain representations in the expected way in VP ellipsis structures, its effect is reportedly weaker in VP *anaphora* structures (Fiengo and May 1994, 107ff.). In VP ellipsis sentences, the VP in the second conjunct is replaced by *did too*; in VP anaphora sentences, it is replaced by *did so too*, or *did it too*, in the case of action verbs. Fiengo and May compare *Mary pampers him, and he does so, too*, with *Mary pampers him, and he does, too*. In their judgment, the former example with VP anaphora more easily allows the overt pronouns to corefer. This follows from the fact that only the VP ellipsis example involves reconstruction of the elided VP. Hence, only the VP ellipsis example will violate Principle B (see Fiengo and May 1994, 110). Our experiment did not attempt to investigate whether children are more likely to accept coreference in VP anaphora structures than in VP ellipsis structures.

12. We say "looks" sloppy here, because in some theories, such as Reinhart's (1983, 1986), sloppy readings are possible only with pronouns that are bound variables. This assumption is not shared by Fiengo and May. Their theory admits sloppy readings with referential pronouns.

13. Fiengo and May (1994, 160) note that if the pronoun in the right-hand clause is stressed, strict and sloppy readings of (i) are possible.

(i) Max said he loves his mother, and Oscar said he does, too.

In their view, stress overrides the condition requiring the structure of both clauses to be parallel, to allow the sloppy reading.

   Also, note that the grammaticality of apparent Principle C violations isn't simply a property of VP ellipsis sentences. We also judge (ii) and (iii) acceptable, in which the second conjunct is an overt coordinate structure. That is, (ii) and (iii) are acceptable even when Superman brushed Superman.

(ii) Perry brushed Superman and HE brushed Superman too.

(iii) Perry brushed Superman and SUPERMAN brushed Superman too.

Chapter 4

1. See McDaniel and Cairns 1996 and Rice, Wexler, and Redmond in press for the use of grammaticality judgment tasks with children.

2. A verb other than *point to* might be preferable, so that a plausible story could be constructed, giving a reason for why Cinderella's sister *might* help Cinderella and why she carries out the relevant action on herself instead. See the discussion of plausible dissent in section 4.2.2.

3. Here, we ignore the possibility of a local coreference interpretation for a matrix sentence like *He dusted Superman.*

4. Control sentences are included for any experiment. If the target sentences are designed to elicit a "No" response, the controls may be designed to elicit a "Yes" response; in this way, "Yes" and "No" responses are balanced, and a response bias is avoided. Since there is always the possibility that a child will not respond as anticipated, several "filler" stories can also be included. The sentence that accompanies these stories is irrelevant to the goals of the experiment. It can be manipulated by the experimenter to elicit either a "Yes" or a "No" response, so that the child's "Yes" and "No" responses can be balanced out.

5. In Chien and Wexler's (1990) experiment, the mismatch picture corresponded to the specific reading. That is, for the test sentence *Every bear is washing her*, the mismatch picture showed no bear washing her (Goldilocks), and each bear washing herself. Nevertheless, the 5-year-old group rejected the sentence 84% of the time. If the picture had also shown one or two of the bears washing Goldilocks,

perhaps the percentage of rejections would have been higher. this wasn't done because of the complexity of the pictorial representation. (The current study shows a 92% rejection on this type of sentence when it is falsified according to the general reading of negation.)

6. This concern for equalizing discourse factors for different types of sentences goes back to the beginning of experimental work on the binding theory with children. Wexler and Chien (1985) and Chien and Wexler (1990) carried out the kind of procedure used here in order to equalize discourse factors (see the works cited for explicit discussion). Failure to equalize discourse factors is another potential artifact suggested by Grimshaw and Rosen (1990).

7. For this particular sentence type, unlike Chien and Wexler (1990), we did not include conditions in which "Yes" would be correct (e.g., in which every reindeer brushed Bert). This is because it had previously been established that children accept this interpretation (see, e.g., Chien and Wexler 1990). Other sentences in our test battery (e.g., ones like (8)) were designed to elicit "Yes" responses.

8. For children who allow local coreference interpretations, the pronoun could in principle also refer to Superman. However, since the story did not make a meaning in which Superman likes himself available, children should not have considered this interpretation.

9. For this structure, it was not possible to have the characters perform a reflexive-like action, as in the stories that tested *Every reindeer brushed him*. This is because the bound variable interpretation rested on the verb *say*, which is a non-action verb.

10. Notice that in this story, the context corresponding to meaning$_1$ comes first, and the context corresponding to meaning$_2$ comes last. The bound variable reading corresponds to meaning$_1$. Presumably, children's acceptance of this meaning could have been boosted by switching the order of events in the story.

11. In retrospect, it would have been better to reverse the two conjuncts of these items so that the quantifier appeared in the first clause of the VP ellipsis structure. Then, the overt pronoun would have to be interpreted as a bound variable.

12. Notice that in this case, the actual outcome is falsified by negating the second conjunct of the VP ellipsis structure. Ideally, since the second conjunct contains the quantifier *every*, the story should have instantiated the negation of the more general reading. That is, it would have been better to have one or two Trolls agree to brush the rock star's hair, and then have them all brush their own. Instead, the story instantiated the negation of the more specific reading. None of the Trolls brushed the rock star's hair. This did not appear to affect the results, however.

13. The ages given are the children's ages at the beginning of the experiment. On average, it took about 4 months to complete the experiment with each child.

14. This was necessary for only two of the children, EX (age 4;10) and BT (age 4;0).

15. The remaining 3 children left the school before they could be tested.

16. Recent versions of the task avoid this problem by having the puppet say, "I know one thing that happened in that story," followed by the test sentence.

17. Other experiments have also found that children sometimes prefer a deictic interpretation of a pronoun over a bound variable one (e.g., Crain and Thornton 1998; Roeper et al. 1985; Thornton 1990). To take an example, in a truth value judgment experiment carried out with 10 children, Crain and Thornton tested the availability of the bound variable interpretation of sentences like *Who thinks he has the best smile?* They also found that children accepted the bound variable interpretation exactly 50% of the time, when this was set up as the "Yes" response. Half of the children overrode any tendency to say "Yes" in order to accept the referential interpretation (which was the "No" response). This is exactly the same percentage as in the present experiment. It is interesting to note that the preference for a referential interpretation of the pronoun seems to be specific to particular structures. When the same children who had a preference for the referential interpretation of the pronoun in *Who thinks he has the best smile?* were tested on structures like *Snoopy said he has the best hat and Donald Duck did too*, many of them chose the sloppy bound variable interpretation. We do not take children's apparent preference for a deictic response to indicate that the bound variable interpretation is unavailable, as Grimshaw and Rosen (1990) have suggested. We believe the literature reviewed in chapter 2 amply proves that children can access these interpretations. The crucial point is that children will not say "Yes" to an ungrammatical interpretation. Sometimes they will say "No" to a grammatical interpretation if another grammatical interpretation is available.

Using an experiment that to our knowledge has not yet been carried out, one could get much closer to testing whether and to what extent children have preferences for constructing referential rather than bound variable interpretations (where the idea that bound variable interpretations are difficult to access is supposed to mean that the construction of *pairs* of interpretations is difficult). This experiment would involve testing an additional sentence. Suppose, for example, that we compared children's responses to *Every Cabbage Patch boy said Superman likes his coat* and *The Cabbage Patch boy said Superman likes his coat*. If Grimshaw and Rosen (1990) are correct, children should have more difficulty accessing the bound variable interpretation in the first sentence, which involves a quantificational NP antecedent, than in the second, which involves a referential NP antecedent. Consequently, their response patterns for the two sentences should be quite different.

18. Actually, since we believe that 3 children had adult knowledge, we should eliminate these children from the data and recalculate the probability of saying "Yes." This results in a probability of .69 that children whose pragmatic knowledge is incomplete will say "Yes." In this case, the probability that children will give three or four "Yes" responses is as follows: $\Pr(3 \text{ or } 4 \text{ yes}) = \Pr(4 \text{ yes}) + \Pr(3 \text{ yes}) = .69^4 + 4 \times .31 \times .69^3 = .23 + .41 = .64$. So we expect $16 \times .64 = 10.24$ subjects to say "Yes" on three or four trials.

19. See Crain and Wexler 1999 and Crain and Thornton 1998 for details on how the grammar and the performance system interact in ambiguous sentences.

Again, it is essential to be clear on the difference between an observed response pattern (say, that some children say "Yes" four out of four times in this experiment) and the statistical inference that we make about the population. We have inferred that there are no children who would always say "Yes" if given enough trials. The children who say "Yes" four times have to be seen as observing this pattern because with an underlying probability of saying "Yes" of .69, we expect a number of children to say "Yes" four times. To show that there really are children who always say "Yes" (in principle), one would have to observe a higher ratio of such children than is expected by chance. This is standard statistical inference, sometimes not observed in the study of language acquisition, but nevertheless correct.

20. As mentioned earlier, since referential pronouns have an additional requirement on them, it would have been better to reverse the clauses of this sentence type, so that the quantificational NP was in the first clause. In this case, both pronouns would have had to be bound variables.

21. For sentence (49), a 21% error rate was attributed to a flaw in the experimental design. However, there do not appear to be any problems with the design of (51). Although some of the errors may be due to true error, it turns out that, in the main, these nonadult acceptances correlate with nonadult acceptances of other sentences. This correlation suggests that the errors are due to a lack of some kind of pragmatic knowledge.

22. Boster (1994) suggests that children's misinterpretations of the sentence are due to a lexical error. These children have miscategorized the pronoun as a reflexive. In addition to the pronoun *him*, they have another lexical entry, *him∅*, that is categorized as a reflexive form. The errors disappear once they rid their grammars of this form. How do they do this? Boster makes the interesting observation that the children who accepted the sloppy readings of sentences like (62) in her experiment were children who had not yet settled on the adult form of the reflexive. These children tended to say *hisself* in their productions, not *himself*. Boster suggests that once *himself* is entered in the lexicon, the tentative lexical entries *hisself* and *him∅* are eliminated. It is not clear that this correlation between reflexive form and allowance of local coreference interpretations holds in all experiments, however. Moreover, if *him∅* exists, the children should accept a pronoun locally bound by a quantifier, but this has not been found to happen in experiments testing English-speaking children.

Koster's (1993, 1994) experiments were based on an act-out task with 43 children ranging from 4 to 8 years of age. Some groups of children enacted a large number of nonadult interpretations of sentences like (62). The 4-year-olds enacted the nonadult interpretation 53% of the time, the 6-year-olds 18% of the time, and the 8-year-olds 40% of the time. It is likely that the higher rate of nonadult interpretations in the act-out task is due to the lack of a clear presentation of possible alternatives, which existed in our truth value judgment task. At any rate, these additional results support our hypothesis that the error is in the pragmatic domain, a difficulty with referential parallelism.

23. This child (JZ) responded like an adult in the present study, as the individual subject data attest. Although JZ's response "and he cleaned him too" might look like a violation of Principle B, we would argue that it is not. Recall that in circumstances where children have been observed to accept a pronoun (e.g., *Bert brushed him*), often a reflexive should have been used instead. However, in JZ's

comment, a reflexive would have induced a sloppy interpretation of the sentence. In the circumstances, then, it seems there is little choice but to use a pronoun, as JZ did. Notice that JZ is exhibiting adultlike behavior by explicit deictic (pointing) reference to Flash Gordon. Clearly, this child is using guises appropriately. The less sophisticated child has the same linguistic behavior but fails to provide the contextual support, that is, pointing, for the deictic guise.

24. Grodzinsky and Reinhart (1993) do not make any explicit predictions about children's behavior on VP ellipsis sentences. However, presumably Rule I applies in both the matrix sentence and sentences like (72).

25. The story contexts controlling for children's acceptance of local coreference were simpler than those used in the main study because they did not also have to incorporate a test of the quantifier *every*. Consequently, it was sufficient to have only two characters instead of four in the stories, one for the subject NP and one for the object NP. In the story leading up to the test sentence *Gumby brushed him*, for example, Gumby takes Gonzo for a ride on his horse. The horse jumps over a big fence and they both fall off into a big haystack. Gonzo stands up indignantly and asks Gumby to brush hay off him. Gumby would like to help, but he decides he can't because he has to brush a lot of hay off himself.

26. It would have been ideal to compare the same children's performance on the two experiments, but this was not possible because too much time had elapsed between the two experiments.

27. In these stories, the friend is always female, in order to avoid a confound for children with nonadult pragmatic knowledge. If the friend had not been female, these children could have taken the pronoun to refer to the friend instead of Kermit.

The design for the stories is as follows:

(i) Sentence: Kermit's friend wiped him and Big Bird did too
   Characters: Kermit, Kermit's friend (Miss Piggy), Big Bird
   *Meaning$_1$, true: Miss Piggy wiped Kermit and Big Bird wiped himself
   Meaning$_2$, false: Miss Piggy wiped Kermit and Big Bird also wiped Kermit

(ii) Background: Kermit's friend wiped *so-and-so* and Big Bird wiped *so-and-so* too
   Assertion: Kermit's friend wiped Kermit and Big Bird wiped Kermit too
   Possible outcome: Kermit's friend (Miss Piggy) and Big Bird wiped Kermit
   Actual outcome: Only Miss Piggy wiped Kermit (Big Bird wiped himself)

Chapter 5

1. The intuition may not be so clear when the quantifier is *every* instead of *no*, as in *The Incredible Hulk brushed HIS hair and every Troll brushed HIS hair too*. These judgments seem to vary across speakers.

References

Akmajian, A., and Jackendoff, R. (1970). Coreferentiality and stress. *Linguistic Inquiry, 1,* 124–126.

Avrutin, S. (1994). *Psycholinguistic investigations in the theory of reference.* Unpublished doctoral dissertation, MIT, Cambridge, MA.

Avrutin, S., and Babyonyshev, M. (1997). Obviation in subjunctive clauses and AGR: Evidence from Russian. *Natural Language & Linguistic Theory, 15,* 229–262.

Avrutin, S., Crain, S., Miyamoto, Y., and Wexler, K. (1992). *Who knows everything about what everyone knows? (A study of quantification in child grammar).* Paper presented at the Workshop on the Acquisition of WH, University of Massachusetts, Amherst.

Avrutin, S., and Thornton, R. (1994). Distributivity and binding in child grammar. *Linguistic Inquiry, 25,* 265–271.

Avrutin, S., and Wexler, K. (1992). Development of Principle B in Russian: Coindexation at LF and coreference. *Language Acquisition, 2,* 259–306.

Avrutin, S., and Wexler, K. (1999). Children's knowledge of subjunctive clauses: Obviation, binding and reference. *Language Acquisition, 8.*

Borer, H., and Wexler, K. (1987). The maturation of syntax. In T. Roeper and E. Williams (Eds.), *Parameter setting.* Dordrecht: D. Reidel.

Borer, H., and Wexler, K. (1992). Bi-unique relations and the maturation of grammatical principles. *Natural Language & Linguistic Theory, 10,* 147–190.

Boster, C. T. (1994). Children's failure to obey Principle B: Syntactic problem or lexical error? In J. Abe, L. Ferro, L. Laporte-Grimes, D. Takahashi, and M. Yamashina (Eds.), *UConn working papers in linguistics 4.* Storrs: University of Connecticut, Department of Linguistics.

Cardinaletti, A., and Starke, M. (1995). The tripartition of pronouns and its acquisition: Principle B puzzles are ambiguity problems. In J. Beckman (Ed.), *NELS 25.* Amherst: University of Massachusetts, GLSA.

Cardinaletti, A., and Starke, M. (in press). The typology of structural deficiency: On the three grammatical classes. In H. van Riemsdijk (Ed.), *Language typology: Vol. 8. Clitics in the languages of Europe.* Berlin: Mouton.

Chien, Y.-C., and Wexler, K. (1990). Children's knowledge of locality conditions in binding as evidence for the modularity of syntax and pragmatics. *Language Acquisition, 1,* 225–295.

Chien, Y.-C., and Wexler, K. (1991). Children's knowledge of pronouns as bound variables in a long-distance context. *Papers and Reports on Child Language Development, 30,* 25–38.

Chien, Y.-C., Wexler, K., and Chang, H.-W. (1993). Children's development of long-distance binding in Chinese. *Journal of East Asian Linguistics, 2,* 229–259.

Chierchia, G. (1995). *Dynamics of meaning: Anaphora, presupposition and syntactic theory.* Chicago: University of Chicago Press.

Chierchia, G., Crain, S., Guasti, M. T., and Thornton, R. (1998). "Some" and "or": A study on the emergence of logical form. In A. Greenhill, M. Hughes, H. Little-field, and H. Walsh (Eds.)., *Proceedings of the 22nd Annual Boston University Conference on Language Development.* Somerville, MA: Cascadilla Press.

Chierchia, G., and McConnell-Ginet, S. (1990). *Meaning and grammar.* Cambridge, MA: MIT Press.

Chomsky, C. (1969). *The acquisition of syntax in children from 5 to 10.* Cambridge, MA: MIT Press.

Chomsky, N. (1981). *Lectures on government and binding.* Dordrecht: Foris.

Chomsky, N. (1986). *Knowledge of language: Its nature, origin, and use.* New York: Praeger.

Chomsky, N. (1993). A minimalist program for linguistic theory. In K. Hale and S. J. Keyser (Eds.), *The view from Building 20: Essays in linguistics in honor of Sylvain Bromberger.* Cambridge, MA: MIT Press.

Chomsky, N. (1995). Categories and transformations. In *The Minimalist Program.* Cambridge, MA: MIT Press.

Chomsky, N., and Lasnik, H. (1993). The theory of principles and parameters. In J. Jacobs, A. von Stechow, W. Sternefeld, and T. Vennemann (Eds.), *Syntax: An international handbook of contemporary research* (Vol. 1). Berlin: Walter de Gruyter.

Chomsky, N., and Miller, G. (1963). Introduction to the formal analysis of natural languages. In R. D. Luce, R. Bush, and E. Galanter (Eds.), *Handbook of mathematical psychology* (Vol. 2). New York: Wiley.

Conway, L. (1997). *Excavating semantics.* Unpublished doctoral dissertation, University of Connecticut, Storrs.

Conway, L., and Crain, S. (1995a). Donkey anaphora in child grammar. In J. Beckman (Ed.), *NELS 25.* Amherst: University of Massachusetts, GLSA.

Conway, L., and Crain, S. (1995b). Dynamic acquisition. In D. MacLaughlin and S. McEwen (Eds.), *Proceedings of the 19th Annual Boston University Conference on Language Development.* Somerville, MA: Cascadilla Press.

Crain, S. (1991). Language acquisition in the absence of experience. *Behavioral and Brain Sciences, 14,* 597–650.

Crain, S., and McKee, C. (1985). The acquisition of structural restrictions on anaphora. In S. Berman, J.-W, Choe, and J. McDonough (Eds.), *NELS 16*. Amherst: University of Massachusetts, GLSA.

Crain, S., and Steedman, M. (1985). On not being led up the garden path: The use of context by the psychological parser. In D. R. Dowty, L. Karttunen, and A. Zwicky (Eds.), *Natural language parsing: Psychological, computational, and theoretical perspectives*. Cambridge: Cambridge University Press.

Crain, S., and Thornton, R. (1998). *Investigations in Universal Grammar: A guide to experiments on the acquisition of syntax and semantics*. Cambridge, MA: MIT Press.

Crain, S., Thornton, R., Boster, C., Conway, L., Lillo-Martin, D., and Woodams, E. (1996). Quantification without qualification. *Language Acquisition, 5,* 83–153.

Crain, S., and Wexler, K. (1999). Methodology in the study of language acquisition: A modular approach. In W. Ritchie and T. Bhatia (Eds.), *Handbook of child language acquisition*. San Diego, Calif.: Academic Press.

Cutler, A., and Fodor, J. A. (1979). Semantic focus and sentence comprehension. *Cognition, 7,* 49–59.

Cutler, A., and Foss, D. (1977). On the role of sentence stress in sentence processing. *Language and Speech, 20,* 1–10.

Cutler, A., and Swinney, D. (1987). Prosody and the development of comprehension. *Journal of Child Language, 14,* 145–167.

Deutsch, W., Koster, C., and Koster, J. (1986). Children's errors in understanding anaphora. *Linguistics, 24,* 203–225.

Evans, G. (1980). Pronouns. *Linguistic Inquiry, 11,* 337–362.

Fiengo, R., and May, R. (1994). *Indices and identity*. Cambridge, MA: MIT Press.

Fodor, J. (1983). *Modularity of mind*. Cambridge, MA: MIT Press.

Fodor, J., Bever, T., and Garrett, M. (1974). *The psychology of language*. New York: McGraw-Hill.

Fox, D. (1998). Locality in variable binding. In P. Barbosa, D. Fox, P. Hagstrom, M. McGinnis, and D. Pesetsky (Eds.), *Is the best good enough? Optimality and competition in syntax*. Cambridge, MA: MIT Press/MITWPL.

Gibson, E., and Wexler, K. (1994). Triggers. *Linguistic Inquiry, 25,* 407–454.

Gordon, P. (1996). The truth-value judgment task. In D. McDaniel, C. McKee, and H. S. Cairns (Eds.), *Methods for assessing children's syntax*. Cambridge, MA: MIT Press.

Grice, H. P. (1975). Logic and conversation. In P. Cole and J. Morgan (Eds.), *Syntax and semantics 3: Speech acts*. New York: Academic Press.

Grimshaw, J., and Rosen, S. T. (1990). Knowledge and obedience: The developmental status of the binding theory. *Linguistic Inquiry, 21,* 187–222.

Grodzinsky, Y., and Kave, G. (1993). Do children really know Condition A? *Language Acquisition, 3,* 41–54.

Grodzinsky, Y., and Reinhart, T. (1993). The innateness of binding and the development of coreference: A reply to Grimshaw and Rosen. *Linguistic Inquiry, 24,* 69–103.

Guasti, M. T., and Chierchia, G. (in press). Reconstruction in child grammar. *Language Acquisition.*

Halbert, A. (1997). *Children's use of prosodic cueing in ambiguity resolution.* Unpublished master's thesis, University of Connecticut, Storrs.

Halbert, A., Crain, S., Shankweiler, D., and Woodams, E. (1995). *Children's interpretive use of emphatic stress.* Paper presented at the Eighth Annual CUNY Conference on Human Sentence Processing, Tucson, Az.

Hamann, C., Kowalski, O., and Philip, W. (1997). The French "delay of Principle B" effect. In E. Hughes, M. Hughes, and A. Greenhill (Eds.), *Proceedings of the 21st Annual Boston University Conference on Language Development.* Somerville, MA: Cascadilla Press.

Hamburger, H., and Crain, S. (1984). Acquisition of cognitive compiling. *Cognition, 17,* 85–136.

Hankamer, J., and Sag, I. (1976). Deep and surface anaphora. *Linguistic Inquiry, 7,* 391–426.

Hawkins, J. (1978). *Definiteness and indefiniteness.* London: Croom Helm.

Heim, I. (1982). *The semantics of definite and indefinite NPs.* Unpublished doctoral dissertation, University of Massachusetts, Amherst.

Heim, I. (1998). Anaphora and semantic interpretation: A reinterpretation of Reinhart's approach. In U. Sauerland and O. Percus (Eds.), *The interpretive tract* (MIT Working Papers in Linguistics 25). Cambridge, MA: MIT, Department of Linguistics and Philosophy. [Originally appeared as SfS-Report-07-93. Tübingen: University of Tübingen, Seminar für Sprach wissenschaft (1993).]

Heim, I., Lasnik, H., and May, R. (1991). Reciprocity and plurality. *Linguistic Inquiry, 22,* 63–102.

Hestvik, A. (1995). Reflexives and ellipsis. *Natural Language Semantics, 3,* 211–237.

Higginbotham, J. (1980). Anaphora and GB: Some preliminary remarks. In J. Jensen (Ed.), *NELS IO.* Amherst: University of Massachusetts, GLSA.

Higginbotham, J. (1983). Logical Form, binding, and nominals. *Linguistic Inquiry, 14,* 395–420.

Hirsh-Pasek, K., Golinkoff, R. M., Hermon, G., and Kaufman, D. (1994). Evidence from comprehension for early knowledge of pronouns. In E. Clark (Ed.), *The Proceedings of the 26th Annual Child Language Research Forum.* Stanford, CA: CSLI. [Distributed by Cambridge University Press.]

Hirsh-Pasek, K., Treiman, R., and Schneiderman, M. (1984). Brown and Hanlon revisited: Mothers' sensitivity to ungrammatical forms. *Journal of Child Language, 11,* 81–88.

Hornby, P. A., and Hass, W. A. (1970). Use of contrastive stress by preschool children. *Journal of Speech and Hearing Research, 13,* 387–394.

Hornstein, N. (1995). *Logical Form: From GB to minimalism.* Oxford: Blackwell.

Hyams, N. (1986). *Language acquisition and the theory of parameters.* Dordrecht: D. Reidel.

Hyams, N., and Wexler, K. (1993). On the grammatical basis of null subjects in child language. *Linguistic Inquiry, 24,* 421–459.

Ingram, D., and Shaw, C. (1981). *The comprehension of pronominal reference in children.* Unpublished manuscript, University of British Columbia, Vancouver.

Jakubowicz, C. (1984). On markedness and binding principles. In C. Jones and P. Sells (Eds.), *NELS 14.* Amherst: University of Massachusetts, GLSA.

Jakubowicz, C. (1991). L'acquisition des anaphores et des pronoms lexicaux en français. In J. Guéron and J.-Y. Pollock (Eds.), *Grammaire générative et syntaxe comparée.* Paris: Editions du CNRS.

Jakubowicz, C., Müller, N., Kang, O.-K., Riemer, B., and Rigaut, C. (1996). On the acquisition of pronominal reference in French and German. In A. Stringfellow, D. Cahana-Amitay, E. Hughes, and A. Zukowski (Eds.), *Proceedings of the 20th Annual Boston University Conference on Language Development.* Somerville, MA: Cascadilla Press.

Kail, M., and Hickmann, M. (1992). French children's ability to introduce referents in narratives as a function of mutual knowledge. *First Language, 12,* 73–94.

Kamp, H. (1981). A theory of truth and semantic representation. In J. Groenendijk, T. Janssen, and M. Stokhof (Eds.), *Truth, interpretation and information.* Dordrecht: Foris.

Karmiloff-Smith, A. (1981). The grammatical marking of thematic structure in the development of language production. In W. Deutsch (Ed.), *The child's construction of language.* London: Academic Press.

Karttunen, L. (1976). Discourse referents. In J. McCawley (Ed.), *Syntax and semantics* (Vol. 7). New York: Academic Press.

Kaufman, D. (1988). *Grammatical and cognitive interactions in the study of children's knowledge of binding theory and reference relations.* Unpublished doctoral dissertation, Temple University, Philadelphia, PA.

Kaufman, D. (1994). Grammatical or pragmatic: Will the real Principle B please stand? In B. Lust, G. Hermon, and J. Kornfilt (Eds.), *Syntactic theory and first language acquisition: Cross-linguistic perspectives. Vol. 2. Binding, dependencies and learnability.* Hillsdale, NJ: Erlbaum.

Keenan, E. (1994). *Creating anaphors: An historical study of the English reflexive pronoun.* Unpublished manuscript, UCLA, Los Angeles, CA.

Kitagawa, Y. (1991). Copying identity. *Natural Language & Linguistic Theory, 9,* 497–536.

Koopman, H., and Sportiche, D. (1982). Variables and the Bijection Principle. *The Linguistic Review, 2,* 139–160.

Koster, C. (1993). *Errors in anaphora acquisition*. Utrecht: Utrecht University, Research Institute for Language and Speech.

Koster, C. (1994). Problems with pronoun acquisition. In B. Lust, G. Hermon, and J. Kornfilt (Eds.), *Syntactic theory and first language acquisition: Cross-linguistic perspectives. Vol 2. Binding, dependencies and learnability*. Hillsdale, NJ: Erlbaum.

Lakoff, G. (1972). Linguistics and natural logic. In D. Davidson and G. Harman (Eds.), *Semantics of natural language*. Dordrecht: D. Reidel.

Lasnik, H. (1972). *Analyses of negation in English*. Unpublished doctoral dissertation, MIT, Cambridge, MA.

Lasnik, H., and Crain, S. (1985). On the acquisition of pronominal reference. *Lingua, 65,* 135–154.

Lebeaux, D. (1983). A distributional difference between reciprocals and reflexives. *Linguistic Inquiry, 14,* 723–730.

Lee, H., and Wexler, K. (1987). *The acquisition of reflexives and pronouns in Korean from the cross-linguistic perspective*. Paper presented at the 12th Annual Boston University Conference on Language Development, Boston, MA.

Lewis, D. (1979). Score-keeping in a language game. In R. Bäuerle, U. Egli, and A. von Stechow (Eds.), *Semantics from different points of view*. Berlin: Springer-Verlag.

Lightfoot, D. (1998). *The development of language: Acquisition, change, and evolution*. Oxford: Blackwell.

Lust, B., and Clifford, T. (1982). The 3D study: Effects of depth, distance and directionality on children's acquisition of Mandarin Chinese. In J. Pustejovsky and P. Sells (Eds.), *NELS 12*. Amherst: University of Massachusetts, GLSA.

Lust, B., Loveland, K., and Kornet, R. (1980). The development of anaphora in first language. *Linguistic Analysis, 6,* 217–249.

Manzini, R., and Wexler, K. (1987). Parameters, binding theory and learnability. *Linguistic Inquiry, 18,* 413–444.

Maratsos, M. (1973). The effects of stress on the understanding of pronominal reference in children. *Journal of Psycholinguistic Research, 2,* 1–8.

Maratsos, M. (1976). *The use of definite and indefinite reference in young children*. Cambridge: Cambridge University Press.

Marcus, G. (1993). Negative evidence in language acquisition. *Cognition, 46,* 53–85.

Matsuoka, K. (1997). Binding conditions in young children's grammars: Interpretation of pronouns inside conjoined NPs. *Language Acquisition, 6,* 37–48.

McDaniel, D., and Cairns, H. S. (1996). Eliciting judgments of grammaticality and reference. In D. McDaniel, C. McKee, and H. S. Cairns (Eds.), *Methods for assessing children's syntax*. Cambridge, MA: MIT Press.

McDaniel, D., Cairns, H. S., and Hsu, J. R. (1990). Binding principles in the grammars of young children. *Language Acquisition, 1,* 121–138.

McDaniel, D., and Maxfield, T. (1992). Principle B and contrastive stress. *Language Acquisition, 2,* 337–358.

McDaniel, D., and McKee, C. (1993). Which children did they show know strong crossover? In H. Goodluck and M. Rochement (Eds.), *Island constraints.* Dordrecht: Kluwer.

McDaniel, D., McKee, C., and Cairns, H. S. (Eds.). (1996). *Methods for assessing children's syntax.* Cambridge, MA: MIT Press.

McKee, C. (1988). *Italian children's mastery of binding.* Unpublished doctoral dissertation, University of Connecticut, Storrs.

McKee, C. (1992). A comparison of pronouns and anaphors in Italian and English acquisition. *Language Acquisition, 1,* 21–55.

McKee, C., Nicol, J., and McDaniel, D. (1993). Children's application of binding principles during sentence processing. *Language and Cognitive Processes, 8,* 265–290.

Miyamoto, Y. (1992). *The collective and distributive interpretation in child grammar: A study on quantification.* General Examination, University of Connecticut, Storrs.

Miyamoto, Y., and Crain, S. (1991). *Children's interpretation of plural pronouns: Collective vs. distributive interpretation.* Paper presented at the 16th Annual Boston University Conference on Language Development, Boston, MA.

Montalbetti, M., and Wexler, K. (1985). Binding is linking. In J. Goldberg, S. MacKaye, and M. Wescoat (Eds.), *Proceedings of the 4th West Coast Conference on Formal Linguistics.* Stanford, CA: CSLI. [Distributed by Cambridge University Press.]

Morgan, J., and Travis, L. (1989). Limits on negative information in language input. *Journal of Child Language, 16,* 531–552.

Padilla, J. (1990). *On the definition of binding domains in Spanish: Evidence from child language.* Dordrecht: Kluwer.

Philip, W., and Coopmans, P. (1996). The double Dutch delay of Principle B effect. In A. Stringfellow, D. Cahana-Amitay, E. Hughes, and A. Zukowski (Eds.), *Proceedings of the 20th Annual Boston University Conference on Language Development.* Somerville, MA: Cascadilla Press.

Pica, P. (1987). On the nature of the reflexivization cycle. In J. McDonough and B. Plunkett (Eds.), *NELS 17.* Amherst: University of Massachusetts, GLSA.

Pinker, S. (1984). *Language learnability and language development.* Cambridge, MA: Harvard University Press.

Pinker, S. (1989). *Learnability and cognition: The acquisition of argument structure.* Cambridge, MA: MIT Press.

Poeppel, D., and Wexler, K. (1993). The full competence hypothesis of clause structure. *Language, 69,* 1–33.

Radford, A. (1990). *Syntactic theory and the acquisition of English syntax: The nature of early child grammars of English.* Oxford: Blackwell.

Reinhart, T. (1983). *Anaphora and semantic interpretation*. London: Croom Helm.

Reinhart, T. (1986). Center and periphery in the grammar of anaphora. In B. Lust (Ed.), *Studies in the acquisition of anaphora* (Vol. 1). Dordrecht: D. Reidel.

Reinhart, T. (1995). *Interface strategies* (OTS-WP-TL-95-002). Utrecht: Utrecht University, Research Institute for Language and Speech.

Reinhart, T. (1997). *Strategies of anaphora resolution* (UIL OTS 97 006/TL-CL). Utrecht: Utrecht University, Utrecht Institute of Linguistics.

Rice, M., Wexler, K., and Redmond, S. (in press). Grammaticality judgments of an extended optional infinitive grammar: Evidence from English-speaking children with specific language impairment. *Journal of Speech, Language and Hearing Research*.

Rizzi, L. (1993). Some notes on linguistic theory and language development: The case of root infinitives. *Language Acquisition, 4*, 371–394.

Roeper, T., Rooth, M., Mallis, L., and Akiyama, S. (1985). *The problem of empty categories and bound variables in language acquisition*. Unpublished manuscript, University of Massachusetts, Amherst.

Rosen, T. J., and Rosen, S. T. (1994). Inferring the innateness of syntactic knowledge. In E. Clark (Ed.), *The Proceedings of the 26th Annual Child Language Research Forum*. Stanford, CA: CSLI. [Distributed by Cambridge University Press.]

Sag, I. (1976). *Deletion and Logical Form*. Unpublished doctoral dissertation, MIT, Cambridge, MA.

Savarese, F. (1999). *Studies in coreference and binding*. Unpublished doctoral dissertation, University of Maryland, College Park.

Schütze, C. (1997). *INFL in child and adult language: Agreement, case and licensing*. Unpublished doctoral dissertation, MIT, Cambridge, MA.

Schütze, C., and Wexler, K. (1996). Subject case licensing and English root infinitives. In A. Stringfellow, D. Cahana-Amitay, E. Hughes, and A. Zukowski (Eds.), *Proceedings of the 20th Annual Boston University Conference on Language Development*. Somerville, MA: Cascadilla Press.

Selkirk, E. (1972). *The phrase phonology of English and French*. Unpublished doctoral dissertation, MIT, Cambridge, MA.

Sigurjónsdóttir, S., and Coopmans, P. (1996). The acquisition of anaphoric relations in Dutch. In W. Philip and F. Wijnen (Eds.), *Amsterdam series on child language development, 5*.

Sigurjónsdóttir, S., and Hyams, N. (1992). Reflexivization and logophoricity: Evidence from the acquisition of Icelandic. *Language Acquisition, 2*, 359–413.

Solan, L. (1978). *Anaphora in child language*. Unpublished doctoral dissertation, University of Massachusetts, Amherst.

Solan, L. (1983). *Pronominal reference: Child language and the theory of grammar*. Dordrecht: D. Reidel.

Solan, L., and Roeper, T. (1978). Children's use of syntactic structure in interpreting relative clauses. In H. Goodluck and L. Solan (Eds.), *University of Massachusetts occasional papers 4: Papers in the structure and development of child language*. Amherst: University of Massachusetts, GLSA.

Sperber, D., and Wilson, D. (1986). *Relevance*. Oxford: Blackwell.

Stalnaker, R. (1979). Assertion. In P. Cole (Ed.), *Syntax and semantics 9: Pragmatics*. New York: Academic Press.

Swinney, D. (1979). Lexical access during sentence comprehension: (Re)consideration of context effects. *Journal of Verbal Learning and Verbal Behavior, 18,* 645–659.

Swinney, D., Nicol, J., and Zurif, E. (1989). The effects of focal brain damage on sentence processing: An examination of the neurological organization of a mental module. *Journal of Cognitive Neuroscience, 1,* 25–37.

Swinney, D., and Prather, P. (1989). On the comprehension of lexical ambiguity by young children: Investigations into the development of mental modularity. In D. Gorfein (Ed.), *Resolving semantic ambiguity*. New York: Springer-Verlag.

Tancredi, C. (1992). *Deletion, deaccenting and presupposition*. Unpublished doctoral dissertation, MIT, Cambridge, MA.

Tavakolian, S. (1977). *Structural principles in the acquisition of complex sentences*. Unpublished doctoral dissertation, University of Massachusetts, Amherst.

Tavakolian, S. (1978). Children's comprehension of pronominal subjects and missing subjects in complicated sentences. In H. Goodluck and L. Solan (Eds.), *University of Massachusetts occasional papers 4: Papers in the structure and development of child language*. Amherst: University of Massachusetts, GLSA.

Taylor-Browne, K. (1983). Acquiring restrictions on forwards anaphora: A pilot study. In *Calgary working papers in linguistics 9*. Calgary, Alberta: University of Calgary, Department of Linguistics.

Thornton, R. (1990). *Adventures in long-distance moving: The acquisition of complex wh-questions*. Unpublished doctoral dissertation, University of Connecticut, Storrs.

Thornton, R. (1991). *Whither Principle B*. Panel discussant. Cognitive Science Colloquium, MIT, Cambridge, MA, November.

Uriagereka, J. (1998). *Rhyme and reason: An introduction to minimalist syntax*. Cambridge, MA: MIT Press.

Varela, A. (1989). *A structural explanation of children's apparent failure to respect Condition B*. Paper presented at the 14th Boston University Conference on Language Development, Boston, MA.

Wexler, K. (1998). Very early parameter setting and the unique checking constraint: A new explanation of the optional infinitive stage. *Lingua, 106,* 23–79.

Wexler, K. (1999). Maturation and growth of grammar. In W. Ritchie and T. Bhatia (Eds.), *Handbook of child language acquisition*. San Diego, Calif.: Academic Press.

Wexler, K., and Chien, Y.-C. (1985). The development of lexical anaphors and pronouns. *Papers and Reports on Child Language Development, 24,* 138–149.

Wexler, K., and Culicover, P. (1980). *Formal principles of language acquisition.* Cambridge, MA: MIT Press.

Wexler, K., and Hamburger, H. (1973). On the insufficiency of surface data for the learning of transformational languages. In K. J. J. Hintikka, J. M. E. Moravcsik, and P. Suppes (Eds.), *Approaches to natural language.* Dordrecht: D. Reidel.

Wexler, K., and Manzini, M. R. (1987). Parameters and learnability in binding theory. In T. Roeper and E. Williams (Eds.), *Parameter setting.* Dordrecht: D. Reidel.

Williams, E. (1977). Discourse and logical form. *Linguistic Inquiry, 8,* 101–139.

Index

Current Studies in Linguistics

Samuel Jay Keyser, general editor